A
PACT WITH THE
DEVIL

Also by Tony Smith

The French Stake in Algeria, 1945–1962 (Cornell University Press)

The Pattern of Imperialism: The United States, Great Britain and the Late-Industrializing World Since 1815 (Cambridge Univesity Press)

Thinking Like A Communist State and Legitimacy in the Soviet Union, China, and Cuba (W. W. Norton)

America's Mission: The United States and the Worldwide Struggle for Democracy in the Twentieth Century (Princeton University Press)

Foreign Attachments: Ethnic Group Power and the Making of American Foreign Policy (Harvard University Press)

A
PACT WITH THE
DEVIL

WASHINGTON'S BID
FOR WORLD SUPREMACY
AND THE BETRAYAL OF THE
AMERICAN PROMISE

TONY SMITH

Routledge
Taylor & Francis Group
New York   London

Routledge
Taylor & Francis Group
270 Madison Avenue
New York, NY 10016

Routledge
Taylor & Francis Group
2 Park Square
Milton Park, Abingdon
Oxon OX14 4RN

© 2007 by Taylor & Francis Group, LLC
Routledge is an imprint of Taylor & Francis Group, an Informa business

Printed in the United States of America on acid-free paper
10 9 8 7 6 5 4 3 2 1

International Standard Book Number-10: 0-415-95245-X (Hardcover)
International Standard Book Number-13: 978-0-415-95245-3 (Hardcover)

Library of Congress Cataloging-in-Publication Data

Smith, Tony.
   A pact with the devil : Washington's bid for world supremacy and the betrayal of the American promise / Tony Smith.
     p. cm.
   ISBN-13: 978-0-415-95245-3
   1. United States--Foreign relations--20th century. 2. United States--Foreign relations--2001- 3. United States--Intellectual life. 4. Intellectuals--United States--Political activity--History. 5. Liberalism--United States--History. 6. Democracy--History. 7. Imperialism--History. I. Title.

E744.S59 2007
327.7309'0511--dc22
                                            2006033031

Visit the Taylor & Francis Web site at
http://www.taylorandfrancis.com

and the Routledge Web site at
http://www.routledge-ny.com

For David Ovalle and Ron Steel
Constant Companions in the Struggle

CONTENTS

Now the serpent was more subtil than any beast of the field
which the Lord God had made. And he said unto the woman:
Yea, hath God not said, Ye shall not eat of every tree of the garden?

...And when the woman saw that the tree was good for food, and that it was
pleasant to the eyes, and a tree to be desired to make one wise, she took of the
fruit thereof, and did eat, and gave also to her husband with her; and he did
eat.

...And the Lord God said...unto the woman...I will greatly multiply thy sor-
row...and unto Adam He said...In the sweat of they face shalt though eat
bread...dust thou art and unto dust shalt thou return...Therefore the Lord God
sent him forth from the garden of Eden...

Genesis 3

PREFACE

If we should perish, the ruthlessness of the foe would be only the secondary cause of the disaster. The primary cause would be that the strength of a great nation was directed by eyes too blind to see all the hazards of the struggle, and the blindness would be induced not by some accident of nature or history, but by hatred and vainglory.

—Reinhold Niebuhr, *The Irony of American History*, 1952

When I arrive at the Pearly Gates, the question from Saint Peter I most fear will be how, given the evidence from the war in Iraq, I myself could have ever been so naïve as to have put so much intellectual stock into supporting Liberal Democratic Internationalism—the belief that fostering human rights and democratic governments abroad should enjoy a prominent role in the making of American foreign policy. I do not think I was ever among the greatest sinners—many of whom this book will mention—liberals with reckless confidence that America's mission was solely to promote universal salvation through democratic government, not only for the sake of foreign peoples but for the purpose of our national security and world peace as well. I always knew there were casualties in the expansion of American power—in the disregard for the victims of economic globalization, in wars like Vietnam, or through interventions such as in Guatemala and Iran—whatever the justification offered that these outcomes were the regrettable by-products of the struggle for the "free world."[1]

I had also always feared that in its self-righteousness the United States might lose an awareness of the limits to its power, an important matter as I never expected that the message of progress through embracing the liberal creed would be greeted elsewhere with the same enthusiasm it met with in countries like the Czech Republic, Hungary, or Slovenia after the fall of the Iron Curtain. Elsewhere, nationalist resistance based on fear of American self-interest, and on pride in ancient ways, would most surely challenge the claim of liberal democracy to be the only legitimate form of government, especially when it was evident that the existence of such a state presupposed basic alterations in social and cultural life. Raw chaos would stand in the way as well if the United States politically decapitated peoples who in their ethno-religious fear and rage could turn upon one another with a vengeance. Given such obstacles to "gunboat democracy," I felt that Washington should be advised to be selective in the importance it gave to human rights and democracy promotion, acting prudently in terms of time and place.

Such an attitude was all the more pertinent with respect to the Middle East. Why should one expect this region to fall under the sway of a doctrine as foreign as liberal democracy when its experience for so long had been one of outside incursions made for strictly self-interested gain? What possible exposure had the populations of the Middle East ever had to U.S. power to make them think the Americans were arriving as liberators rather than as conquerors? Even with some Arab intellectuals favorably disposed to the idea of liberalizing politically, socially, and economically, what likelihood was there that these peoples could easily transform themselves in such a radical fashion? Might it not happen that in their efforts to replace narrow authoritarian regimes by broad-based democratic government, a form of populist, militarist, nationalist neofascism could instead emerge rather than a liberal constitutional order friendly to American interests and values?

Such considerations inoculated me against taking seriously the pretensions of the Bush Doctrine, from which the Iraq War was drawn as surely as Eve from the rib of Adam, and from which other wars could be anticipated to follow. The determination to use, unilaterally and preemptively, what the Bush administration in 2002 repeatedly described as American military power "beyond challenge" in order to push the expansion of democratic government and open market economies as "the single sustainable model" for peace and progress in world affairs, struck me as an exaggerated claim to make on History's patience.

Despite being a liberal myself, I had already become worried by what I sensed was an intoxicating ideological conviction being formulated by liberal internationalists well outside the Republican party during the 1990s. Thanks to conceptual innovations they made during these years in their understanding of history and politics, these neoliberals, many of whom later metamorphosed into "liberal hawks" and supported the invasion of Iraq in March 2003, developed the heartfelt conviction that with the collapse of Soviet communism the tide of history was with them. Not so much the United States as liberal democratic internationalism had triumphed with the fall of the Berlin Wall in 1989. Now was the moment to agitate for Washington to pursue the global spread of human rights and democratic government to create what the late eighteenth century German philosopher Immanuel Kant had envisioned as "perpetual peace," even if the mission required the use of force.

Gathering at home were the storm clouds of what Samuel Huntington had warned us of in the mid-1990s, a "clash of civilizations" based on a deep sense of cultural and creedal divisions.[2] Might democracy promotion be an instance of fostering such a clash? The "civilized" world of Kantian principles would take on the "barbarians" living in the Hobbesian state of nature, both to protect itself from the enemy hordes and to save these peoples themselves from their cruel fate living under despotism. An irony of history was in the making with liberals feeding the very problem of world disorder that they claimed they knew how to cure.

After 9/11, when the Taliban refused to cooperate with Washington to deliver Osama bin Laden, invading Afghanistan was legitimate, indeed imperative. But why take on Iraq? The reasons given—that Saddam Hussein had weapons of mass destruction or that he was in league with Al-Qaeda—should not detain us. Virtually no one today believes that such was the root cause for America to go to war, even if some high officials may have suspected these weapons or contacts existed. Here, rather, was a pretext for the affirmation of American supremacy, a primacy in world affairs that Washington maintained was not only military, but also ideological, with the blueprint it possessed for winning the peace that would follow winning the war.

Combining the conviction that America enjoyed unrivalled power with the self-righteous, self-serving, and self-blinding assurance that it had a master plan with which to remake foreign domestic orders, and as a consequence perhaps to reconfigure the entire international system, the Bush Doctrine was a manifest case of imperial hubris. As the United Nations inspection team under Hans Blix found no weapons of mass destruction in Iraq by early 2003, and as the world community asked why the rush to war, the decision nonetheless to invade began to appear to me to be certifiably megalomaniac.

The difference between taking on Serbia in the 1990s—a policy I supported and felt President Bill Clinton should have undertaken earlier than he did—was thus quite different than taking on Iraq. Not only was Iraq a considerably more difficult task to tackle than the Balkans (which itself was no cakewalk), but it was linked to notions of remaking the "Broader Middle East" and thereby securing a hammerlock on political developments even further afield—a foolhardy ambition that vastly exaggerated both foreign susceptibilities and American capabilities. The decision to depose Saddam was therefore of a very different magnitude altogether than the decision to depose Slobodan Milosevic.

Nevertheless, as the argument spread that "the future of freedom" was what was at stake, the Democratic Party swung into line behind the Iraq War with a vengeance. Hillary Clinton, Joseph Biden, Joseph Lieberman, and Richard Holbrooke (along with many other luminaries) were supported by the spectacularly misnamed Progressive Policy Institute, the self-described think tank of the Democratic Leadership Council. This combination of Democrats joined in criticizing the Bush administration for botching the Iraq invasion—but *not* for organizing it in the first place, nor for thinking of further conquests thereafter. These Democrats seemingly had no doubts that the battle cry had to be as the Bush administration had defined it—for an American victory defined as the democratization of Iraq and carrying the banner of freedom beyond. Their aim in 2002, and still through 2006, remained affirming American supremacy worldwide under the auspices of this country's military primacy and its blueprint for order based on the enlargement of the sphere of market democracies.

The intellectual background of these Democratic leaders' convictions was independent of the neoconservative thinkers surrounding President Bush. Indeed, many of the seemingly most sophisticated arguments backing war for the sake of democracy promotion came not from official Washington, where the phrases offered by the neocons were well-turned, yet scarcely original. They arose instead from neoliberals in their think tanks, universities, and non-governmental organizations. Here during the 1990s, neolib scholars, scholar-activists, and activists had honed to perfection an argument for liberal imperialism just waiting to be used when a team with the will to power took over in Washington. The administration of Bill Clinton had avoided the temptation their arguments offered—or was so stymied by its own internal problems that it simply failed to act—one that the trigger-happy administration of George W. Bush, wanting to leave its mark on history, embraced with alacrity.

My focus in the pages that follow concerns the responsibility of those liberal internationalists of the center and the left—as much as the more publicly known neoconservatives—for providing the intellectual underpinnings for an invasion based on democracy promotion. These neoliberals, or neo-Wilsonians as we might call them in honor of the Democratic President Woodrow Wilson (1913–1921), who first advanced a global design for democracy promotion, proposed a powerful set of interlocking reasons in the 1990s to think democracy's moment had finally arrived worldwide. With the end of the Cold War, neoliberals could step forward and spread their wings. No longer relegated to a back seat by containment policy, they could proclaim in the early Clinton years a global mission to promote the "enlargement of market democracies."

During the 1990s, neoliberals working in international relations theory elaborated reasons in the aftermath of the Cold War as to why American security would be enhanced if democratic governments were to expand worldwide. Democratic peace theory, as their premise was called, was a pseudo-scientific account of world affairs that saw itself as the intellectual harbinger of a new age in human history, one that would usher in an era of enduring peace based on democratic governments, open and integrated economic markets, and participation in multilateral organizations. That this position could claim scientific standing for its pretensions, and that it could don the cloak of Kantian philosophy, was no small element of its appeal—or of its danger.

During the same period, neo-Wilsonians working in the field of comparative political development assured us that the democratization of people under authoritarian governments was an easier undertaking than an earlier generation had believed. Democracy had a universal appeal, they claimed. When great ideas were adopted by great leaders at critical historical junctures, momentous change could be the result.

Finally, neoliberal international jurists told us that the concept of sovereignty as it stood in international law did not provide immunity from attack to states engaging in systematic human rights abuses or amassing weapons of mass destruction. Instead, these were "outlaw" states, pariahs to be attacked by democratic coalitions with a warrant to take them on and liberalize their politics.

Neoliberals in effect divided the world into three spheres. First came the zone of democratic peace inhabited by "post historic" liberal market democracies, peoples freed of living in the state of nature that had hitherto typified human affairs and so capable of enjoying an enduring peace. As the first among equals in this "Community of Democracies," as the Clinton administration had come to label this grouping, the United States enjoyed a hegemonic status. That is, Washington did not need to impose its views on the members of this "pacific union" for our partners would recognize a collective interest in following American leadership.

A second zone was more problematic. States within it gave signs of moving toward being market democracies, but the transition would take time.
Washington should do what it could to help these lands make their historic
transition, with the understanding that their conversion was in everyone's
interest.

A third zone consisted of states and organizations actively hostile to the
world of market democracies. These enemies were not to be trusted and might
be attacked and forcibly converted into democratic regimes under the terms
of a new doctrine of "just war" set forth by neoliberal intellectuals. In these
instances, America would obviously be acting imperialistically, making foreign
peoples subject to forms of political organization spelled out by Washington.[3]

As we shall see in Chapters 4 through 7, this three-part conceptualization
of the world scene is not a mental map I have imposed on neoliberal thought.
Thus, John Rawls, probably the most eminent liberal political philosopher the
United States has produced, in 1999 divided the world into regimes that were
liberal and capable of being law-abiding members of a "Society of Peoples,"
"relatively decent hierarchies," and "outlaws." While he counseled goodwill
toward the "relatively decent hierarchies" and their treatment as equal members of the world community, his assumption was that war might be called for
by the liberal democracies against the outlaws, to be followed by their forced
conversion to liberal democratic ways.[4]

Rawls was not just speaking for himself. His tripartite ranking of the
world's states flowed directly from a much greater river of neoliberal discourse
in the aftermath of the Cold War that fundamentally conditioned his philosophical conclusions. Rawls died in 2002, and there is no necessary reason to
think he might have favored the Iraq War. Surely he would have been scandal-
ized by the actual conquest of that country, from its plundered public offices
to its American-run torture chambers. That said, Rawls's ideas obviously lent
themselves to appropriation by the war party.[5] Following in these footsteps
were neoliberals aplenty who still today condemn the Bush administration's
conduct of the war without at the same time rejecting either the idea of the
invasion itself or the notion that Iraq was just the first in a series of progressive
imperialist acts the United States might engender.

What the account in the following chapters reveals is that under neoliberal
auspices a comprehensive and coherent ideology for liberal imperialism was
born in the 1990s. The neoliberal perspective on how to run an imperial order
was far more tightly argued than anything the neoconservatives, who ran the
foreign policy establishment in Washington after the inauguration of George

W. Bush in 2001, came close to articulating. To be sure, these neolibs lacked
the ability to justify unilateral action on the part of a Washington possessed of
their beliefs. That was an argument provided by the neoconservatives.

Under the national trauma following the attack of September 11, 2001, a
marriage between first cousins was arranged. The opening round in the growing interaction between the neocons and the neolibs had already occurred in
disputes about what to do with Milosevic. The neoconservative insistence that
nothing would happen without American leadership was persuasive, for it did
indeed take determined action by Washington to oust the Serbian dictator.
But somewhat less persuasively, the neoliberals could point to multilateral
cooperation as key to the success of the mission. The second round, post-9/11,
was over the question of Saddam. Here again, the neocons had a game plan
ready, one that many liberals endorsed, even if most of them with a certain
reluctance. America would effectively act alone.

However, the neocons were not acting alone. In intellectual terms, their
wedding had taken place with the neoliberals, a fusion of ideas whose product
was the Bush Doctrine, articulated in 2002 in the aftermath of 9/11. There
are reasons, we might appreciate anew, that marriage between first cousins is
outlawed in the United States today. As the terms of the doctrine suggest, the
probability of genetic mutations in the offspring of such unions is too high to
warrant the risk.

Did the neoliberals realize just what they had produced intellectually and
where they were headed politically? Perhaps not. Certainly many of them were
washing their hands of any involvement within two years of the invasion. But
others stayed the course. And they did so with good reason, for the result
of their labors over the preceding decade had been to fashion an elaborate
justification for what might be called a modern version of both just war and
wars of national liberation. Now Washington would be a revolutionary force,
determined to make use of the window of opportunity it had in military and
ideological terms to create a structure of world affairs capable of protecting
American security and providing through war what it was confident would be
an extended era of peace.

The result was the laying of the intellectual foundation for a bipartisan
political consensus based on a common ideological agenda. That leading elements of the Democratic Party could sign on to the mission impossible laid
out by the Bush Doctrine only underscores the role of ideology in organizing American foreign policy. As Thomas Friedman, the country's most widely
read foreign correspondent, put it in the *New York Times* on March 3, 2006, "A

XVIPREFACE

majority of Americans, in a gut way, always understood the value of trying to produce a democratizing government in the heart of the Arab-Muslim world. That is why there has been no big antiwar movement."

A Pact With the Devil

A pact with the Devil occurs if we exchange control over our immortal soul to a sinister force in the expectation of realizing a powerfully desired goal that except for this agreement could not be obtained. Or in secular terms, we risk the farm thanks to a will to power with its tricks of self-deception that places us on the wrong side of history. But ambition proves its own undoing. History trips up those who would place it under their control; God will not be mocked. In the event, the serpent wins the day.

Whether the Faustian bargain is conducted for personal fame and fortune or for a more selfless common good, in every case, those who make such wagers calculate that once they obtain their heart's desire, they may outsmart the Devil. Their gamble invariably fails. Satan ultimately wins the soul of those who make such a pact because he knows he can count on God, or on history, to punish the sin of pride.

The reason is familiar. Whatever the motives lying behind such a pact, its signatories inevitably pay a terrible price for wanting what the nature of our condition will never permit. Adam and Eve expelled from the Garden, the humbling of the builders of the Tower of Babel, King David confronted by Nathan for thinking he was above divine law—such are the lessons of our religious tradition for the punishment of arrogant pride, lessons that in secular terms, too, are imminently comprehensible.

This book recounts two such pacts. The first, without parallel in this country's foreign policy tradition, came in the form of the Bush Doctrine, which looked to exploit America's military superiority over any conceivable rivals, and the ideological primacy of the appeal of open market capitalism—globalization—and liberal democracy, so as to dominate the international system for generations to come. Here was a pact with the Devil if ever there was one. As the subtitle of this book puts it, in Washington's bid for world supremacy lay the betrayal of the American promise. America gave in to the temptations of a superpower to overplay its hand, to gamble with fate that it could make a lasting mark on world events.[6] Rushing into the Iraq War to bring global history under control was as perfect an illustration for our day as exists of the adage that pride comes before the fall.

The second pact occurred when neoliberal hawks, who had for the most part not initially supported this Republican president, nonetheless made common cause with him. Many of these hawks were political independents. But the most influential of them brought their ideas from America's leading universities into the Democratic Party, whose intellectual high ground they effectively controlled. These neoliberals were the functional equivalent for the Democrats of the neoconservatives within the Republican Party, a pro-war faction able to articulate in seemingly persuasive fashion why America's moment of unrivalled power meant embracing a mission that would echo through the ages for its vision and its courage.

The result? A stunning setback not only for America but as well for liberal internationalism with its call for human rights and democracy promotion as a doctrine of human betterment. A noble idea was tainted. Whatever the outcome of this war, America will remain a superpower. But its doctrine of hegemonic and imperial domination for the sake of pursuing progressive ends has suffered a reversal from which it will likely never recover. To be sure, some liberal individuals and organizations opposed the war and were individually spared from the contamination. But the well has been poisoned. By making liberal internationalism the doctrine of American nationalism in an era of imperialism, too many articulate spokespersons have hopelessly compromised the future of this once progressive doctrine.

How these ideas of empire were formulated on the basis of liberal democratic internationalist thinking, why they were mistaken, and what lessons a more sobered country can draw from the experience, are the subjects of this book.

A WORD OF THANKS

In the course of writing this book, I was enormously aided by several longtime friends. Ronald Steel and David Fromkin, two historians who have never had the slightest truck with liberal internationalism, saw the conceits and misuse of this ideology within months after 9/11. So, too, did my colleague Jeffrey Taliaferro, a political scientist specializing in American foreign policy and a master of the theories guiding the discipline today as it seeks to grasp the logic of world events. Stanley Hoffmann—ever the gadfly, a liberal in the company of realists, a realist in the company of liberals—likewise saw immediately the self-destructive course liberalism had set itself upon when it came to be the standard-bearer of war in the Middle East.

Mario Bettati—a Frenchman and the original author, along with Bernard Kouchner, of the concepts of a "right to intervene" and a "duty to intervene," and hence a liberal with every bone in his body—was nonetheless from the beginning a critic of the war in ways that afforded me special insights. So, too, was Toni Chayes, a liberal lawyer specializing at the Fletcher School in the international law of humanitarian intervention. Justin Vaisse, another Frenchman, was a precious source of information on the first two decades of the neoconservative movement. I also appreciate the encouragement of David Rieff. Rieff was virtually the only liberal internationalist who, *well before* the Iraq War, recognized how destructive the exercise of American power would be both to world order and to progressive politics, if it camouflaged its wide range of imperial interests by flying the banner of human rights and democracy promotion worldwide. Michael Kerns acted ably as editor of the book as did Suzanne Lassandro as project manager; thanks to them as well.

Other friends were equally encouraging. I would especially like to thank David Ovalle, Bill Barnes, Sylvan Barnet, Bonnie Cronin, Roger Fauroux, Nadia Georges, Arthur Goldhammer, Hyman and Lillian Goldin, Inge Hoffmann, Marla Joel, Barbara Leaver, Gary Tinterow, Ann Tucker, Hubert Vicente, John Wong, and Henri Zerner. What these friends have in common is an everyday wonder at the foibles of human vanity. All possess the common sense to see folly for what it is, and so labeled the call for the invasion of Iraq as exactly what it was from its first day: an act of hubris—excessive pride based on moral arrogance, a cause for national shame.

I am grateful for a Tufts' Faculty Research Awards grant for time to complete this manuscript. Vickie Sullivan and Rob Devigne were a tremendous help as were a number of undergraduate students, most especially Jorge Rueda and Philip Moss.

To all of them, I would like to express my appreciation for their support in writing this "biography of an ideology," an attempt to explain how an idea with such promise—that the world would be a better place if human rights and democratic government were but expanded—could come to contribute to such a tragic turn of events.

Tony Smith, Boston, November 2006

INTRODUCTION: THE WAR OF IDEAS

Winning the war on terror means winning the war of ideas, for it is ideas that can turn the disenchanted into murderers willing to kill innocent victims.

National Security Strategy of the United
States, March 2006 (section III, C)

Fighting a War of Ideas is not for sissies. It requires insight into the target audience, their interests and their values. It involves creating messages that resonate, penetrate and are remembered. It entails finding ways to deliver those messages, repeatedly, to the ears and eyeballs of those who need to understand.

Clifford May, Chairman of the Foundation for the
Defense of Democracies, March 17, 2005

The preliminary battles of the war on terrorism were the military invasions of Afghanistan, then Iraq. Once these conquests of arms were achieved, the difficult political part followed: winning the peace. President George W. Bush's administration planned to consolidate its military victories by democratizing the two countries and, as a consequence of these successful missions, spreading the model of free market democracies to more of the Muslim world, perhaps even further, to China.

To undertake such an historic mission required what official Washington and its supporters tirelessly called "a war of ideas." How these ideas were structured into a coherent policy for action called the Bush Doctrine, where they came from, and why they were badly mistaken in their first premises as goals for the United States are the subjects of this book.

One may legitimately doubt, of course, that ideas matter that much in the course of human events. Emotions, especially a will to power in the case we are considering, most certainly count enormously in the making of history. Still, passions need organization and direction; they need explanations in conceptual terms for how what is desired may actually be achieved. The course of the American Revolution may not have depended solely on the thinking of men like Jefferson and Franklin, Paine and Hamilton, Adams, Madison, and Monroe; basic material interests and human emotions were involved and should not for a moment be discounted. Yet that this Revolution would occur and take the course it did in establishing not only the independence of the United States but even more importantly the Constitution by which it continues to be governed, requires turning to the ideas of the Founders, seeing their thinking as an independent force that gave interest and passion a concrete political form. In a word, ideas matter, often decisively so.

After the attack of September 11, 2001, the decision to invade Afghanistan is understandable in terms that are not highly ideological. America was acting in outraged self-defense in a way that requires no special interpretation. However, the same can not be said with respect to the decision to invade Iraq. That Saddam Hussein had weapons of mass destruction, or that he might act in league with Al-Qaeda, are today widely acknowledged as pretexts for an undertaking whose essential mission was justified in highly ideological terms: the assertion of American primacy in world affairs by bringing not simply Iraq but the Middle East more generally under Washington's control. Justification for such an unprecedented undertaking was the task of the Bush Doctrine, which I will argue was the most explicit and ambitious official declaration of this country's place in the world in the entire history of American foreign policy. Here ideas matter.

Persuading the public both at home and abroad to rally to the terms of this presidential doctrine was no small feat. Hence the necessity of invoking Saddam's alleged possession of weapons of mass destruction and supposed contacts with international terrorism. But the actual goals the Bush Doctrine pursued were extraordinary, of a measure altogether greater than the charges made against Saddam. When the Bush administration hoisted the flag of its intentions in invading Iraq in 2002, its imperial idea was that democratic regime change there would create a new order not only in that country but throughout what it called the "Broader Middle East." Once this mission was accomplished, the entire structure of world affairs would likely be decisively altered in America's favor. Here was a grand design presented by Washington without precedent in American history.

A part of such reasoning was that terror, and anti-Americanism in general, stemmed from authoritarian governments and violent religious factions that turned popular sentiments in the region against the United States and the democratic world in general, including especially Israel, the United States' premier ally in the region. The remedy to the problem could not simply be the military defeat of hostile states in the Muslim world. The underlying conditions giving rise to this behavior needed to be addressed. The solution, then, was Iraq's democratization, assumed to be a pacifying political formula for reasons this book will investigate, and with it liberalizing reforms adopted by other parts of this region critical in world affairs, either by demonstration of what could be accomplished in Iraq alone or by further armed intervention.

But could such a gargantuan project be pulled off? Under the terms of the Bush Doctrine, military triumph alone over religious fundamentalism in Afghanistan and secular despotism in Iraq was not nearly enough. What Washington looked forward to after the conquest of Kabul and Baghdad was the remaking of these defeated political orders, as well as the civil societies over which they presided, in ways that would make them market democracies and so provide for their incorporation into the international system in a way that would contribute to what with pride might be thought of as the *Pax Americana*, or the American Peace.[1]

It was at this point that the war of arms necessarily gave way to the war of ideas. The undertaking would be heroic for its goal was to make history by radically altering the political and social organization of a major region of the world. Peoples who had never known democratic rule would find themselves possessed of new political institutions resting on the consent of the governed. Civil orders that had never negotiated a social contract among their various factions—be they ethnic, religious, or linguistic (or all these and even more)—would be called upon for measures of trust and cooperation that they had never before exhibited. Economic arrangements that had favored unaccountable patronage and privilege would give way to market forces. Ancient cultural practices sanctified by familiarity and religious belief would reorder themselves by evolving new ways of seeing individual and group rights and responsibilities. And this impressive agenda would unfold under the terms of a set of ideas and institutions promoted by the benevolent compulsion of American power. For all the dire warnings in 2005–2006 from the neoconservatives and

President Bush that what the "Islamofascists" wanted was a "global caliphate," their own assumptions of their self-appointed historical mission to rework human affairs were if anything even more ambitious.

Once this many-faceted process of democratization had successfully occurred, the countries in question would presumably find themselves exposed to levels of freedom and prosperity that would make them willing members of an international community of market democracies led by the United States. As America had done in Japan and Germany after World War II, as was occurring in Central Europe and other parts of the world after the U.S. victory in the Cold War, so now peace with freedom thanks to American efforts would spread in turn to the Middle East.

If we can expect difficulties in bringing the Arab and Muslim worlds into line with these ideas, then we should expect problems garnering support for them at home as well. Most Americans reading this bill of sale would quite understandably find it a tall order. Pursuing a government alleged to harbor weapons of mass destruction that it would use against us was one thing. But successful completion of a mission such as what the Bush Doctrine envisaged required the achievement of many long-term, intrinsically difficult, perhaps impossible, tasks. The public might well ask how realistic it was that such an agenda would ever be accomplished. Manipulating the trauma of the terrorist attack of 9/11 into a grandiose battle plan might work for a while, but in due course a sense of security had to be heightened, not lessened, by American actions overseas. By explaining to the peoples of the Middle East why the attack on Iraq of March 2003 was justified and what the United States hoped to achieve thereby, the partisans of the war were laying out to the American people as well why they should make what the Bush administration often called "a generational commitment" to the effort.

As the war went badly, however, more and more Americans, like more and more people abroad and especially in the Middle East, began to question with increased vehemence what the thinking was that lay behind this conflict in the first place. They were right to ask the question.

The Government Invigorates "Public Diplomacy"

"The propagandists have done a better job of depicting America as a hateful place, a place wanting to impose our form of thought and our religion on people," President George W. Bush announced on CNN on January 16, 2005. "We're behind when it comes to selling our own story and telling people the truth about America...I'll continue to be straightforward and plainspoken about my view that freedom is necessary for peace and that everybody deserves to be free." On March 27, 2006, Secretary of Defense Donald Rumsfeld wondered if much had changed. Given this country's noble purpose, why all this anti-Americanism, why do they call *us* a "rogue state," why do they hate us? "If I were grading, I would say we probably deserve a D or a D-plus as a country as to how well we're doing in the battle of ideas that's taking place in the world...I'm not going to suggest that it's easy, but we have not found the formula as a country for countering the extremists' message."

To conduct the war of ideas more effectively, the U.S. government decided to emphasize "public diplomacy," a term that goes back to the early 1960s. According to a State Department definition issued in 1997, public diplomacy "seeks to promote the national interest of the United States through understanding, informing and influencing foreign audiences." Most governments engage in such practices, but given the ideological character of the Iraq War, the United States had to be especially vigilant, concerned that the Muslims of the Middle East understood what we hoped to achieve and that our citizens at home also supported the historic endeavor. Given the enormity of the task, trusting to America's reputation for sound leadership was not enough. A vision needed to be projected, explained, and defended. A moral purpose was at issue: freedom and peace were at stake above all else.

The person in charge of this multi-million dollar U.S. government public diplomacy undertaking, at the time of this writing, was the Under Secretary of State for Public Diplomacy and Public Affairs, Karen Hughes. Speaking before the Council on Foreign Relations on May 10, 2006, Hughes defined "our transformational public diplomacy" as a "comprehensive strategy that's based on three strategic objectives."

> First, we must offer people throughout the world a positive vision of hope and opportunity that is rooted in our belief in freedom, equality, justice and opportunity for all.... Our second strategic objective is to isolate and marginalize the violent extremists and confront their ideology of tyranny and hate...[third we must] foster a sense of common interests and common values between Americans and people of different countries and cultures around the world.

As the under secretary's final objective specifies, public diplomacy targets an American audience as well as that overseas. It is at home that the administration's effort must be persuasive too, for as the partisans of the war warn, should anti-war sentiment grow, then not only will the conquest of Iraq likely turn into a defeat, but the entire global enterprise of American supremacy in world affairs will come under question. Given the stakes the Bush White House and its supporters have put on this historic gamble, America must be mobilized for victory.

We should note with special interest that it was not just the party in power that advocated this agenda; leading elements of the Democratic Party backed the notion of a war of ideas without the slightest reservation. Indeed, as we shall see in Chapter 6, the center-left could easily wax as eloquent on the necessity of such a war as anyone in the Bush administration or its neoconservative allies. Thanks to the enduring legacy of Democratic President Woodrow Wilson (1913–1921), the center-left was the home of the earliest supporters of human rights and democracy promotion abroad, so that when President George W. Bush hoisted the flag of exporting liberal rights and responsibilities to Iraq and the Broader Middle East, many outside the Republican party were among the first to salute.

The result was bipartisan support for the war of ideas, which had particularly devastating consequences on the ability of the public at large to see the Iraq invasion at all correctly given the perceived lack of responsible anti-war arguments. Rather than seeing the invasion of Iraq as a self-interested power grab as old as human history, many to the left of the Bush administration would instead justify the war so making opposition to it a matter of protests on the fringes of American political life. For example, as early as 2003, George Packer, a writer for the *New Yorker* and certainly to the left of the Republican party, edited a book called *The Fight Is for Democracy: Winning the War of Ideas in America and the World*. Packer described his fellow contributors as people to the left, having in common: "an attachment to the ideals of American democracy, a dissatisfaction with its current practice, and a belief that we are engaged in a war for world opinion, a war of ideas. No one should doubt that we are losing it." Why? Because we Americans "have no ardor for democracy." What we must come to grips with is that:

> the fight against political Islam isn't a clash of civilizations and it isn't an imperialist campaign…it is a conflict of ideologies and they come down to the century old struggle between totalitarianism and liberal democracy. There is no possibility of a negotiated peace, because the ideologies are incompatible— they can't coexist…America has to persuade people around the world that this is their fight too, that the side of liberal democracy is where their hope lies.[2]

Packer was not at all an isolated voice. Many individual Democrats and Independents to the left echoed these sentiments rather exactly. On the issue of American military intervention in the Middle East, the Progressive Policy Institute (PPI) of the Democratic Party's National Leadership Council and the neoconservative Project for the New American Century (PNAC) were effectively mirror images of one another.

As we shall see in Chapter 6, these Democrats' embrace of an imperialist strategy for American supremacy internationally began soon after 9/11. It did not end there. In 2006, the PPI brought out *With All Our Might: A Progressive Strategy for Defeating Jihadism and Defending Liberty*, whose first part was entitled "winning the war of ideas." Among its contributors were several this book will discuss as "neo-Wilsonians" and "neoliberals" or "neo-Kantians," all of whom became "liberal hawks." At about the same time, Peter Beinart, an editor of the *New Republic*, brought out a volume specifically targeting the Democratic Party to rally it to the war. Its title reveals its contents: *The Good Fight: Why Liberals—and Only Liberals—Can Win the War on Terror and Make America Great Again.* Here were intellectuals of the left who unequivocally embraced the Iraq War and American domination of international affairs beyond. Their only problem was with the highly unsatisfactory way the Bush administration had conducted what they agreed was this sacred mission. Or consider again The Euston Manifesto issued by a British group in the spring of 2006. To read these so-called "progressives," to stand for the rights of women, gays, labor, or the environment, was to be "for democracy," offer "no apology for tyranny," endorse "human rights for all," and, of course to stand "united against terror" and for "a new internationalism" that ultimately would lead in due course to support for whatever advanced freedom at the expense of dictatorship the world around. In a word, here was another group of "progressives" who favored "self-defensive" liberal imperialism in the Middle East. [3]

A War of Ideas on Three Fronts

The effort to grasp the logic of the Bush administration's war of ideas necessarily operates on three levels, which I will call the *popular*, the *elite*, and the *priestly*. Each level has its own structure of argument and its own political goal.

At the popular level, propaganda is put forward on a daily basis from a variety of individuals and organizations that constitute the war party. This aspect of the war of ideas relies on simple propositions, assenting to which implies endorsing American imperialism. You oppose terror, for example, or you understand the universal appeal of freedom, and within short order, by following up an initial agreement with a second and third, you fall down a slippery slope and are made to think you should back the deployment of troops to the Middle East.

The elite level of the war of ideas, by contrast, is a more sophisticated matter contained within the parameters of the argument set forth by the Bush Doctrine. Unlike the structure of argument at the popular level, the doctrine is an integrated set of ideas that adds up to a coherent whole, a political grand design. Its focus is on persuading the international foreign policy elite as to the logic of American purpose. Scholars, journalists, professional political activists, and government officials both at home and abroad are attuned to the nuances of this level of argument.

The third level of the war of ideas, the priestly, is the hardest to maneuver, the most difficult to penetrate. Its precincts are guarded by academic celebrants of international relations and political science theory whose sometimes arcane formulations may be difficult for the uninitiated to comprehend. Yet the effort must be made. For here lies the core ideology itself, the coherent but complex set of concepts we should see as the fount of both popular and elite arguments. From this inner sanctum emerged the terms of the Bush Doctrine and popular propaganda as well. Understanding its logic is fundamental to grasping how power justifies itself in Washington. Here is the center of gravity giving intellectual unity to popular messages and elite behavior. Neither the Bush Doctrine, nor popular propaganda championing the war, could stand close examination were it not for the fire of these ideas, which must be extinguished if finally the dragon of liberal imperialism is to be slain.

Each of the three dimensions of the war of ideas is reflected in this book. The first two chapters are focused on the elite level of argument, that is, with terms of the Bush Doctrine, the domain of official doctrine wherein a highly elaborated, authoritative statement of American purpose is set forth. Chapter 3 sets the doctrine within the context of the historical evolution of the school of American thinking on world affairs to which it belongs, that of liberal democratic internationalism.

Chapters 4 through 7 deal with the core ideology, the domain of the high priests of international liberalism who guard the sacred fires from which the Bush Doctrine could be derived and the arguments of popular propaganda produced. This central creedal arena, with its complex but coherent doctrine, is the principal focus of this book. Here is the dragon's lair.

Because so much of the book deals with the elite and priestly levels of the war of ideas, let us look more closely in this introductory chapter at how arguments to support the Bush Doctrine are pitched at the popular level. At its crudest, this aspect of the war reduces to public marketing. Ideas are thrown up by individual writers, orchestrated through institutional channels whose boards of directors often are interlocking, then finally argued to the public at large. Focus groups are the most obvious expression of this approach, but everything from techniques practiced by Madison Avenue marketing, or by Hollywood horror films and thrillers, may play a role. The bottom line is to control the domestic political process by controlling the terms of the debate.

The Case of the Foundation for the Defense of Democracies

Consider, for example, the part played by the neoconservative Foundation for the Defense of Democracies (FDD) in the war of ideas. Its role is to shape popular, not elite, opinion, and its audience is as much the home market as that abroad. As the FDD's chairman, Clifford May, described his job in a citation that opened this introduction, it is most certainly "not for sissies," for it "involves creating messages that resonate, penetrate and are remembered. It entails finding ways to deliver those messages, repeatedly, to the ears and eyeballs of those who need to understand."[4]

The FDD described itself on its website in the summer of 2006 as a "tax exempt, non-profit and non-partisan institution. We do not seek to advance any political party or views."[5] Yet it most certainly has a political agenda, one that it advances not only with privately donated funds, but also with State Department and Agency for International Development (AID) financial support and through co-sponsorship of political events with the National Endowment for Democracy (NED), whose president since 1983 is Carl Gershman, a well-known neoconservative.

"We focus our effort where opinions are formed and ultimately where the war of ideas will be won or lost: in the media, on college campuses, and in the policy community at home and abroad," the FDD announces. So far as the media is concerned, for example, the FDD has as major objectives both "shutting down terrorist media" while at the same time "shaping the media" at home and abroad so as "to fight terrorism and promote democratic values" through "producing documentary films and radio programs" (in part with grant money from the Corporation for Public Broadcasting) for distribution *in the United States*.

So far as higher education is concerned, the FDD is eager to spread its message "at a time when college campuses are under the sway of apologists for terrorism." As part of its campaign, the FDD put out flyers in 2006 advertising

Undergraduate Fellowships on Terrorism, "for students interested in combating the terrorist threats to our democratic way of life." After attending seminars in Israel and the United States, a student is expected to become "a campus leader by shaping events that promote democracy and educate peers on terrorism: Bring terrorism experts and government officials to campus for lectures; promote democratic reformers from Algeria, Iran, Iraq, and Syria; support our troops abroad and foster democratic development in the Middle East."[6]

Another FDD concern is to expose the malfeasance of the United Nations. Despite its claim that it is "non-partisan" and does "not advance any political party or views," consider the words of the organization's journalist in residence Claudia Rosett, opinions that the FDD's website heartily endorsed:

> The United Nations was founded as a forum of governments.... Now the UN, in contravention of its own charter, is rapidly evolving into something larger, more corporate, and more menacing: a predatory, undemocratic, unaccountable, and self-serving vehicle for global government. Like the Soviet Union of old, the UN is unwieldy, gross, inefficient, and incompetent. It is also so configured as to reach deep into the national politics of its member states.... There will never be enough John Boltons to counter all of this—not that it was easy to come up with even one.[7]

As yet another of its multifaceted approaches "to winning the war of ideas internationally," the FDD has linked up with like-minded groups abroad. Its website reports that it works in a "partnership with the European Foundation for Democracy, an anti-terrorism, pro-democracy think tank and advocacy group headquartered in Brussels, as well as through relationships with similar organizations in Paris, London, Berlin and other European capitals." One of the groups the FDD lists is the Henry Jackson Society, located in Great Britain. This "registered charity" described itself on its website in the summer of 2006 in ways quite compatible with the FDD:

> The Henry Jackson Society is a non-profit and non-partisan organization that seeks to promote the following principles: that liberal democracy should be spread across the world; that as the world's most powerful democracies, the United States and the European Union—under British leadership—must shape the world more actively by intervention and example; that such leadership requires political will, a commitment to universal human rights and the maintenance of a strong military with global expeditionary reach; and that too few of our leaders in Britain and the rest of Europe today are ready to play a role in the world that matches our strength and responsibilities.[8]

Illustrative as the FDD is as to how the war of ideas is being waged, it is only the tip of the proverbial iceberg. Not only do quite a range of neoconservative organs exist promoting much the same line as the FDD, but so too are there Democratic groups, which, attacks on the UN aside (Democrats have remained for the most part loyal to international institutions) are ideologically indistinguishable from their right-wing counterparts.

As I have indicated, the American government is well mobilized to conduct a war of ideas to persuade public opinion at home and abroad through official channels such as the NED, the AID, and the office of the under secretary for diplomacy and public affairs at the State Department. Estimates are that American government sponsored democracy programs cost over $2 billion annually, of which actual propaganda is presumably a relative small part.

In addition, the Bush administration also worked with self-described "non-partisan" groups like the Foundation for the Defense of Democracies. The foundation's usefulness to the promotion of the Bush Doctrine was that it could present itself as an independent voice and that it could generate on its own ideas that might gain more general currency.

One of these concepts was the notion that although the terrorists behind the attack of 9/11 were Islamic extremists, most Muslims are not any more represented by these people than most Christians are represented by the Ku Klux Klan. As a consequence, the FDD has an outreach program to the Arab and greater Muslim world, trying to establish links around common interests and values that oppose terrorism.

The result is that the FDD plays a role in establishing the mental picture of "us" and "them" that is indispensable to the conduct of the war of ideas at the popular level. The effort is to split the Muslim world into those who would collaborate with "us" and those extremists whom "we" (that is, we Americans and those friendly Muslims) would marginalize or destroy. Thus, we can work with "moderate" Muslims, and we will help them in their struggle against the extremists, usually described as "totalitarians," (or, the word of choice in 2005–2006, "Islamofascists"). We are not imperialists, we are liberators. Our arrival in their lands is an invasion, to be sure, but we are acting in self-defense. And we will help moderate Muslims to act in their self-defense as well. Like us, the forces we favor in the Middle East are moderate, progressive, modern, and like us they are in danger of being attacked by the same forces that hate us, whether they be theocratic or secular in the despotism they are trying to impose.

Thus, the Iraq War is not a "clash of civilizations," a term to be avoided at all costs. Rather, the struggle is progressive modernity in conflict with obscurantism and despotism. And when the war is won, it will be a victory not so much for America's power position in the world thanks to its control of a very valuable piece of geo-strategic territory, but a victory for freedom and peace for us all. Our conquest is not in our narrow self-interest—and should not be confused with oil, Israel, or securing a power position in the Middle East that allows us to dominate global affairs. Our victory is a win for the general cause of humanity expressed in two key words, "freedom" and "peace."

The Example of Thomas Friedman

Consider as an example of how this line is promoted, the many editorials of America's most widely read foreign correspondent, a man generally considered supportive of the Democratic Party, Thomas L. Friedman of the *New York Times*. As early as December 19, 2001, Friedman was in print calling for a unilateral attack on Iraq to prosecute what he had called "World War III" as early as September 13.[9] Again and again in the years that followed, he invoked the "war of ideas" defining it as an effort to support "moderate" Muslims against the extremists.

A high point came in a series of six editorials Friedman published in January 2004, all entitled "the war of ideas." In the opening lines of the first installment on January 8, Friedman declared that the "global war on terror… amounts to World War III—the third great totalitarian challenge to open societies in the last 100 years.… What we can do is to partner with the forces of moderation within these societies to help them fight the war of ideas. Because ultimately, this is a struggle within the Arab-Muslim world, and we have to help our allies there, just as we did in World Wars I and II." In his final lines of the sextet on January 25, Friedman concluded: "The war of ideas among Arabs and Muslims can only be fought and won by their own forces of moderation, and these forces can only emerge from a growing middle class with a sense of dignity and hope for the future. Young people who grow up in a context of real economic opportunity, basic rule of law and the right to speak, and write what they please don't usually want to blow up the world. They want to be part of it."

A sample from other Friedman editorials conveys the same message, that a common Western and moderate Muslim "us" must stand shoulder to shoulder against an extremist, totalitarian "them." As he put it on October 3, 2004, what mattered was "a decent outcome in Iraq, to help move the Arab-Muslim world off its steady slide toward increased authoritarianism, unemployment,

overpopulation, suicidal terrorism and religious obscurantism." Reflecting on
the Iraqi elections of January 30, 2005, he could declare on February 3 that
he was "rooting for the good guys...I am thrilled that things have come this
far." Or again, "What threatens America most from the Middle East are the
pathologies of a region where there is too little freedom.... The only way to
cure these pathologies is with a war of ideas within the Arab-Muslim world, so
those with bad ideas can be defeated by those with progressive ones." On April
20, 2005: "For me, the war in Iraq was always about democracy and the necessity of helping it emerge in the Arab-Muslim world." On July 8, 2005, he chose
as his essay's title: "If It's a Muslim Problem, It Needs a Muslim Solution."

As for the Iraq War's reverses, Friedman repeatedly blamed the calamities
on the hapless Secretary of Defense Donald Rumsfeld, but not for a moment
on the idea of the invasion itself, which Friedman consistently supported.
Thus, on May 6, 2004, Friedman published "Restoring Our Honor," in which
he called for the secretary's removal so as to "rebuild our credibility as instruments of humanitarian values, the rule of law and democratization in Iraq and
elsewhere." Otherwise, Friedman sadly concluded, "we are in danger of losing
America as an instrument of moral authority and inspiration in the world."

Friedman's approach was paralleled by many others, and not just the FDD.
Since democracy and open markets represent modernity, prosperity, freedom
and peace, and so have a universal appeal, the war party patiently explained,
resistance to American power was not a clash of civilizations, or even a struggle between "us" and "them" in simpler cultural terms, so much as a struggle within the Middle East between the past and the present, tradition and
modernity, oppression and freedom, with us on the progressive side. Hence
the confidence with which the well-known writers Ian Buruma and Avishai
Margalit could assert:

> the West is not at war with Islam. Indeed, the fiercest battles will be fought
> inside the Muslim world, not strictly between religionists and secularists, but
> between those who favor civil liberties and freedom of thought and those who
> wish to impose a theocracy.... There is indeed a worldwide clash going on, but
> the fault lines do not coincide with national, ethnic, or religious boundaries....
> The war of ideas is in some respects the same as the one that was fought several
> generations ago, against various versions of fascism and state socialism.

Accordingly, America's conquest accomplished, we can rest easy, for
Buruma and Margalit reassure us, "the other intellectual trap to avoid is the
paralysis of colonial guilt."[10]

Do we have reason to doubt the good faith of Friedman or of Buruma and Margalit? I assume that they wish the best for the Muslims of the Middle East and can make a good argument that many inhabitants of the region wish, much as they do, to see individual freedom and responsible government there. In a word, these men are not camouflaging their desire to see American power expand by cloaking it in the rhetoric of benevolence; they mean what they say. They are saints, not scoundrels.

But there are reasons, we have learned, to keep our distance from saints. For these three men are quite sophisticated politically. They know well enough that if they wish the end—a democratic future for the Muslim Middle East— they have willed the means as well—the American invasion of Iraq and perhaps beyond. Given their long experience in the region, they also know well enough that to keep its power position, the United States will have as its first concern maintaining its hold politically, an enterprise that may well put the benevolent ends our authors would see served in considerable jeopardy. The naïveté of saints on this score, if not their hypocrisy, is the cause of their perdition, and of ours too if we follow their well-meaning counsels.

The reason that saints are so often naïve is that they fail to see that power has as its first rule its self-preservation. To be liberators, the Americans must first be conquerors. As with conquerors before them, they are likely to have a host of demands placed on them not least of which are a series of self-interested goals that may conflict with whatever noble intentions they have proclaimed to world opinion. What then happens to the promise of freedom is anyone's guess. It is naïve to think this war is about liberation when first it is about conquest. Or are these three authors hypocrites, knowing very well that what they are saying is only for public consumption, and that for them, too, the success of the American conquest is what matters most? In either case, whether naïve or hypocritical, these saints may usefully serve the ends of scoundrels.

A further reason to be leery of Friedman, Buruma, and Margalit's contribution to the war of ideas is that their assertions arise from a deeper complex of liberal internationalist ideology, what I referred to as the priestly arguments, which is problematic in its formulation. That is, these three men are articulating a position that they did not arrive at alone—in fact, their position is preached on every street corner by partisans of the Iraq War—but that has its origins in theoretical arguments of democratic peace theorists and the democratic transition literature, whether or not they are aware of these elaborate theoretical arguments generated at the priestly level of the war of ideas.

That is how ideologies work; the core structure can generate conclusions or debating points in seeming independence of their germinal base. Because, as I shall show in Chapters 4 and 5, these intellectual origins are themselves suspect, so also are arguments derived from them. What comes of bad seed cannot bear good fruit.

The War of Ideas in the Middle East

I am aided in my undertaking to conduct a war against the "war of ideas" by the following apparent twin facts: for the most part, neither the public abroad nor the public in America appears to buy in to the educated arguments of the intellectuals who are working overtime like Friedman or the FDD to persuade them of the necessity of invading Iraq. Perhaps humanity's common sense may escape the traps set to ensnare them by an elite at the service of power.

Let us consider first the war of ideas as it is fought in the Middle East. Peoples with histories as old, proud, and experienced with foreign invasions as those of this region most certainly did not view the arrival of hundreds of thousands of American and coalition troops in Iraq as coming for other than self-interested reasons. To be sure, there were Arabs, Iranians, and Turks (to which we might add minority populations like Kurds and Berbers) who surely did hope to constitute liberal democratic governments in their lands in keeping with their national aspirations for progressive change. They understood well enough that theocratic or secular totalitarians were their enemies. For instance, the United Nations' *Arab Human Development Report* (its third edition appeared in 2005) made it clear that an important group of Arab intellectuals supported liberalizing change.[11] However, the idea that the liberation of Arabs was basically what prompted American imperialism was more difficult to believe. Oil might be one factor, Israel another. What seemed most apparent was that the United States, like imperial powers as old as history, was seeking to augment its power position over international affairs generally by establishing a commanding position for itself in the Middle East. If it succeeded, its conquest would complement its already predominant position in Europe, Northeast Asia, and the Western hemisphere and so give it undisputed domain over all of world affairs. As for democracy—well, that is a separate question.

What I surmise to be the thinking of mainstream Arab opinion appears to be corroborated by work done by professor Shibley Telhami of the University of Maryland and the Brookings Institution. In a series of three respected polls conducted over a number of years in six Arab countries, Telhami has shown that it is American and Israeli *policies* that anger the great majority of Arab peoples, *not* Western values and ways. Accordingly, majority Arab opinion did not oppose democracy so much as it feared American self-aggrandizement. Where Al-Qaeda was supported, only a small minority endorsed its theocratic teachings and its terrorist practices. What was most admired was that Al-Qaeda confronted the United States.[12]

The Pew Research Center for the People and the Press has also polled the Arab world. Its findings tend to corroborate Telhami's. Arabs for the most part do not have a hostile attitude toward democracy, to the extent they genuinely understand what such a system of politics implies, and they fear extremists in their midst. However, they most certainly distrust deeply the United States, seeing its policies as self-aggrandizing, not aiding local peoples.[13]

What, then, of the war of ideas at home? The American public may have been genuinely persuaded that its government was acting in the country's self-defense when it began military operations against Afghanistan, then Iraq. But a majority has never signed on to the arguments about democracy promotion in the Muslim world for the sake of national security, whatever the arguments that encouraged them to do so thanks to the war of ideas beginning in 2002.

Tracing public opinion polls from 1976 through 1996, professor Ole R. Holsti found democracy promotion abroad to be a low priority among Americans of all political persuasions. Even among those who defined themselves as "very liberal," only 25 percent in 1996 thought this end was "a very important foreign policy goal." Only 10 percent of those questioned felt that "the U.S. should not hesitate to intrude upon the domestic affairs of other countries in order to establish and preserve a more democratic world order."[14]

The attack of 9/11 and the invasion of Iraq only slightly altered these figures. In August 2004, the Pew Research Center released a public opinion poll that had asked respondents to rank a list of 19 foreign policy "top priorities." Human rights promotion came in sixteenth, democracy promotion eighteenth. A poll released by the Chicago Council on Global Affairs in September 2005 asked whether respondents favored "promoting democracy by military force," and found that 35 percent did while 55 percent did not. The experience of trying to democratize Iraq made 72 percent of respondents less positive about using military force in the future to promote democracy, and only 26 percent agreed that "when there are more democracies, the world is a safer place" (versus 68 percent who disagreed). Nevertheless, the CCGA did find that if the role of military force were dropped and the priority of democracy promotion reduced from being "very important" to "somewhat important" as a goal, then public support increased. Only 19 percent were prepared to disregard democratization altogether as a priority for the country's foreign policy.[15] Finally, in July 2006, a New York Times/CBS poll found that 59 percent of the public "did not believe the United States should take the lead in solving international conflicts in general," while 31 percent said it should. Three-fourths of Republicans supported the Iraq War, three-fourths of Democrats did not, with Independents effectively split.

As this evidence suggests, Americans tend to be a "show me" people. Public opinion before 2001 did not for the most part see democracy promotion as important to the country's national security, nor did the public convert to this notion en masse after 9/11. Americans are not highly ideological. What this means is that they are seldom interested in large-scale intellectual constructions of the logic of history that contain in them specific policy recommendations based on deductions from theories that are holistic or "big picture." Americans tend to be pragmatic problem solvers reasoning inductively from common sense observations backed up by proof close at hand. In this, the American public is like most other peoples worldwide who have a free press—too smart to be long deceived by a manipulative war of ideas.

In a word, the elaborate ideological justifications the intellectual mandarins set forth for democracy promotion, then put into simpler sloganeering by the spin masters, do not suit the temperament of the American people or people in the Middle East. It is not the value of liberal democracy that is put in question so much as the motives of the Bush administration. The progressive ends sought are either discounted as rationalizations for other ambitions or are seen as unrealistic in the context of the conquest of a leading country in the Arab world. Once again, common sense has it right.

But common sense is not enough. What is called for is an examination of the ideas themselves that not only justified this war but contributed as well to the optimistic forecast it could be won on grounds Washington specified. One could blame what increasingly came to be seen as a fiasco of historic proportions on poor Secretary Rumsfeld and the Pentagon's botched conduct of the invasion if one wished. But the sentiment grew stronger that more than this was at the basis of this calamity, that the mission itself was failing in good measure by virtue of its first premises—the ideology that had given it birth.

The Liberal Internationalist Pathology

The purpose of this book is to get at these first premises by laying out the reasoning behind the Bush administration's adoption of democracy promotion as a solution to America's security dilemma in the Middle East. The book thus revolves around the analysis of an ideology, one usually called "Wilsonianism" or "liberal internationalism." Elements of what can be called "progressive imperialism" can be traced back to the American Revolution. Features of the national culture that elevate the importance of the democratic creed reinforce such a worldview. So, too, do Christian evangelical groups with their insistence on moral purpose in the country's foreign policy and their emphasis on missionary activities create a mind-set favorable to evangelizing democracy as well.

However, it was only in the twentieth century that liberal internationalism became more formally organized as a coherent framework for pursuing the national interest. Woodrow Wilson was the first American president to put together in a single package the importance to this country of democracy for others (hence the term "Wilsonianism" as synonymous with liberal internationalism). During the Cold War, liberal internationalism played a powerful role in sustaining the West in containing the Soviet Union. Yet it was only in the 1990s that this approach to world affairs can genuinely be called an *ideology*. Now for the first time, American nationalism could be expressed as a liberal internationalist worldview based on a complex reading of history, resting on a variety of empirical proofs offered by American social scientists, one even extolled by prominent philosophers, all of which gave the United States a purposeful mission to exercise in world affairs.

Neither the administration of George H. W. Bush nor that of Bill Clinton adopted what could now be called liberal internationalist imperialism as the fulcrum of its foreign policy, however. Although both presidents made efforts to promote human rights and democracy abroad, Bush senior made the famous remark that he did not have "the vision thing." Clinton's hallmark was a prudent reserve that took each issue on its own merits and looked for preexisting public support.

George W. Bush, by contrast, was possessed of a compulsion to show that leadership mattered and that he was a leader. He and his foreign policy team were also driven to show that, unlike Clinton, they knew that America had the power to make a long-term difference in world affairs. The attack of 9/11 was thus their invitation to act, to show by deeds, and not by words alone, what greatness meant.

Might a Republican-dominated Congress have endorsed something like the Bush Doctrine without 9/11? Surely the administration was already planning something like an invasion of Iraq before this historic date. Yet without such terrorist aggression, it is unlikely that the American Congress and public could have been convinced to take on a mission as practically ambitious and ideologically grandiose as the Bush Doctrine presented for the country to pursue. But under the pressure of this traumatic attack, normal restraints were put aside. The nation was ready to march and liberal internationalist ideology directed the campaign. A sentiment mixing self defense with a will to power drove American policy, all of it to be cloaked in a self-righteous and self-assured crusade that liberal internationalism as an ideology was by now quite able to provide. The result was "grand strategy" on a scale hitherto unknown to the American tradition.

Like all such vainglorious ambitions, it was foredoomed to failure. Had it not been blocked in Iraq, it might have been at its next stop (Damascus), or at the stop thereafter (Tehran or Riyadh). Certainly the idea of many neoconservatives that China and Russia could be democratized by an American crusade staggers the imagination. America simply did not have the power, or the appeal, to achieve what it wanted. Meanwhile, its high-energy update of liberal internationalism encapsulated in the Bush Doctrine generated both a fear and a hope that were the stuff of the "fog of war" itself. The fear was of the enemy, the hope for a better tomorrow. The character of each was badly misunderstood, which only compounded the problem of retreat.

The danger of the liberal internationalist worldview is far from ended. Ideologies have a way of blocking an accurate perception of reality, of maintaining individuals and groups on a self-defeating course that more pragmatic people would move to abandon. And so it may come to be with a secular creed like the Bush Doctrine that has deep undertones of religion to it. Many Christians see Armageddon, it must be recalled, as a period of creative destruction, only after which can a golden age be born. Right-wing Zionists see the continuation of the war and its expansion in July 2006 by an Israeli invasion of Lebanon in response to Hezbollah attacks as vital to an Israel that they see as under siege. Some liberal fundamentalists are no less committed to seeing this war through, however bitter the struggle may be. Even some realists conclude that, although embarking on the war was a mistake, now that Iraq has been conquered, the United States can only go forward. The war of ideas is thus far from over.

There is drama in the study of ideas when they are possessed of momentous human consequence. What we shall review here was the thinking that moved a mighty nation at the height of its power to throw itself in to the kind of crusade it would previously have avoided. Here is a "grand design" made-in-America if ever one was. Here is the drama of arrogance, of hubris, in a word of pride that leads to its own undoing. Here is a tragedy, one that can be spelled out by names, dates, and events, but whose essence nonetheless lies in the manner that a group of intellectuals, armed with what they believed were powerful ideas, set out to change history and so better the world. In their downfall lies a lesson for all who think about world affairs. Our task is to learn from their misguided thinking, and from a consideration of the primitive passions that surrounded it, what we may of America's role in world affairs.

The definition of megalomania well suits the Bush Doctrine. Its delusion of omnipotence rested on its belief that America enjoyed both military primacy and a blueprint for world order thanks to its global experiences fostering "free market democracies." As a consequence, the United States could remake foreign countries—their state institutions, economic and civil orders, and basic cultural arrangements—so as to engender a peaceful international order under American control, a terror-free tomorrow. And because a brutal war was launched on the terms of this doctrine, a conflict that has benefited no one involved in it and is far from ended, the stated grounds for war have shown themselves to be pathological as well.

The greatest of the American theologians who has addressed the issues of world affairs remains Reinhold Niebuhr. In *Beyond Tragedy*, Niebuhr reflected on the wide canvas of human history and asserted the ruin to which pride can bring us all: "man is constantly tempted to forget the finiteness of his cultures and civilization and to pretend a finality for them which they do not have. Every civilization and every culture is thus a Tower of Babel."

> The pretensions of human cultures and civilizations are the natural consequence of a profound and eradicable difficulty in all human spirituality.... This pride is at least one aspect of what Christian orthodoxy means by "original sin".... [T]he tragic self-destruction of civilizations and cultures, records of which abound in the annals of human history, are partially caused by this very defect.
>
> One of the most pathetic aspects of human history is that every civilization expresses itself most pretentiously, compounds its partial and universal values most convincingly, and thus claims immortality for its finite existence at the very moment when the decay which leads to death has already begun.[16]

The Bush Doctrine and the Bid for World Supremacy

We are led by events and common sense to one conclusion: The survival of liberty in our land increasingly depends on the success of liberty in other lands. The best hope for peace in our world is the expansion of freedom in all the world... So it is the policy of the United States to seek and support the growth of democratic movements and institutions in every nation and culture, with the ultimate goal of ending tyranny in our world.

President George W. Bush, Second Inaugural
Address, January 20, 2005

Cromwell, I charge thee, fling away ambition: By that sin fell the angels.

Shakespeare, *Henry VIII* (3.2)

Presidential doctrines define the parameters of national security. Doctrines may lay out the framework for American policy toward specific regions of the world or toward international events in general. What they have in common is that they are declarations of presidential purpose that stake out the grounds potentially for making war.

Over the years, many of these doctrines have proved insubstantial. The Eisenhower, Johnson, Nixon, or Carter Doctrines are cases in point. By contrast, the Reagan Doctrine had genuine importance, but only for a limited period. Yet other doctrines have proved to be significant statements of America's place in the world. If the greatest of these is surely Washington's Farewell Address of 1796—an enduring formulation of this country's proper role in world affairs that weighed on our country's policy making through World War I, and that still has important lessons to be heeded today—one might also consider the Monroe Doctrine (1823), which asserted American primacy in the Western hemisphere, and the Truman Doctrine (1947), which defined "containment" as the framework for American policy in the Cold War. Although they were not called "doctrines," we should also place in this category Wilson's Fourteen Points (1918), which laid out American grand strategy after World War I, and FDR's Atlantic Charter and Declaration on Liberated Europe (1941, 1945), which stated American policies for international order after World War II, as milestones in the assertion of America's place in world politics.[1]

The origins of the Iraq War similarly lie in a landmark foreign policy declaration, the Bush Doctrine, a presidential proclamation of purpose likely to rank in historical significance with any of its predecessors save the Farewell Address. With it, President George W. Bush set out a framework for American conduct in security terms in world affairs in a series of statements beginning in June 2002 in his commencement address at West Point and culminating in the publication of the National Security Strategy (NSS) of the United States in September 17, 2002. Three and a half years later, in the National Security Strategy of March 2006, President Bush reconfirmed his policy orientation. In terms of originality and boldness, what was quickly known as the Bush Doctrine took its place with the hallmark declarations of purpose in the American foreign policy tradition, a point that needs to be insisted upon against those who would label it as no more than updated Wilsonianism. The fact that the Bush Doctrine, unlike its illustrious predecessors such as the Monroe or Truman Doctrines, was manifestly an exaggerated statement of American power and purpose that led to a calamitous policy outcome with the Iraq War, makes it no less significant in the annals of this country's engagements in world affairs, no less likely to be an object of analysis and debate for generations to come.

By the formulations of this doctrine, the United States declared its dominance of the full spectrum of leading issues in world affairs. In military terms, Washington announced its primacy would be maintained against all comers. Protected by an unrivalled security umbrella, America would foster its blueprint for a world order, one composed of democratic states with open market economic systems, an order whose prospect was that of a golden age of global harmony.

In order to obtain its ends, the United States would work collaboratively where it could, but it was prepared to act with armed force unilaterally and preemptively if a threat to the American peace appeared genuine. In the aftermath of battle, America would reincorporate that part of the world recalcitrant to its model for proper behavior back into the international system on the basis of restructuring it as a market democracy.

The result of this exercise of American preeminence, so far as its authors were concerned, would be not only to enhance this country's national security but also to provide to the world community in general the promise of a future of peace, prosperity, and freedom. Absent the deliberate exercise of this power to secure these ends, the Bush administration warned that global anarchy would intensify. The stark choice was between a "benevolent" American hegemony over the international system, with imperialism against those who thwarted America's grand design, or chaos and the march of the barbarians.

Given these unprecedented suppositions so far as the traditions of American foreign policy were concerned (although certainly not unprecedented in the history of the world's empires), to understand the Iraq War it is critical to understand the logic of the Bush Doctrine. Those closest to the making of this doctrine understood the doctrine in exactly such terms. Thus, the editors of the neoconservative publication *Commentary* introduced a "Symposium" of the opinions of 36 well-known students of world affairs assessing the doctrine in November 2005 by calling it a "sweeping redirection of policy," "a historically stunning move" that quite obviously had led to the invasion of Iraq and that held more promise waiting to be realized.[2]

These observers were correct. To be sure, aspects of the Bush Doctrine echoed earlier pronouncements in the American foreign policy tradition, especially when links are pointed out between it and the worldview of Woodrow Wilson, who left the presidency in 1921, 80 years before Bush took office. Yet, after the Wilsonian credentials of the doctrine are acknowledged, the position staked out by the Bush White House in 2002 was without easy historical precedent. Never before had the United States enjoyed a position as the sole undisputed superpower, in both military and economic terms, allowing it to declare its predominance over the entire international system. Nor had an American administration ever affirmed so confidently its faith in a master plan for domestic and international order as it did with its invocation of open markets and democratic government worldwide for the sake of freedom and prosperity. If the term "grand strategy" means anything when speaking of a policy with respect to world affairs, then the Bush Doctrine most surely qualifies for membership in this league.

Here was what I would call a pact with the Devil: the proud assertion that this country had a formula it was prepared to implement by military force for world freedom, prosperity, and peace. Washington was ready to throw the iron dice, mindless of the powerful riptides of history that had destroyed so many examples of overweening self-confidence before it. Perhaps the Bush administration had not reached the dimension of megalomania that moved Philip II of Spain to announce as his motto: "the world is not enough." Yet the hubris of Washington's stance in world affairs had never been so pronounced as in the statements and actions of the team that took office in January 2001. Assured of America's paramount military position, its leaders would ultimately reveal the country's actual weakness and make it more vulnerable. Confident in what they immodestly called their "moral clarity," they would soon give evidence of their moral arrogance at the cost of hundreds of thousands of deaths and hundreds of billions of dollars. Committed to bending history to their will so as to give proof to the transforming power of courage and conviction in human affairs, they instead gave witness once again, should it be needed, of the undying danger of vainglorious pride.

The Bush Doctrine's Two Pillars: Power and Purpose

Let us look more closely at the Bush Doctrine to appreciate in detail the grand scope of its design. While the doctrine extolled the power position the United States enjoyed by virtue of its military preeminence in world affairs, it had a sense of purpose as well, a conviction that its blueprint of market economies and democratic governments worldwide could provide stability both for domestic and international affairs.

The Republicans who took office in 2001 were adamant that the preceding decade had been precious time lost because of American leaders' failure of vision and courage. Policy in Washington with respect to world affairs had been *piecemeal, reactive,* and *short term.* America and the world needed policy to be *comprehensive, proactive,* and *long term.* As the authors of the Bush Doctrine recognized, purpose without power was impotent, while power without purpose was ephemeral. When properly combined, however, power and purpose on a scale such as America enjoyed together could monumentally swing the course of human events.

The Pillar of Power

The military pillar of the Bush Doctrine asserted that it was in the collective interest of world peace that American primacy be maintained. If the United States could persuade the world's states that any effort to match American power was preordained to failure—that this country's strength was "beyond challenge," as Washington repeatedly put it in 2002—then regional conflicts might be minimized and total world military expenditures decreased. Even though American military spending would have to rise, maintaining primacy was far cheaper than fighting a foreign war would be.[3]

In President Bush's words at the United States Military Academy at West Point on June 1, 2002, "Competition between great nations is inevitable, but armed conflict in our world is not...America has, and intends to keep, military strength beyond challenge, thereby making the destabilizing arms races of other eras pointless, and limiting rivalries to trade and other pursuits of peace."[4] Three months later in the NSS, the president reaffirmed "the essential role of American military strength":

> We must build and maintain our defenses beyond challenge.... The United States must and will maintain the capability to defeat any attempt by an enemy—whether a state or non-state actor—to impose its will on the United States, our allies, or our friends. We will maintain the forces sufficient...to dissuade potential adversaries from pursuing a military build-up in hopes of surpassing, or equaling, the power of the United States.

Then-National Security Advisor Condoleezza Rice expressed her endorsement of the approach on October 1, 2002:

> The United States will build and maintain twenty-first century military forces that are beyond challenge. We will seek to dissuade any potential adversary from pursuing a military build-up in the hope of surpassing, or equaling, the power of the United States...surely clarity is a virtue here. Dissuading military competition can prevent potential conflict and costly global arms races.... What none of us should want is the emergence of a militarily powerful adversary who does not share our common values.

Contrary to popularly held notions, these bold words of 2002 were not born of the attack of 9/11, but of concepts formulated by neoconservative political activists that handily predate it. For the foreign policy team that came into office in 2001, "fecklessness" and "dithering" were words routinely used to describe the Clinton years, a period when Washington seemed "embarrassed" by its relative power position and quite unsure of how to convert its "unipolar moment" into the sustained political advantage of a unipolar epoch.[5] They leveled much the same charge at the presidency of George H. W. Bush. With the inauguration of George W. Bush on January 20, 2001, all this would change.

The template for national security that the new team brought with them into office had been forged over the preceding decade. Following the instructions in late 1991 of the then-Secretary of Defense (later Vice President) Richard Cheney, the then-Under Secretary of Defense for Policy (later Deputy Secretary of Defense) Paul Wolfowitz had drawn up briefing points on what American defense strategy should look like to be used as a basis for the Defense Department's biannual budgetary report eventually to be submitted to Congress. Wolfowitz in turn delegated the job of writing a final report on the basis of his briefing paper to I. Lewis Libby (who from 2001 to late 2005 was chief of staff to Vice President Cheney) and Zalmay Khalilzad (who was appointed to a senior position in the National Security Council in 2001 before being named ambassador to Afghanistan in 2003 and ambassador to Iraq in 2005).[6] The product of their labors came to be known as the Defense Policy Guidance (DPG) of 1992.

The first point of the DPG of 1992 asserted, in terms obviously related to the Bush Doctrine of a decade later, that the United States should consider itself preeminent militarily in world affairs and work to establish a general recognition that "world order is ultimately backed by the U.S." Woe to those who would challenge America's position:

> Our first objective is to prevent the re-emergence of a new rival...the U.S. must show the leadership necessary to establish and protect a new order that holds the promise of convincing potential competitors that they need not aspire to a greater role or pursue a more aggressive posture to protect their legitimate interests...we must maintain the mechanisms for deterring potential competitors from even aspiring to a larger regional or global role.

The document avoided any mention of working collectively with other states through the United Nations (UN) or the North Atlantic Treaty Organization (NATO). Instead, the DPG indicated the need for the unilateralism that we find a decade later in the Bush Doctrine: "we should expect future coalitions to be ad hoc assemblies, often not lasting beyond the crisis being confronted and in many cases carrying only general agreement over the objectives to be accomplished." Where what would later be called "coalitions of the willing" were impossible to assemble, "the United States should be postured to act independently when collective action cannot be orchestrated." In addition to opening the door to unilateral action, the DPG also speculated that preemption could be called for in situations where weapons of mass destruction existed. Not only did the document insist on the need to maintain preeminence with respect to Russia and China, but any European ambition to act independently of Washington was soundly rejected. So far as NATO was concerned, while it "continues to provide the indispensable foundation for a stable security environment in Europe...we must seek to prevent the emergence of European-only security arrangements which would undermine NATO, particularly the alliance's integrated command structure."[7]

When the DPG was leaked in March 1992 there was an outcry from many in Washington that it exaggerated the power at America's disposal and was too aggressive for an era that wanted to take shelter in the "peace dividend" with the Cold War over. Although the critics implicitly included President Bush senior and his National Security Advisor Brent Scowcroft, who never expressly endorsed it, Secretary of Defense Cheney nonetheless reworked the report and published it under his name in January 1993, just days before Bill Clinton was sworn in as president.

Cheney's apparent purpose was to leave for posterity a finalized, public version of the DPG, which he renamed "Defense Strategy for the 1990s: The Regional Defense Strategy" (DS). Once again the "zone of peace" created and led by the United States was invoked, but this time with more emphasis on playing the democratic against the non-democratic world. While Cheney expressed concern that issues like nuclear proliferation might tempt American allies such as Germany and Japan to "renationalize" their security politics should the U.S. umbrella seem uncertain, he repeatedly singled out the "non-democratic powers" as the likely source of future problems.

As in the DPG of 1992, so the DS of 1993 anticipated no threats of a global nature from a power that could possibly threaten the United States. Instead problems would be, as the subtitle of the report indicated, regional. Except for sub-Saharan Africa and South Asia, all other areas of the world were considered of vital importance to the United States for one reason or another. Because the best defense is a good offense, "precluding regional threats and challenges can strengthen the underpinnings of a peaceful democratic order in which nations are able to pursue their legitimate interests without fear of military domination...we must not stand back and allow a new global threat to emerge or leave a vacuum in a region critical to our interests." And because some of these regional issues might not seem vital to our closest democratic allies, "We will, therefore, not ignore the need to be prepared to protect our critical interests and honor our commitments with only limited additional help, or even alone, if necessary."[8]

The neoconservative branch of the Republican Party kept alive the idea of the importance of American primacy in security matters as it was expressed in the DPG and the DS during the Clinton years. Through *The Weekly Standard*, founded in 1995, and the Project for the New American Century (PNAC), founded in 1997—both handsomely backed up by, among others, the conservative think tank, the American Enterprise Institute—William Kristol and Robert Kagan were particularly instrumental in articulating ideas that were faithful to this design of 1992–1993.

In the summer 1996 issue of *Foreign Affairs,* Kristol and Kagan published their most widely read piece on the need to maintain American primacy, a key statement still today of the intellectual origins of the Bush Doctrine.[9] Like Reagan, whose tradition they invoked, Kristol and Kagan "refused to accept the limits on American power imposed by the domestic political realities that others assumed were fixed.... Having defeated the 'evil empire' the United States enjoys strategic and ideological predominance. The first objective of U.S. foreign policy should be to preserve and enhance that predominance." Focusing largely on defense issues, Kristol and Kagan concluded, "American hegemony is the only reliable defense against a breakdown of peace and international order. The appropriate goal of American foreign policy, therefore, is to preserve that hegemony as far into the future as possible." What was their principal worry? Americans might "absentmindedly dismantle the material and spiritual foundations on which their national well-being has been based...the main threat the United States faces now and in the future is its own weakness."

In 2000, Kristol and Kagan published what they referred to as an update of their influential 1996 essay in a volume they edited entitled *Present Dangers: Crisis and Opportunity in American Foreign and Defense Policy.* In their introductory chapter, the editors repeated the charge that the leading present danger "is one of declining military strength, flagging will and confusion about our role in the world. It is a danger, to be sure, of our own devising." The authors dismissed the years of the previous Bush and Clinton administrations as "a squandered decade," a "holiday from history," the "lost decade," where instead of respecting the obligation after the Cold War "to prolong this extraordinary moment...preserving and reinforcing America's benevolent global hegemony" the United States had failed to come up with a grand design for world order. They lamented the lost opportunities of the 1990s when "a passive worldview encouraged American leaders to ignore troubling developments which eventually metastasized into full-blown threats to American security." Should the United States step up to the plate, such an undertaking would now involve augmenting military spending (an increase of about 25 percent was indicated). At the same time, PNAC brought out a companion analysis on America's military needs entitled "Rebuilding America's Defenses," specifically linking its analysis back to the Defense Department documents of 1992–1993.[10]

Given this established mode of thought, the neoconservative response to the attack of 9/11 fit like a glove the hand of the American mood. Accordingly, American weakness had provoked the attack. The welcome, if overdue, assertion of American strength would prove the basis of a new alignment of international relations that should have been undertaken years before.

Some compared the American power position after the Cold War to Britain's during the Pax Britannica only to maintain that America's relative sway was greater.[11] Others preferred comparisons with the Roman empire. The best known of the pundits to conceptualize America's position was the neoconservative Charles Krauthammer with his concept of the unipolar epoch. As late as 2004, whatever the evidence accumulating from Iraq, Krauthammer was still reaffirming that with the death of the Soviet Union "something new was born, something utterly new—a unipolar world dominated by a single superpower unchecked by any rival and with decisive reach in every corner of the globe. This is a staggering new development in history, not seen since the fall of Rome."[12]

Many echoed Krauthammer's comparisons, but no one doing so with intellectual stature was quite so effusive as senior Yale University historian Paul Kennedy. After having first been celebrated for his 1987 book *The Rise and Fall of the Great Powers* with the argument that "overstretch" had been the ruin of most empires and threatened to be that of the United States, Kennedy had been lambasted as a "declinist" for failing to foresee the collapse of the Soviet Union and so to anticipate the moment when American power would be fully revealed in all its splendor.[13] No longer a declinist, Kennedy in 2002 in effect recanted his earlier position and now weighed in as a leading academic expert on world history to describe America's international power position in terms that outdid even Krauthammer.

Writing in the *Financial Times* in 2002, Kennedy compared the extent of American military power relative to that of other states and concluded:

> Nothing has ever existed like this disparity of power, nothing.... The Pax Britannica was run on the cheap. Britain's army was much smaller than European armies and even the Royal Navy was equal only to the next two navies—right now all the other navies in the world combined could not dent American maritime supremacy. Charlemagne's empire was merely western European in its reach. The Roman empire stretched father afield, but there was another great empire in Persia, and a larger one in China. There is, therefore, no comparison.[14]

Among the reasons to think that America's moment of world supremacy might endure was its economic base, which Kennedy declared meant keeping preponderant military primacy was so inexpensive that "being the world's single superpower on the cheap is astonishing." He then listed such American achievements as garnering a disproportionate number of Nobel prizes thanks to the glory of our research universities ("that is leaving everyone else—the Sorbonne, Tokyo, Munich, Oxford, Cambridge in the dust, especially in the experimental sciences"), cited the vigor of our banks, our industry, and our cultural power from the English language to media and youth culture; and concluded that, as with America's relative military position, on these other chessboards too "the same lopsided picture would emerge...there is no point in the Europeans or Chinese wringing their hands."

The relationship between this analysis of U.S. power and the Bush Doctrine was abundantly apparent. Kennedy closed referring to "the historical irony that the republic whose first leader cautioned against entangling alliance and distraction is now, a quarter way into its third century, the world's policeman."

These confident assertions notwithstanding, the Bush Doctrine was much more than simply arrogant boasting about America's military dominance in world affairs. To be sure, America's relative power position was indeed a comfort, but official Washington in 2001 was aware that power without purpose could simply be reactive to historical events, not formative. What was obviously required was a political complement to the raw muscle at America's disposal. America had to be more than simply "the world's policeman." The need was for an agenda for structuring world order such that the unipolar epoch could be maintained after the eventual decline of this country's military position thanks to the structural changes introduced into the world system during America's moment of unquestioned paramountcy.

The Pillar of Purpose

Although the Pentagon statements of 1992–1993 that were reviewed above focused essentially on American military planning, they also expressed the Wilsonian (or Reaganite) notion that the expansion of a liberal internationalist framework for world order would be in keeping with national security concerns. Democracy and open markets would ensure freedom, prosperity, and peace. Hence, we find formulated a decade prior to the Bush Doctrine its other pillar, its ambition to restructure world affairs in accordance with a master plan calling for the expansion of "free market democracies."

Thus, in its opening section, the DPG of 1992 spoke of how "the integration of Germany and Japan into a U.S.-led system of collective security and the creation of a democratic 'zone of peace'" contributed handily to "the collapse of the Soviet Union, the disintegration of the internal as well as the external empire, and the discrediting of communism as an ideology with global pretensions and influence." In the DS, which appeared under the name of Defense Secretary Cheney in January 1993, the message was reaffirmed:

> Our alliances, built during the struggle of containment, are one of the great sources of our strength in this new era. They represent a democratic "zone of peace," a community of democratic nations bound together by a web of political, economic, and security ties.... Together with our allies, we must preclude hostile non-democratic powers from dominating regions critical to our interests.... Precluding regional threats and challenges can strengthen the underpinnings of a peaceful democratic order in which nations are able to pursue their legitimate interests without fear of military domination.... We can secure and extend the remarkable democratic "zone of peace" that we and our allies now enjoy, preclude threats, and guard our national interests.[15]

Although the Soviet Union was no more, the DPG identified terrorism, drug trafficking, access to vital raw materials (primarily from the Persian Gulf), and the proliferation of weapons of mass destruction as remaining challenges of high-profile importance. It followed logically that, just as this country should aim in areas recently freed from Soviet domination to promote open market economies and liberal democratic states, so too in order to consolidate American regional interests elsewhere Washington should "address sources of regional conflict and instability in such a way as to promote increasing respect for international law, limit international violence, and encourage the spread of democratic forms of government and open economic systems." The end to be sought, as we might expect, was not military domination for its own sake but to serve "our fundamental belief in democracy and human rights."

So the American hegemonic sphere could be expanded. With communism dead, "Our goal should be to bring a democratic Russia and the other new democracies into the defense community of democratic nations so that they can become a force for peace, democracy, and freedom not only in Europe but also in other critical regions of the world."

The political purpose to be served by American muscle could not be reactive, short term, or piecemeal as it had been during the presidencies of Bush senior and Clinton. America had a window of opportunity to act more concretely to provide stability. Simply to respond as problems arose, to settle them each in their own terms without thought for an overarching architecture of order, was not acceptable. What the United States needed was a *grand strategy* that was proactive, long term, and comprehensive, a political formulation for world order behind which Washington could put America's formidable military muscle. Here were the certainties fervently expressed in the early 1990s by the men whose thinking became the basis of the Bush Doctrine in 2002.

Just as the insistence on American military primacy announced in 1992–1993 was kept alive by the neoconservatives during the Clinton years, so too they insisted on the promotion of market democracies and active campaigns against rogue states. In Kristol and Kagan's 1996 *Foreign Affairs* article (referenced above), China and Iraq came in for particular attention, but Russia, Serbia, Iran, Cuba, and North Korea drew mention as well. And in *Present Dangers* in 2000 the same authors concluded that "even an ally such as France" may not be above trying to thwart "a prolonged period of American dominance."

Kristol and Kagan's vision in 1996 was that the United States would preside over what they entitled a "benevolent hegemony," although they expected some to find this "either hubristic or morally suspect." Military primacy was thus not an end in itself but should be dedicated to the role of "actively promoting American principles of governance abroad—democracy, free markets, respect for liberty." Hence, "actively pursuing policies—in Iran, Cuba, or China, for instance—ultimately intended to bring about a change of regime" was called for as "the policy of putting pressure on authoritarian and totalitarian regimes [has been shown to have] had practical aims and, in the end, delivered strategic benefits."

Accordingly, Kristol and Kagan in their 1996 essay looked forward to a Washington that would issue the equivalent of the Truman-era NSC-68, which called for "an all-out effort to meet the Soviet challenge that included a full-scale ideological confrontation and massive increases in defense spending." A major benefit would be that "an elevated patriotism" could serve the contemporary task of "preparing and inspiring the nation to embrace the role of global leadership... The re-moralization of America at home ultimately requires the re-moralization of American foreign policy."

> Because America has the capacity to contain or destroy many of the world's monsters, most of which can be found without much searching, and because the responsibility for the peace and security of the international order rests so heavily on America's shoulders, a policy of sitting atop a hill and leading by example becomes in practice a policy of cowardice and dishonor.

In the book they edited in 2000, Kristol and Kagan made the vision more explicit:

> when it comes to dealing with tyrannical regimes, especially those with the power to do us or our allies harm, the United States should seek not coexistence but transformation...how utopian is it to imagine a change of regime in a place like Iraq? How utopian is it to work for the fall of the Communist Party oligarchy in China.... With democratic change sweeping the world at an unprecedented rate over these past thirty years, is it "realistic" to insist that no further victories can be won?

As we can see from this review of neoconservative thinking in the decade before 9/11, the two pillars of the Bush Doctrine—the primacy of American power and the promise of its purpose of peace—were very much in place prior to the attacks, prior to the election of George W. Bush as president, indeed prior to the neoconservatives even deciding whom to support in the 2000 election. With the election and the attack, with a nation asking itself what to do aside from military action to answer to the threat to its security, their vision was waiting to be adopted.

And adopted it was. As it is phrased in the opening words of the basic text that most clearly lays out the Bush Doctrine, the NSS of September 2002:

> The great struggles of the twentieth century between liberty and totalitarianism ended with a decisive victory for the forces of freedom—and a single sustainable model for national success: freedom, democracy, and free enterprise.... We seek instead to create a balance of power that favors human freedom.... We will defend the peace by fighting terrorists and tyrants.... We will extend the peace by encouraging free and open societies on every continent.

Even more forcefully, in his Second Inaugural Address of January 20, 2005, the president announced that America had lit the "untamed fire of freedom" that "warms those that feel its power [but] burns those who fight its progress." As he declared in widely cited phrases that immediately summoned up Wilson's pledge on the eve of America's entry into World War I nearly ninety years earlier to work for a world order that made future wars impossible:

> We are led by events and common sense to one conclusion: The survival of liberty in our land increasingly depends on the success of liberty in other lands. The best hope for peace in our world is the expansion of freedom in all the world.... So it is the policy of the United States to seek and support the growth of democratic movements and institutions in every nation and culture, with the ultimate goal of ending tyranny in our world.

The ideological basis of the doctrine was the conviction that the promotion of what was repeatedly called "free market democracies" the world around would bring the peace we all desire. The concept of American order might take root of its own accord—as one could see in Central Europe after the fall of the Iron Curtain, for example—as the benefits of liberty and prosperity became increasingly obvious. However, should the American Peace be resisted by authoritarian or despotic elites in other parts of the world, especially should these reactionary forces mount an attack on the Pax Americana, they would be subject to military defeat and "regime change" so as to bring the blessings of modern government and economic relations to people too long denied them.

In His Own Words: The President and His Doctrine

If the immediate architects of the Bush Doctrine were the neoconservatives, no one has better stated its meaning than the president himself. From June 2002 through November 2006, he was consistently on message as to what its terms meant in a way that showed he had well internalized his convictions as a liberal internationalist. To those unschooled in the rhetoric of liberal internationalism, Bush's speeches may seem little more than well-put, boilerplate appeals to American patriotism. To those with a sense of the history of American foreign policy and of the academic work on the relationship between democratic government and world peace, however, the speeches are a plausible rendering of a sophisticated ideology.

Speculations vary as to when George W. Bush incorporated liberal internationalist thinking into his own worldview. By June 2002 at the latest, the president was firmly on message that democracy promotion worldwide was not only an American value but an American interest. Yet at the beginning of 2000, Condoleezza Rice had made it clear in an article in *Foreign Affairs* that the United States would not be "the world's 911," that the American military was for war fighting, not walking children to school.[16] And in the presidential debate that October, candidate Bush stressed his reluctance to get involved in human rights promotion and nation-building abroad. "We know freedom is a powerful, powerful, powerful force, much bigger than the United States of America," Bush declared, "but I think the United States must be humble and must be proud and confident of our values, but humble in how we treat nations that are figuring out how to chart their own course." And again, "If we're an arrogant nation, they'll resent us. If we're a humble nation, but strong, they'll welcome us."[17]

While it is tempting to date the president's embrace of liberal internationalism to the months following the attack of 9/11, in fact his conversion may have come substantially earlier. Perhaps because talk of human rights, democracy promotion and nation building appealed more to the American left than to American conservatives, Bush had simply shaded his message in the October 2000 debate. Certainly by November 1999, when he made his first foreign policy speech as a candidate for the presidency, Bush was capable of being articulate on the subject.

Entitling his 1999 address "A Distinctly American Internationalism," Bush saluted the fall of Soviet communism but warned, "The Empire has passed, but evil remains." Invoking Natan Sharansky, Václav Havel, Lech Walesa, and Nelson Mandela, Bush declared, "The most powerful force in the world is not a weapon or a nation but a truth: that we are spiritual beings and that freedom is 'the soul's right to breathe'." Noting that by Freedom House's count there were a dozen democracies in the world at the time of Pearl Harbor but 120 at the end of the century, the Republican presidential candidate announced, "There is a direction in events, a current in our times.... Some have tried to pose a choice between American ideals and America interests—between who we are and how we act. But the choice is false. America, by decision and destiny, promotes political freedom—and gains the most when democracy advances." Hence the "distinctly American internationalism" would be: "Idealism without illusions. Confidence without conceit. Realism in the service of American ideals.... America's values are always part of America's agenda."

For our purposes it is not critical to know exactly when Bush became a liberal internationalist—whether in 1999 or after 9/11—nor who opened his mind to this approach of reflecting on world affairs. My own speculation is that he was in fact capable of being on-message by late 1999, and that the primary agent in his conversion to this mode of thinking was Paul Wolfowitz, who along with Condoleezza Rice was his chief foreign policy advisor by the fall of 1998, and a committed liberal internationalist for many years at this time.

Still, in the immediate aftermath of the attack of September 11, 2001, the president did not articulate a noticeably Wilsonian vision of future American policy. As an initial reaction to 9/11 and the question "why do they hate us," it was soon standard fare for many in the United States to reply as the president did on September 20, 2001 before a joint session of Congress: "They hate what they see right here in this chamber—a democratically elected government. Their leaders are self-appointed. They hate our freedoms—our freedom of religion, our freedom of speech, our freedom to vote and assemble and disagree with each other." And it was equally soon that many commentators here agreed that the aggressors were, as the president was among the first to put it, "the heirs of all the murderous ideologies of the 20th century. By sacrificing human life to serve their radical visions—by abandoning every value except the will to power—they follow in the path of fascism, and Nazism, and totalitarianism."

The force of these statements notwithstanding, they are not adequate to qualify President Bush as a liberal democratic internationalist in the Wilsonian tradition. To say that terrorists struck the United States because of its way of life was to invoke the idea of democracy and freedom as a rallying call for an armed patriotism. But it was a giant step indeed to go from this understandable reaction to 9/11 to the notion that the essential remedy for terrorism was to accompany the force of arms with which it would be answered with the promise of democratic government for Iraq and the "Broader Middle East" thereafter. America would go on the offensive not only militarily but ideologically as well. Iraq, and quite surely its neighbors, were to be restructured politically so that their governments were not only more progressive for their own peoples but so that they no longer troubled the peace of the world. When Bush eventually made these kinds of pronouncements, he had become a liberal in the way that term is conventionally used to describe a historical tradition and a recognized form of political discourse concerning world affairs.

The first clear public sign of Bush's embrace of liberalism, in the classical sense that this book uses the term, came in the assertion at West Point on June 1, 2002, that, "we will extend the peace by encouraging free and open societies on every continent." Here was the harbinger of an approach to world affairs that had clear precedent in the history of American foreign policy and that was increasingly recognized in the American academy as a legitimate assertion of the proper ends for American power in the world of the early twenty-first century. Affirming what was to be a leitmotif of the liberal internationalist argument, Bush declared that these values and the nation's essential interests were one, and that with our democratic allies the consensus was firmly established that peace depended on freedom.

Essentially, "regime type mattered." Unlike authoritarian governments, democracies were able to relate to each other peacefully so that for a new day to dawn in world affairs, democratic institutions needed to be spread worldwide. Hence, this country "will defend the peace that makes all progress possible," a democratic peace.

> The 20th century ended with a single surviving model of human progress, based on non-negotiable demands of human dignity, the rule of law, limits on the power of the state, respect for women and private property, and free speech and equal justice and religious tolerance.... When it comes to the common rights and needs of men and women, there is no clash of civilizations. The requirements of freedom apply fully to Africa and Latin America and the entire Islamic world. The peoples of the Islamic nations want and deserve the same freedoms and opportunities as people in every nation. And their governments should listen to their hopes.

The president's daring vision, first stated publicly in June 2002, was followed in a consistent manner thereafter. Never did he stray from the message that the goal of American policy in Iraq (and beyond) was to provide not only for a better life for Muslims living under cruel and corrupt dictatorships, but also for an end to the terrorist threat to the United States and the democratic world through the expansion of a form of government that could give the most evidence of an ability to serve the common good of working for a peaceful world order. Making democracy the guarantee of a country's good conduct in world affairs, promising peace as a result of regime change, and linking American security internationally to these domestic developments abroad—these have traditionally been the hallmarks of liberal internationalism. Woodrow Wilson speaking nearly a century earlier with respect to Latin America or Europe could not have said it better than George W. Bush phrased it with regard to the Middle East and world order more generally.

Over time the president expanded on his original message. On the first anniversary of 9/11, Bush welcomed what he thought he saw as signs that both Russia and China were liberalizing and declared that such "shared commitments bring true friendship and peace." He reaffirmed his grand design as "a just peace where repression, resentment and poverty are replaced with the hope of democracy, development, free markets and free trade." And he concluded his speech saluting "the new opportunities we have for progress. Today, humanity holds in its hands the opportunity to further freedom's triumph over all its age-old foes. The United States welcomes its responsibility to lead in this great mission."

Nowhere was the president's "great mission" for the country more strongly cast than in NSS 2002, passages from which were cited above. To be sure, the overwhelming superiority of the country's military force would be maintained without question. Yet as the liberal framework specified, ultimately in order to win the peace America so desired, the conversion of leading countries to democracy was called for. Accordingly, the NSS welcomed signs of liberalization in China and Russia as evidence that they were coming to share common values and interests with the United States. It saluted this country's fellow democracies as fitting partners in the struggle to globalize freedom. It warned the world's tyrants that "freedom is the non-negotiable demand of human dignity; the birthright of every person—in every civilization." It announced yet again that Washington "welcomes our responsibility to lead in this great mission," which was to "further freedom's triumph."

The direct application of this general framework to Iraq had already been intimated on September 14, 2002, when the president addressed the UN General Assembly. Citing the long list of serious human rights violations of the Saddam Hussein regime, Bush asked for an end to the "silent captivity" of the Iraqi people: "Liberty for the Iraqi people is a great moral cause and a great strategic goal. The people of Iraq deserve it; the security of all nations requires it. Free societies do not intimidate through cruelty and conquest, and open societies do not threaten the world with mass murder.... The people of Iraq can shake off their captivity. They can one day join a democratic Afghanistan and a democratic Palestine, inspiring reforms throughout the Muslim world." Here Bush clearly offered an interlinked promise: that the region could be democratized for the betterment of the Iraqi people, and that with democracy in the Middle East the zone of peace internationally would be expanded ultimately for the well-being of America too. As he later eloquently phrased it on February 21, 2005, "the advance of freedom within nations will build the peace among nations."

By the time President Bush addressed the American Enterprise Institute on February 26, 2003, scarcely two weeks before the invasion of Iraq, his vision that American security depended on the democratization of the Middle East could be emphatically laid out. "The current Iraqi regime has shown the power of tyranny to spread discord and violence in the Middle East. A liberated Iraq can show the power of freedom to transform that vital region, by bringing hope and progress into the lives of millions. America's interests in security, and America's belief in liberty, both lead in the same direction: to a free and peaceful Iraq." Then, in words that spelled out his ambitions more broadly perhaps than ever before, the president declared:

> There was a time when many said that the cultures of Japan and Germany were incapable of sustaining democratic values. Well, they were wrong. Some say the same of Iraq today. They are mistaken. The nation of Iraq—with its proud heritage, abundant resources and skilled and educated people—is fully capable of moving toward democracy and living in freedom.
>
> The world has a clear interest in the spread of democratic values, because stable and free nations do not breed the ideologies of murder. They encourage the peaceful pursuit of a better life. And there are hopeful signs for freedom in the Middle East...from Morocco to Bahrain and beyond, nations are taking genuine steps toward political reform. A new regime in Iraq would serve as a dramatic and inspiring example of freedom for other nations in the region.

Once the capture of Baghdad had been achieved, there was little more of substance to add to the president's words. The message became a mantra. Addressing the UN General Assembly on September 23, 2003, Bush asserted:

> Success of a free Iraq will be watched and noted throughout the region. Millions will see that freedom, equality and material progress are possible at the heart of the Middle East. Leaders in the region will face the clearest evidence that free institutions and open societies are the only path to long-term national success and dignity. And a transformed Middle East would benefit the entire world by undermining the ideologies that export violence to other lands. Iraq, as a dictatorship, had great power to destabilize the Middle East. Iraq, as a democracy, will have great power to inspire the Middle East.

Addressing the National Endowment for Democracy on November 6, 2003, Bush announced that the country, "has adopted a new policy, a forward strategy of freedom in the Middle East.... As in Europe, as in Asia and in every region of the world, the advance of freedom leads to peace." Explicitly exonerating Islam as a faith from terrorism as a practice or from an inability to have the cultural values necessary to support a democratic state, the president concluded by observing, "The failure of Iraqi democracy would embolden terrorists around the world...Iraqi democracy will succeed—and that success will send forth the news from Damascus to Teheran—that freedom can be the future of every nation. The establishment of a free Iraq at the heart of the Middle East will be a watershed event in the global democracy revolution."

Speaking in London in November 2003, the president spoke at length of his faith in "the global expansion of democracy" as both a possible and a highly desirable undertaking: "We cannot rely exclusively on military power to assure our long-term security. Lasting peace is gained as justice and democracy advance." In February 2004, at the Library of Congress, the president reiterated, "We seek the advance of democracy for the most practical of reasons: because democracies do not support terrorists or threaten the world with weapons of mass murder."

As the 2004 election drew closer, President Bush remained consistently on message. But with his victory in the balloting in November, his expression of liberal convictions grew, if it were possible, more insistent, more rhetorically charged. As we have seen, Bush's Second Inaugural Address was replete with Wilsonian phrases, as was his State of the Union Address delivered on February 2, 2005.

From the first months of 2005, the president used his approach to appeal to the Europeans to work with the United States so that, "together we can once again set history on a hopeful course." Speaking on March 8, 2005, at the National Defense University, Bush went so far as to criticize past American policy toward the Middle East: "By now it should be clear that decades of excusing and accommodating tyranny in the pursuit of stability have only led to injustice and instability and tragedy. It should be clear that the advance of democracy leads to peace, because governments that respect the rights of their people also respect the rights of their neighbors." Emboldened perhaps by the successful national elections in Iraq held on January 30, 2005, the president delved more deeply into the history and politics of that region than was customary, but drawing his usual optimistic conclusions.

> Parts of that region have been caught for generations in a cycle of tyranny and despair and radicalism. When a dictatorship controls the political life of a country, responsible opposition cannot develop, and dissent is driven underground and toward the extreme...dictators place blame on other countries and other races and stir the hatred that leads to violence. The status quo of despotism and anger cannot be ignored or appeased.... The entire world has an urgent interest in the progress, and hope, and freedom in the broader Middle East.

Nor did the message change in the president's State of the Union Address on January 31, 2006. Once again, no mention was made of the United States working with other countries. Instead, Washington would provide the leadership to save the world from chaos: "we've been called to leadership in a period of consequence. We've entered a great ideological conflict we did nothing to invite…. Lincoln could have accepted peace at the cost of disunity and continued slavery…. Today, having come far in our own historical journey, we must decide: Will we turn back or will we finish well?"

As for the struggle itself, "Abroad, our nation is committed to an historic, long-term goal—we seek the end of tyranny in our world…the future security of America depends on it…. Every step toward freedom in the world makes our country safer—so we will act boldly in freedom's cause." A next target? Perhaps Iran, "a nation now held hostage by a small clerical elite…our nation hopes one day to be the closest of friends with a free and democratic Iran."

The analysis of President Bush's liberal democratic internationalism over more than a four-year period suggests two important features. First, he remained consistent over time. His message may have varied over the years that followed June 2002—for example, I find his rhetoric about the "evil" of the insurgency in Iraq reaching a high point in October–November 2005, just as there was a new emphasis on combating "tyranny"—but it does not falter. Whether in terms of historical tradition or current academic discourse, his arguments are clearly and coherently liberal. They place the democratization of foreign states through regime change at the center of the American agenda for world order and thus for national security. This suggests that the president was relying less on his advisors and speechwriters to shape his words than on his own intuitive understanding of and commitment to the notion that, as he put it at Freedom House on March 29, 2006, "the only path to lasting peace is the expansion of freedom and liberty."

Second, over time the president's rhetoric developed a more fully coherent argument for democratization. His position came to resemble more closely what I will call in later chapters neo-Wilsonian democratic peace theory and democratic transition theory—the first emphasizing the desirability of democracy's spread, the second its "universal appeal," which suggests the ease with which its ways will be disseminated. In a word, Bush became more complexly and fervently ideological. As he put it in a salute to Hungary on March 15, 2006:

I believe freedom is universal. I believe the example of Hungary proves that freedom is universal. I believe everybody desires to live in freedom. I believe there is an Almighty, and I believe the Almighty God's gift to each person in this world is liberty. And I believe the United States and I believe Hungary, and I believe other free nations have the responsibility to help other people realize their freedom, as well.

In the aftermath of the 2004 election, there were those who said that the neoconservative moment had ended, and that a more realistic discourse would be emerging from Washington in due course. That was not to be. The president had clearly internalized his argument and would give no quarter in pushing it forward. Indeed, on March 16, 2006, three years almost to the day after the invasion of Iraq (and three and a half after the publication of NSS 2002), the White House released amidst great fanfare an updated version of the Bush Doctrine, labeled simply National Security Strategy 2006.

NSS 2006 was organized in terms of the same divisions of concern as its predecessor. Its opening lines declared a dedication to democracy promotion abroad as a vital element of American security in a way that was repeated throughout the document and that summoned up four years of such assertions:

> It is the policy of the United States to seek and support democratic movements and institutions in every nation and culture, with the ultimate goal of ending tyranny in our world. In the world today, the fundamental character of regimes matters as much as the distribution of power among them. The goal of our statecraft is to help create a world of democratic, well-governed states that can meet the needs of their citizens and conduct themselves responsibly in the international system. This is the best way to provide enduring security for the American people.

As the president put it yet once again in an address before Freedom House on March 29, 2006, "the only path to lasting peace is the expansion of freedom and liberty...the advance of freedom is a vital aspect of our strategy to protect the American people, and to secure the peace for generations to come."

From the fall of 2005 through the spring of 2006, the neoconservatives were critical of the Bush administration's handling of the Bush Doctrine. Was the United States in retreat? Was rhetoric now replacing substance? But with the Israeli attack on Lebanon in July 2006 strongly endorsed by the president, the neoconservatives could relax. "Lebanon is the latest flashpoint in a broader struggle between freedom and terror that is unfolding across the region," the president declared on July 29. "The only way to secure our nation is to change the course of the Middle East—by fighting the ideology of terror and spreading the hope of freedom." Here, then, was "a moment of opportunity for broader change in the region" which might witness the birth of what Secretary Rice was calling a "new Middle East." In answering a question for the press a day earlier, Bush had been clear on the matter:

we have a foreign policy that addresses the root causes of violence and instability.... You defeat it with a more hopeful ideology called freedom.... The
notion of democracy beginning to emerge scares the ideologues, the totalitarians, those who want to impose their vision.... And so what the world is seeing
is a desire by this country and our allies to defeat the ideology of hate with an
ideology that has worked and that brings hope...I'm as determined as ever to
continue fostering a foreign policy based upon liberty. And I think it's going
to work unless we lose our nerve and quit. And this government isn't going
to quit.

The president repeated his argument on August 14, 2006, explicitly linking
the Israeli attack on Lebanon with the American war on terror in Iraq. "Forces
of terror see the changes that are taking place in their midst. They understand
that the advance of liberty, the freedom to worship, the freedom to dissent,
and the protection of human rights would be a defeat for their hateful ideologies.... So the terrorists are striking back with all of the destructive power they
can muster. It's no coincidence that two nations that are building free societies in the heart of the Middle East, Lebanon and Iraq, are also the scenes of
the most violent terrorist activity." Eventually terrorism would be destroyed
because, "we know and understand the unstoppable power of freedom. In a
Middle East that grows in freedom and democracy, people will have a chance
to raise their families and live in peace and build a better future...there will
be no room for tyranny and terror, and that will make America and other free
nations more secure." Then, once again, he repeated the mantra that ensured
the success of his undertaking: "I believe that freedom is a universal value.
And by that I mean people want to be free. One way to put it is, I believe mothers around the world want to raise their children in a peaceful world. That's
what I believe."

Here, then, is an outline of the terms by which the Bush Doctrine would
function. While it demonstrated flexibility as to tactics and timing, it was
obviously about far more than the conquest of Iraq. As a blueprint for global
order and American hegemony, its assumptions were spelled out with a preci-
sion rare in American foreign policy pronouncements. Given the importance
of the developments it inspired, the doctrine is sure to be studied for generations to come by those who would understand this country's sense of its role
in world affairs in the aftermath of the Cold War and in response to the attack
of 9/11.

CHAPTER 2

The Intellectual Origins of the Bush Doctrine

I don't have the foggiest idea of what I think about international policy.

> Then-Governor of Texas, George W. Bush, late 1997,
> cited by Bob Woodward, *State of Denial*

*For if the trumpet give an uncertain sound, who shall prepare himself
to the battle?*

> 1 Corinthians 14:8

If President George W. Bush were fully committed to the terms of the doctrine that bore his name in 2002, there is, nevertheless, no reason to attribute to him the original authorship of the ideas his position statements purveyed. Bush had never shown particular interest in world affairs before entering office, and one reason that he was able to assemble the foreign policy team he did was that most of its members found him not simply a man who might win the election in 2000 but that he was educable to their point of view as well. To say this is not to suggest that the president was an empty vessel waiting for others to assign him a mission, so much as to indicate a compatibility between his preexisting orientation toward world affairs, which held that America alone had the ability to provide order in a world badly in need of leadership, a leadership that only Republicans of his mettle seemed capable of providing, and the more conceptually refined focus the team he assembled to advise him had of how American power should be exercised.[1]

It is widely agreed that the immediate source of the ideas expressed in the Bush Doctrine came for the most part from neoconservative intellectuals surrounding the president. As we shall see, to assent to this proposition does not mean that Bush and other members of his war cabinet were reluctant for their own reasons to make a bid for world supremacy, nor to suppose that the neoconservatives alone had a monopoly on the concepts that set forth to guide American foreign policy. President Bush, Vice President Cheney, Secretary of Defense Rumsfeld, and National Security Advisor Rice very much had their own minds when it came to thinking about America's role in the world. Moreover, the arguments the neoconservatives made resonated with preexisting currents in American political thought and practice. These allowances made, it is nonetheless persuasive to see the neoconservatives as possessed of a coherent doctrine for world power in the aftermath of the attack of September 11, 2001, and as determined to make their framework for action the marching orders adopted by the Bush administration. Any discussion of the intellectual origins of the Bush Doctrine must pay special attention to their arguments.

The Neoconservative Agenda

In September 1995, with the financial support of Rupert Murdoch, William Kristol (aided by Robert Kagan, John Podhoretz, and Fred Barnes) became the founding editor of the neoconservative flagship publication *The Weekly Standard*, a political magazine that in short order was to be the main mouthpiece for the dissemination of the viewpoints we reviewed in the preceding chapter that ultimately were to culminate in the Bush Doctrine. Then in June 1997, Kristol (again accompanied by Kagan) founded the Project for a New American Century (PNAC). Much as two decades earlier, when the neoconservatives had tried to revitalize the Democratic Party to purge it of McGovernites (through the Coalition for a Democratic Majority) and rouse the country to the menace of Soviet totalitarianism (through the Committee for the Present Danger), so now PNAC's project was to revitalize the Republican party by reminding it of its combative Reaganite credentials.

By the late 1990s a synergistic interaction of *The Weekly Standard*, PNAC, and the American Enterprise Institute had become the center of gravity for a wide and ever-expanding network of neoconservative individuals, publications, TV and radio outlets, and think tanks devoted to calling for the kind of framework for America's role in the world that was eventually made manifest in the Bush Doctrine. With some justice, Stefan Halper and Jonathan Clarke call this development the emergence of "a dynamic shadow defense establishment" capable of providing an aggressive new direction to American policy should a new administration in Washington adopt their outlook.[2]

The neoconservatives who had articulated the Pax Americana framework during the 1990s moved into high office after the election of 2000. One measure gives a telling sense of their influence. In 1998, PNAC had submitted a letter to then-President Clinton calling for Saddam's forcible ouster from power. On October 1, 2001, Kristol and Kagan pointed out in *The Weekly Standard* that:

> The signatories of that 1998 letter are today a Who's Who of senior ranking officials in this administration. Secretary of Defense Donald Rumsfeld, U.S. Trade Representative Robert Zoellick, Deputy Secretary of State Richard Armitage, Deputy Secretary of Defense Paul Wolfowitz, Undersecretary of State John Bolton, Undersecretary of State Paula Dobrinsky, Assistant Secretary of Defense Peter Rodman and National Security Council officials Elliott Abrams and Zalmay Khalilzad. If those Bush administration officials believed it was essential to bring about a change of regime in Iraq three years ago, they must believe it is even more essential today. Last week we lost more than 6,000 Americans to terrorism. How many more could we lose in a world where Saddam Hussein continues to thrive and continues his quest for weapons of mass destruction?[3]

In fact, as Gary Dorrien and as Stephan Halper and Jonathan Clarke document, the presence of members of the neoconservative movement was substantially more pervasive than Kristol and Kagan stated it.[4] Among those Kristol and Kagan omitted who also signed the letter, for example, were Jeb Bush, Dick Cheney, I. Lewis Libby, and Richard Perle.

Whence the origin of the ideas that inspired the neoconservatives and gave them their unity as an intellectual movement? Our concern is not so much with the personalities that typified this school as with the main concepts that guided its members' thinking. To be sure, the neoconservatives were never organized in any kind of disciplined party structure. Yet despite referring to themselves as a "persuasion" or a "sensibility" rather than a more fixed movement, certain key concepts emerge as fundamental to their political argument.

The first of the neoconservative axioms, laid down long before the early 1970s when it gained its name as a movement, was that totalitarian states were deadly enemies of all that liberal democracies quite rightly cherish. The progenitors of neoconservatism were young, leftist, New York City Jewish intellectuals who came to these conclusions in the late 1930s and 1940s, first in debates on the left over the relative merits of Stalin and Trotsky (and the relationship of each to Lenin), later in confronting Hitler and the awful fact of the Holocaust.

As a consequence, early partisans of this movement had vigorously supported America in World War II to destroy fascism. Thereafter, they became dedicated Cold Warriors of the left, eager to take on the arguments of communist movements backed by the Soviet Union so as to win the contest with Moscow on terms favorable to the West. It was here in this earlier forum that they learned the importance waging a war of ideas and of a network of international democratic activists to keep the communist menace at bay. After the Cold War, in keeping with their deep-set distrust of totalitarian movements, the neoconservatives were quick to denounce the communist governments of North Korea, Cambodia, Cuba, and China as well as populist militarist governments, often with a fascist air, as in Serbia under Slobodan Milosevic, in Venezuela under Hugo Chavez, and in Iraq under Saddam Hussein.[5]

This school's second axiom also has a pedigree taking us back to the 1940s. It holds that whatever the shortcomings of liberal democracies, they represent the highest political order we have produced, so that the preservation of this human accomplishment is an imperative moral duty of all citizens. Nevertheless, neoconservatives typically despair that their fellow citizens, especially liberals, are equal to the task. In campaigns against American leftists, most neoconservatives (even if they did not gain their name until the early 1970s) approved of Senator Joseph McCarthy's search for communists in the American government in the early 1950s; fought the anti-war movement for what they felt was its anti-Americanism during and after the Vietnam War; and opposed the Civil Rights movement when it called for constructive relations with radical foreign movements like the Palestinian Liberation Organization, an appeal which many felt concealed an anti-Semitic bias. Likewise, in their opposition to Richard Nixon and Henry Kissinger, the neoconservatives lambasted détente with the Soviet Union and the opening toward China as morally ungrounded and practically dangerous.

A number of corollaries flow naturally from these two axioms. First, world affairs are heavily charged morally: totalitarianism is evil and liberal democracy virtuous. "Moral clarity" on this score is an essential point of departure for all serious political analysis. "Moral equivalence" and "relativism" are signs of unclear thinking or a dubious character.

Second, in such circumstances, where evil is on the prowl to destroy liberal freedoms, American military primacy is a non-negotiable imperative. Under no conditions should it be surrendered.

Third, the fate of liberal democracy worldwide depends on American leadership. If the dependence of Israel on American power holds a place of special importance for the neoconservatives—the wars between the Jewish State and its Arab neighbors in 1967 and 1973 galvanized their concern just as did the 2006 war between Israel and Hezbollah in Lebanon—it is nonetheless the case that democracy *everywhere* depends on American resolve, a determination they pledge to stiffen.

It is commonplace these days to attribute the fundamental principles of neoconservative thought to the political philosopher Leo Strauss (1899–1973), a German Jewish refugee from Nazi Germany who for many years taught at the University of Chicago where many of the neocons were either his students or (as with Allan Bloom) students of his students. Yet while the "axioms and corollaries" I have described certainly were compatible with Strauss' thinking, it is quite possible to subscribe to these concepts without ever having been exposed to Strauss.[6] The first generation of thinkers of what came to be called neoconservatism, apparently arrived at these conclusions without Strauss's mediation, even if, like Irving Kristol, many of them came to recognize the power of his thinking. His influence was more marked on those who came of age not in the 1940s but in the 1960s.

But in just what ways did Strauss matter to the formulation of American foreign policy after the Cold War? One aspect of his teachings as it was interpreted by some of his followers was to create something of an intellectual honor society, complete with the conviction that their thinking was necessarily superior to that of the public at large. In order to guide policy, leaders therefore must be ready to tell "noble lies," for the danger of democracy, whatever its comparative advantages, was the short-term, self-interested, and emotional basis of mass politics. Indeed, a leading argument among Straussian scholars is whether he was genuinely committed to democratic government, or whether he saw it as the least menacing from of political organization for it allowed philosophers relative freedom to pursue their task of nailing down the truth. Seen from this latter perspective, Straussians needed to protect democracy from itself—from traditional conservatives, who lacked the intellectual heft to understand the course of history, and from liberals who systematically failed to take the enemy as seriously as they should. To the extent Straussians and neoconservatives were one, then we may speak of a cabal, taking over a series of high offices in January 2001 with a clear idea of what they intended to achieve that they rather carefully concealed from public view.

Such a belief may have played a role in persuading some Bush administration officials to misrepresent the threat of Saddam's weapons of mass destruction (WMD) in the run-up to the invasion of Iraq. It may also have reinforced the belief of some officials that executive powers needed to be strengthened in a time of national emergency (and then preserved thereafter). The anti-democratic elitism of Straussian thinking—to save democracy it is necessary to subvert certain elements that make it dangerous to itself—deserves our attention.

But so far as the Bush Doctrine itself is concerned, Strauss' influence is harder to perceive. Indeed, his thinking would have implicitly warned *against* that aspect of the doctrine that emphasized the perfectibility of humanity through the spread of market democracy worldwide. Whatever his belief in reason and his arguments in favor of universal natural rights, Strauss was convinced that notions of individual and social perfection grew out of an Enlightenment fallacy that put more stake on the possibility of "progress" than was prudent. Reason alone could not rule human decisions, nor would it have had perfect insight were it able to predominate. Other interests and emotions might well turn rational argument into self-serving agents of destructive ambitions.

Thus Francis Fukuyama, who was a student of Allan Bloom and considered himself both a neocon and a Straussian through 2003, writes that while Strauss was a staunch defender of liberal democratic government, he was also aware of how difficult it was for such political orders to take root. It would therefore be impossible to attribute to Strauss the idea that democracy promotion worldwide would be a realistic undertaking for U.S. foreign policy. Fukuyama writes:

> A correct understanding of the Straussian interpretation of regime would have raised red flags over the American effort to bring about regime change. Regimes, by this understanding, are not just formal institutions and authority structures; they shape and are shaped by the societies underlying them. The unwritten rules by which people operate, based on religion, kinship, and shared historical experience, are also part of the regime.... If there is any central theme to Strauss's skepticism about the modern Enlightenment project, it is the idea that reason alone is sufficient to establish a durable political order or that nonrational claims of revelation can be banished from politics.[7]

Steven B. Smith, one of Strauss's most insightful interpreters, also maintains that the neoconservatives should be seen as quite distinct from their supposed mentor. "Evil is a theme Strauss mentions several times throughout his writing, always in the context of warning against radical expectation in politics." Hence for Strauss, Smith writes:

> Evil is a permanent disposition of the human heart. The task of the statesman is not to try to eradicate the causes of evil, something that would require a permanent war against human nature, but to mitigate its worst effects. Aware of "the limits set to all human action and all human planning," the philosopher statesman will be modest in his expectations from politics. "He will try to help his fellow man by mitigating, as far as in him lies, the evils that are *inseparable from the human condition*".... The dangers of arrogance and imperial overreach exhibited by Periclean Athens should be a sobering counter-example to neoconservatism's assertion of national greatness.[8]

Without doubting that speculation on Strauss' influence is a path worth following, to understand the Bush Doctrine, it does not seem to me necessary to go further than the neoconservatives themselves, who were quite articulate in saying what they believed. Later marginal additions to their intellectual package to be noted, these two axioms and their three corollaries defined the major features of the political character of the neoconservative movement from its origins until today. In terms of their political identities, the neoconservatives could be called super-patriotic Americans, convinced of the rightness and the necessity of this country's leadership role in world affairs. They might also be considered cosmopolitans, for they saw liberal democracy wherever it flourished as something they would support, just as they saw totalitarianism wherever it appeared, as a force they would combat. And they were Zionists, committed to the defense of democratic Israel, which they saw as a moral ward of the Western world.

Seemingly always in opposition, the neocons' fortunes began to change in 1976, the year they founded the Committee on the Present Danger and discovered in Ronald Reagan a man they could support for the presidency. Having started on the far left in the 1940s, the neoconservatives had moved to the socialist left, then into the Democratic party, until finally with Reagan's move into the White House in 1981 they found a president on the right whose convictions were also theirs.

During the Reagan years, the neoconservatives added three additional arguments to their battery of concepts on world affairs. First, they perfected a profound suspicion of multilateral alliances unless American leadership were acknowledged, fearing that our Lilliputian allies or our authoritarian opponents might tie down the great Gulliver, who must count on his own wits to do the world's battles. Part of their concern was based on considerations of the sanctity of American sovereignty that were widely shared on the American right. Part of their suspicions grew from their perception of the ineffectiveness of international institutions. Part of it reflected their reaction to the way aggressive Third World countries were using the United Nations to their own purposes hostile to the United States and Israel. NATO still held a place of honor, to be sure, but the UN was seen as an obstacle to American goals in world affairs, and unilateral initiatives by the United States were correspondingly to be encouraged.[9] Accordingly, the multilateral approach to foreign policy that appealed to liberals was always seen as something of a trap to the neoconservatives.

A second clear lesson during this period was that fundamentalist Christian groups played an essential role in the election of Republicans to political office, and that their commitment to notions of Biblical prophecy made them willing supporters of right-wing Zionist movements at home and in Israel. Because neoconservatives tended to favor the political stands of the Likud party in Israel (including the expansion of Jewish settlements in lands these Zionists referred to as "Judea and Samaria," and a policy of "peace through strength with Israel's neighbors) the attitude of the Christian right was seen as constructive of a Republican open-ended commitment to Jerusalem to support that country in world affairs, whatever policy it chose to adopt. The Jewish and Christian right in world affairs thus could make common cause, whatever the tensions that might nonetheless persist.[10]

The third lesson this school learned during the Reagan years was that democracy might flourish among virtually any people on Earth, and that where it came into existence American security interests were served. Although a hallmark of neoconservative thinking had always been its embrace of liberal democracy as the best form of government, prior to the Reagan years there was no sense of optimism that such a political regime would easily sink roots in many parts of the world. What certain neoconservatives learned from President Reagan, however, was that liberal democratic government might be possible for all peoples, a development that could be seen both as a good in itself and as a contribution to increased national security.

Speaking before the British Parliament in June 1982, Ronald Reagan gave what most observers consider to be his most eloquent address on world affairs during his eight years in office. For most neoconservatives, it marked an intellectual turning point as well, a moment when their faith in liberal democracy for the West could be seen as a creed that could be extended to all the world.

"Regimes planted by bayonets do not take root," Reagan declared in a rebuke to Nazi as well as to Soviet totalitarianism, evoking "the great purge, Auschwitz and Dachau, the Gulag, and Cambodia.... Must freedom wither in a quiet, deadening accommodation with totalitarian evil?" Focusing on Poland's Solidarity movement particularly, the president concluded, "democracy is proving itself to be a not-at-all-fragile flower." Whereas previous Republican presidents had attacked Moscow in the name of democratic national self-determination, Reagan went further, declaring that a "democratic revolution is gathering new strength" and mentioning its vigor in countries as different as India, Nigeria, and El Salvador. "We must be staunch in our conviction that freedom is not the sole prerogative of a lucky few, but the inalienable and universal right of all human beings."

> The objective I propose is quite simple to state: to foster the infrastructure of democracy, the system of a free press, unions, political parties, universities, which allows a people to choose their own way to develop their own culture, to reconcile their own differences through peaceful means. This is not cultural imperialism. It is providing the means for genuine self-determination and protection for diversity. Democracy already flourishes in countries with very different cultures and historical experiences. It would be cultural condescension, or worse, to say that any people prefer dictatorship to democracy. Who would voluntarily choose not to have the right to vote, decide to purchase government propaganda handouts instead of independent newspapers, prefer government to worker-controlled unions, opt for land to be owned by the state instead of those who till it, want government repression of religious liberty, a single political party instead of a free choice, a rigid cultural orthodoxy instead of democratic tolerance and diversity?[11]

We can debate which experiences in democratization most influenced the members of the Reagan administration. For the president himself, it was most probably El Salvador and Poland where democratic forces looked likely to unseat communist regimes. For others, especially those connected to the National Endowment for Democracy established by 1983, it was more likely the Philippines, Chile, or South Korea, where democracy movements might oust authoritarian allies of the United States. In terms of sophisticated thinking, we might reflect on "constructive engagement" with respect to South Africa, a position that apartheid had to end and black majority rule occur in order to blunt the appeal of communism in southern Africa. In every case, the point was the same: democracy seemingly had a universal appeal and the defense of freedom required the advance of freedom not only against the Soviet Union but more broadly still in world affairs.

Perhaps the place the president's ideological offensive was most effective was the Soviet Union itself, with Mikhail Gorbachev's "new thinking." By its terms—*glasnost* and *perestroika,* or political and economic liberalization— profound reforms were proceeding apace under the terms of ideas that the first secretary was cobbling together from a wide variety of sources, which included in some measure his contacts with the U.S. president and Secretary of State George Schultz. Not just the threat of American arms, but also the seduction of American ideas, helped to bring about the peaceful collapse first of the Soviet empire in 1989, then of the Soviet Union itself in 1991, in the immediate aftermath of the Reagan presidency.[12]

The neoconservatives were, of course, front row center for what appeared at the time to be a dramatic change in world political consciousness. With the eventual collapse of the Soviet Union, not only Václav Havel, but Boris Yeltsin and even Mikhail Gorbachev, could claim to be liberal democrats. Small wonder that a historic wind seemed to be blowing that in due course would sweep the globe. The dramatic fall of the Berlin Wall in November 1989, the lightning American victory in the Persian Gulf in February 1991, and the collapse of the Soviet Union that December left no doubt as to America's supremacy in world affairs. Woodrow Wilson's day had finally arrived, to be inaugurated by the first Republican administration to make his confidence its own that to make the world safe for democracy, the world would best be democratized.

However, at the very moment of victory, retreat seemed to set in from the neo-conservative point of view. President George H. W. Bush (1989-1993) had called for a "new world order," but he had done very little indeed from their perspective to do much about implementing any such design, even when presented with a golden opportunity in the form of victory in the 1991 Gulf War. The neocons in charge of Pentagon policy planning set out to rectify this omission. As we have seen in the preceding chapter, the result was in effect the first draft of what came to be called the Bush Doctrine. In it, the traditional neoconservative argument that the United States should strive to maintain its military primacy was now joined to what had been learned during the Reagan years: power's purpose was the regional, and perhaps worldwide, expansion of liberal democratic government.

The Neoconservatives and Iraq

The neoconservatives not only authored the essential arguments of the Bush Doctrine, they also interpreted it to justify an attack on Iraq. Indeed, the evidence suggests it was not so much the Bush Doctrine that legitimized the invasion of

Iraq as it was instead the determination to be rid of Saddam, and thereby to control the Middle East, which led to the formulation of the doctrine.

Since the Gulf War of 1991, Saddam Hussein had been in the crosshairs of the neoconservative movement, whose members repeatedly call for action to oust the despot, especially after 1995 when PNAC was created. The website for the Project for a New American Century in the spring of 2006 continued to make available a host of statements documenting the organization's longstanding determination during the Clinton presidency to find "A Way to Oust Saddam," as a *Weekly Standard* editorial of November 1998 by Robert Kagan put it. If PNAC's letter to President Clinton of January 1998 was its most notable public statement during that presidency, it was far from alone. During the Clinton years, PNAC publications included "A 'Great Victory' for Iraq," "Bombing Iraq Isn't Enough," and "How to Attack Iraq," all by Kagan and William Kristol; "Adrift in the Gulf" and "The UN Rewards Saddam" by John Bolton; "Saddam Wins—Again" by Kagan; and a number of "project memoranda" to the same end by Gary Schmitt.[13]

The consensus today is that in terms of official Washington, Paul Wolfowitz was the best connected and most influential of the neoconservatives. He was therefore more likely than any other member of this school to appear before congressional committees detailing how to remove Saddam by force, an argument summed up by him in "Overthrow Him" in *The Weekly Standard* of December 1, 1997. Since the late 1970s, Wolfowitz had been working on the challenge posed by the Saddam regime, and by 1996 he was active in organizing the crescendo of demands that the tyrant be ousted, offering specific military plans that could bring this about. By 1997 (perhaps much earlier), he had made contact with Ahmad Chalabi, the head of the Iraqi National Congress (INC), and could pin his hopes on this individual and his movement—styled "the democratic opposition"—to be the fulcrum of an eventual assault on Saddam. In 1998, when Congress passed the Iraq Liberation Act, the INC was granted $97 million to work for Saddam's removal—in good measure thanks to Wolfowitz's unending pressure.[14]

Given this background, it should come as no surprise that the neoconservatives called instantly for an attack on Iraq in the aftermath of 9/11. Indeed, like Wolfowitz and PNAC member and former CIA Director James Woolsey, some wanted to forego an attack on Afghanistan altogether, seeing it as a sideshow to the major theater of action: the Middle East, with Iraq as the lever for American policy.[15]

While concern with China and calls for its liberalization ran wide and deep in neoconservative circles, Iraq was a more promising case to demonstrate

what American primacy could accomplish. Saddam was a universally acknowledged despot whose crimes against humanity were the most notorious of any
person in the 1990s. His military force was weak. He had flouted repeated UN
resolutions. He was widely believed to possess weapons of mass destruction or
was actively seeking to acquire and use them.

Moreover, conquest of the country could provide extra dividends in that
Iraq was blessed with enormous oil deposits, which suggested the occupation
could be paid for locally while the international oil cartel would come under
renewed pressure from Washington. Geo-strategically, Iraq was central in the
Middle East. American bases in Iraq meant that U.S. troops could be withdrawn from Saudi Arabia, where their presence was causing domestic difficulties. These bases could also reassure Israel so that it would be more inclined
to making concessions for peace in its relations with the Palestinians. Syria
and Iran would feel the heat of nearby American military bases while Jordan
and Lebanon might feel comforted. Finally, the assumed disaffection of the
population with the tyrant's rule over what Kanan Makiya has aptly called the
Republic of Fear, where hundreds of thousands of citizens were killed by their
own government, suggested that democracy might take root in Iraq and serve
as a model to transform the region politically.[16]

Hence crisis was opportunity. Although Afghanistan was necessarily the
first target of response after 9/11, Iraq was logically the second. Iran or Syria,
perhaps Saudi Arabia, might follow soon enough thereafter.

Iraq as an End in Itself and as a Means to a Greater End

We can understand in light of the logic of the Bush Doctrine that attacking
Iraq was both an end in itself, given that country's grim human rights record
combined with its undeniable aggressive ambitions, and a means to a greater
purpose given Iraq's place in the Middle East and the place of the Middle East
in the international balance of power. There were then, three chessboards on
which the plan of attack of March 2003 was carried forward: national, regional,
and international.

Hence the relative unimportance of Afghanistan. To be sure, the Taliban
regime had to be destroyed and with it as much of the Al-Qaeda terrorist network
as possible. But critics of the administration who maintain that it was a fundamental strategic blunder to re-deploy quickly from Afghanistan to Iraq, and who
may be correct to say so, nevertheless need to answer the argument that any effort
to restructure Afghanistan in a stable way was a quixotic mission, and that in any

case the central front was not in this remote part of Central Asia but rather in the Middle East. Why divert energy to a peripheral issue that itself presented a host of difficulties when victory on the main front needed to be gained?

As anyone who grasped the logic of the Bush Doctrine would understand, when ultimately the decision was made to attack the Taliban, it was generally understood that Iraq was next in line to be dealt with, by an invasion that this time would not stop short of Baghdad. As the liberal hawk Thomas L. Friedman explained in the *New York Times* on June 4, 2003, the "real reason" Iraq was invaded was "Because We Could."

> After 9/11 America needed to hit someone in the Arab-Muslim world. Afghanistan wasn't enough because a terrorism bubble had built up over there—a bubble that posed a real threat to the open societies of the West and needed to be punctured. This terrorism bubble said that plowing airplanes into the World Trade Center was OK, having Muslim preachers say it was OK was OK, having state-run newspapers call people who did such things 'martyrs' was OK and allowing Muslim charities to raise money for such 'martyrs' was OK…. The only way to puncture that bubble was for American soldiers, men and women, to go into the heart of the Arab-Muslim world, house to house, and make clear that we are ready to kill, and to die, to prevent our open society from being undermined…we hit Saddam for one simple reason: because we could, and because he deserved it and because he was right in the heart of that world.

As was so often the case, Friedman's thinking closely paralleled that of the neoconservatives. On September 20, 2001, a long list of signatories organized by the Project for a New American Century sent a letter to President Bush entitled "Toward a Comprehensive Strategy." Its forthright conclusion: "It may be that the Iraqi government provided assistance in some form to the recent attack on the United States. *But even if evidence does not link Iraq directly to the attack,* any strategy aiming at the eradication of terrorism and its sponsors must include a determined effort to remove Saddam Hussein from power in Iraq. Failure to undertake such an effort will constitute an early and perhaps decisive surrender in the war on international terrorism" (emphasis added). The PNAC statement also called for threats of action to be issued to Syria and Iran, while Israel should be reassured that the United States considered that it "has been and remains America's staunchest ally against international terrorism." Again, in November 2001, the neoconservative Richard Perle gave a widely noted address entitled "Next Stop, Iraq."[17] It was old hat, then, on January 21, 2002, for Robert Kagan and William Kristol to declare in *The Weekly Standard*:

It is necessary to stabilize Afghanistan.... But none of this precludes dealing with Iraq.... The United States can, after all, walk and chew gum at the same time. The Iraqi threat is enormous.... A devastating knockout blow against Saddam Hussein, followed by an American-sponsored effort to rebuild Iraq and put it on a path toward democratic governance would have a seismic impact on the Arab world—for the better.

Here was the challenge to act that neoconservatives had been looking for since the early 1990s if not much earlier. The attack of 9/11 crystallized as nothing else could an opportunity to deal with a spectrum of difficulties involved in organizing the oil-rich Middle East into the international system on American terms. Long determined to find the occasion to overcome the pussyfooting it saw in the administration of President Bill Clinton, eager to exercise what it flattered itself was its historically unprecedented military power in terms of an American promise to spread freedom, official Washington in 2001 had many proponents of acting decisively to reshape international politics when the upsurge of fear and anger kindled by 9/11 offered the nationalist support to act decisively to settle a range of long-simmering problems.

As William Kristol put it in *The Weekly Standard* on April 28, 2003, the attack of 9/11, "was the product of two decades of American weakness in the face of terror and three decades of American fecklessness in the Middle East." Consequently, Iraq was an end in itself and a means to a greater end.

But that era—in which the American stance was one of doubt, weakness, and retreat, in which we failed to affirm our most cherished principles or even stand up for ourselves—came to an end on September 11, 2001. The United States committed itself to defeating terror around the world. We committed ourselves to reshaping the Middle East.... The battles of Afghanistan and Iraq have been won decisively and honorably. But these are only two battles. We are only at the end of the beginning in the war on terror and terrorist states.

In short, the logic of the Bush Doctrine's formulations meant that control over this valuable piece of real estate would make the United States the predominant power in the Middle East. Moreover, such a position would handsomely complement the dominant military positions the United States already enjoyed in Europe and Northeast Asia, the other two strategic zones in world affairs, so making this country the undisputed center of power globally.

Still, there was good reason to think that such an enormous ambition might not be sold to the American public, whatever its concern over 9/11. Asserting that Saddam threatened the world with his WMD was thus a convenient pretext for waging a war whose rationale depended on strategic calculations on a far greater chessboard. Deputy Secretary of Defense Wolfowitz's interview in *Vanity Fair* summed it up when he conceded, "Iraq's supposed cache of WMD had never been the most compelling casus belli. It was simply one of several. For bureaucratic reasons we settled on one issue, weapons of mass destruction, because it was the one reason everyone could agree on." As the Ten Downing Street "secret memo" of July 2002, reported, senior officials in the British government understood, "Military action was now seen as inevitable. Bush wanted to remove Saddam through military action, justified by the conjunction of terrorism and WMD. But intelligence and facts were being fixed around the policy." As Paul Pillar, the CIA national intelligence officer for the Near East and South Asia from 2000–2005, wrote, "intelligence on Iraqi weapons programs did not drive [the] decision to go to war...[the] decision to topple Saddam was driven by other factors—namely, the desire to shake up the sclerotic power structures of the Middle East and hasten the spread of more liberal politics and economics in the region."[18]

With respect to the WMD, there is every reason to think that Pentagon officials, mightily aided by Vice President Cheney, did what they could to find evidence that these weapons existed and in their zeal intimidated intelligence officials, deliberately slanted the evidence, and knowingly disregarded information they might have considered that doubted Saddam had much of an arsenal. Not for a moment should we doubt that these actions were deliberate, nor should we disregard the gravity of these matters for the public life of a democracy or the toll this took on American trustworthiness in world councils. Assertions such as that Saddam could launch his missiles in 45 minutes (Tony Blair) or that if we did not act now it would be too late when a "mushroom cloud" brought us to our senses (the president and National Security Advisor Condoleezza Rice) were simply instrumental to bringing about a war that was in the national interest, weapons of mass destruction or no.[19]

In sum, the WMD were not the reason the White House wanted the Iraq War. They were only a pretext. The purpose of invading Iraq was to seize a valuable piece of real estate in its own right and to use this conquest as a fulcrum to move history. Anyone informed by the logic of the Bush Doctrine would understand that far more than deposing a single despot hostile to the American peace was at stake.

Freed from the seemingly necessary spins of evidence that official Washington was engaged in, some leading neoconservatives were refreshingly ready to tell it like it was. In *The War Over Iraq: Saddam's Tyranny and America's*

Mission published on the eve of battle by William Kristol and Lawrence Kaplan, we have what still remains today, nearly four years after its publication, the best single statement of what we may assume the administration's case for war actually was.[20]

As we might expect from straight-shooters like Kristol and Kaplan, they are quite frank that the Iraq invasion is only part of a much vaster game plan. They open their book declaring, "we stand at the cusp of a new historical era." The "holiday from history" is over and their book promises to explain the "new era for which we need a new roadmap." The invasion, they declare on their opening page, "is so clearly about more than Iraq. It is about more even than the future of the Middle East and the war on terror. It is about what sort of role the United States intends to play in the world in the 21st century." The very last lines of their book dramatically convey their intent:

> The mission begins in Baghdad, but it does not end there…America cannot escape its responsibility for maintaining a decent world order. The answer to this challenge is the American idea itself, and behind it the unparalleled military and economic strength of its custodian. Duly armed, the United States can act to secure its safety and to advance the cause of liberty—in Baghdad and beyond.

The logic of Kristol and Kaplan's book should come as no surprise although its frankness may. They reassert the two pillars of American strength presumed by the Bush Doctrine—its military and ideological preeminence in world affairs—and defend yet again the decision to maintain this preeminence by a preemptive, unilateral policy that will expand the boundaries of American leadership. Thus, "the United States remains the hinge of the international system. And when it sits idly by in the face of threats to that system international order erodes. Quickly." Making the by-now obligatory comparisons to Rome and the British empire, they duly find, as a host of their intellectual kinfolk also do, that America's relative position surpasses all that went before so that what is to be feared is not action but inaction.

Told they are "glorifying the notion of dominance," Kristol and Kaplan reply, "Well, what is wrong with dominance in the service of sound principles and high ideals?" They declare their "belief in the uniqueness and virtue of the American political system that, when translated into foreign policy terms, offers the United States as a model for the world." Finally, they salute the Bush Doctrine as "grand strategy" and assert in terms we should take seriously:

A humane future, then, will require an American foreign policy that is unapologetic, idealistic, assertive and well funded. America must not only be the world's policeman or its sheriff, it must be its beacon and guide...The alternative to American leadership is a chaotic, Hobbesian world, where there is no authority to thwart aggression, ensure peace and security or enforce international norms. That is what it means to be a global superpower with global responsibilities.[21]

In the aftermath of the American conquest of Baghdad, Kristol urged the troops ever forward. Already in an editorial in *The Weekly Standard* of January 21, 2002, Kristol and Kagan had insisted in line with the logic of the argument they had been making for years at this point that the fate of Saddam—not what happens in an insignificant place like Afghanistan—"will shape the contours of the emerging world order, perhaps for decades to come. Either it will be a world order conducive to our liberal democratic principles and our safety, or it will be one where brutal, well-armed tyrants are allowed to hold democracy and international security hostage." By May 13, 2003, after President Bush had announced the invasion a success, Kristol wrote that the victories in Afghanistan and Iraq were "merely battles," a prelude to war with Iran.

We are already in a death struggle with Iran over the future of Iraq. Iran is the tipping point in the war on proliferation, the war on terror, and the effort to reshape the Middle East. If Iran goes pro-Western and anti-terror, positive change in Syria and Saudi Arabia will follow much more easily.... On the outcome of the confrontation with Tehran, more than any other, rests the future of the Bush Doctrine—and quite possibly, the Bush presidency—and the prospects for a safer world.

If this prospect sounds daunting, in *The Weekly Standard* just a week earlier Max Boot had published a piece calling for "a much broader neo-Wilsonian vision of foreign policy" that included exercising control not only over Syria, Saudi Arabia, and Iran, but also over Egypt and Pakistan.

Later events in the Middle East were not to disturb these elements of the war party's thinking. On July 24, 2006, William Kristol published an editorial in *The Weekly Standard* on the Israeli invasion of Lebanon entitled "It's Our War." In it, Kristol maintains that the real enemy Israel and "liberal democratic civilization" face is not so much Hezbollah as Iran.

No Islamic Republic of Iran, no Hezbollah. No Islamic Republic of Iran, no one to prop up the Assad regime in Syria...no Shiite Iranian revolution, far less of an impetus for the Saudis to finance the export of the Wahhabi version of Sunni

Islam as a competitor to Khomeini's claim for leadership of militant Islam—
and thus no Taliban rule in Afghanistan, and perhaps no Hamas either....

For while Syria and Iran are enemies of Israel, they are also enemies of the
United States. We have done a poor job of standing up to them and weaken-
ing them. They are now testing us more boldly than one would have thought
possible a few years ago. Weakness is provocative. We have been too weak,
and have allowed ourselves to be perceived as weak.... [W]e might consider
countering this act of Iranian aggression with a military strike against Iranian
nuclear facilities. Why wait? Does anyone think a nuclear Iran can be contained.... Yes, there would be repercussions—and they would be healthy ones,
showing a strong America that rejected further appeasement.

The Bush Doctrine: Pinning It on the Neocons?

By late 2005, when American fortunes in the Middle East were going poorly,
voices were raised on every side assigning primary responsibility for the
war on neoconservative ideas. If victory has a thousand fathers but defeat
is an orphan, in John F. Kennedy's words, then the Iraq War, by general
consensus, had been fathered by the neoconservatives, who deserved all
the blame.

To compound the charge, many neoconservatives had claimed no less
themselves than to have authored the framework for U.S. foreign policy that
brought the debacle about. Thus, Max Boot had called the National Security Strategy (NSS) of 2002 "a quintessentially neoconservative document."
Joshua Muravchik had explained that 9/11 revealed what his school had
understood all along: "a sharp change of course was required" in American foreign policy, "and the neoconservatives, who had been warning for
years that terror must not be appeased, stood vindicated.... Not only did
the neocons have an analysis of what had gone wrong in American policy,
they also stood ready with proposals for what to do now." Or as Kristol had
written in *The Weekly Standard* on March 17, 2003, "Our policy specified
in 1997 is now official. It has become the policy of the U.S. government....
History and reality are about to weigh in, and we are inclined simply to let
them render their verdicts." Indeed, as late as the summer of 2005, Charles
Krauthammer was continuing to maintain that whatever minor disagreements might exist, everyone was now a neoconservative. "The remarkable
fact that the Bush Doctrine is, essentially, a synonym for neoconservative

foreign policy marks neoconservatism's own transition from a position of dissidence...to governance."

> What neoconservatives have long been advocating is now being articulated and practiced at the highest levels of government by a war cabinet composed of individuals...[whose] differences have, if anything, narrowed...it is the maturation of a governing ideology whose time has come.[22]

Part of the evidence of the justice of the neocon position came from the president himself. William Kristol, as discussed above, had said on July 24, 2006, that the Israeli invasion of Lebanon could be summed up as "It's Our War" and that we should go to the source of the problem in Iran. On August 14, 2006, Bush declared himself of the same mind: "The conflict in Lebanon is part of a broader struggle between freedom and terror that is unfolding across the region.... So we've launched a forward strategy of freedom in the broader Middle East.... The world must now recognize that it's Iranian sponsorship of Hezbollah that exacerbated the situation in the Middle East...Hezbollah has been emboldened because of its state sponsors." By late summer, official opinion was more and more of the conviction that Washington and Israel were engaged in a common cause in their struggles against what they identified as terrorism in the Middle East, for the most part based on Islamic fundamentalism. Ultimately the crux of the matter lay in Tehran's behavior.[23]

But is attributing the content of the Bush Doctrine solely, or even largely, to the neoconservatives in fact a fair assessment even if they claim authorship? To some extent they certainly bear responsibility. We have seen the way their distinctive ideas and organizational acumen led them to have real influence in the Bush White House, influence they used to considered purpose to respond to the crisis of 9/11. The way in which they drove policy thereafter should leave not the slightest doubt that the terms of the Bush Doctrine, the course of the Iraq War, and the decision that Iran's development of advanced nuclear technology was unacceptable, should be laid in good measure directly at their doorstep.

However, it would be a serious mistake to exaggerate the importance of the neoconservatives. Michael Lind, as well as Ivo Daalder and James Lindsay, have persuasively maintained the autonomy of the president and his closest policy-making advisors from the neoconservatives. If the neoconservatives did indeed pour a poison of unlimited expectations into the president's ear, along with those of Vice President Cheney and Secretary of Defense Rumsfeld, these men were more than ready to heed the tempters' message. Anyone who knows the stories of the political stances these men had taken over the twenty-five-year period or more before 2001, would have no doubts about the matter. Like Ronald Reagan, they had come to a view of world affairs that dovetailed with that of neoconservatives long before these various people had become acquainted. And then there is Tony Blair, a man ready to march against Saddam despite a total lack of contact with the neocons.

If we accept the relative autonomy of the War Cabinet from the neoconservative councilors, and I certainly think we should, then the door is open to canvassing other intellectual origins of the Bush Doctrine. To what extent did neoconservatives borrow concepts from other sources about the proper conduct of American foreign policy? To what extent were the members of the War Cabinet listening to other voices altogether? The end result of such deliberations may well be to diminish the role neoconservative thinking played in formulating the terms of the Bush Doctrine and its broad public acceptance.

In this spirit, Jonathan Monten has pointed out the many ways neoconservative thinking, with respect to expanding American power after the Cold War, might be seen as standard fare for a country that sees itself in such an enviable power position as the United States after the Cold War. Would any country faced with the temptations of a superpower not have found a pretext to act as Washington did?

As for democracy promotion, Monten includes in his survey the predispositions of evangelical Christianity to act with missionary purpose in world affairs against the forces of evil. He considers as well the secular mode of thinking in the Age of Reason that contributed to the American Revolution and to the process of elaborating a national constitution thereafter. Here in the American Enlightenment were notions of universal truths and values not restricted in their relevance to the continent of North America. He speculates too on latter-day influences of the character of the American Founding, with its insistence that the American national identity be a highly creedal affair, based on the virtues of freedom through self-government. Finally, Monaten discusses Progressivism as a politics of reform in the early twentieth century whose spirit may still be with us today.

As a result, the Bush Doctrine, which Monten defines as the "operationalization of neoconservatism...is not unique and its nationalist vision of the United States as a redeeming force in international politics provides an essential point of continuity with preceding generations of grand strategy."[24] Surely this argument is to some extent correct. The neoconservative appeal could not have been as great as it was without finding resonance in older and varied sources of American culture and belief.

Other observers have plausibly linked the Bush Doctrine to traditions in the actual exercise of American foreign policy that antedate the Iraq War. For example, William Kristol and Lawrence Kaplan invoke the mainstream tradition of Teddy Roosevelt, Harry Truman, John Kennedy, and Ronald Reagan when speaking of the doctrine. Paul Berman harkens back to Abraham Lincoln reflecting on the meaning of America to the world during the Civil War. Michael Ignatieff links the Iraq War, and so the doctrine, to nothing less than Thomas Jefferson's remarks days before his death as he reflected on the significance of the American Revolution to world affairs. Whatever the reference, the point is the same: the war and its antecedent doctrine are but another expression of a "distinctly American internationalism," one interpreted in a unique way by President Bush and his foreign policy team, to be sure, but nonetheless very much within the established parameters of American foreign policy.[25]

President George W. Bush agreed that his policy is in the mainstream American tradition. However, he was more likely to speak of historical analogies, such as the occupations of Germany and Japan or the taking of the Philippines, rather than of actual administrations (most of which were democratic) when pointing out the precedents for his war. When speaking of her support for the Iraq War, Secretary of State Condoleezza Rice also frequently referred back to the golden era of the 1940s when the United States established a security framework for world affairs that eventually faced down Soviet communism. However, she was more likely still to recall the legacy of the presidencies of Ronald Reagan and George H. W. Bush, the latter of whom she served as first the Soviet Empire, then the Soviet Union itself, collapsed—so providing her the inspiration for her later mission.

Yet why not go back before the 1940s if we want to try to establish the historical *bona fides* of the Iraq War? The most serious contender for the title of having authored a "distinctly American internationalism," most historians would surely agree, was Woodrow Wilson (1913–1921) at a moment when the United States for the first time appeared on the world stage with a blueprint for world order. True, Wilson was a Democrat and is associated in contemporary conservative minds with what they frequently call "fuzzy-minded" multilateralism. But the Wilsonian master plan for world order had as its primary tenet the hope to spread democracy worldwide. Since that policy framework was used extensively (in modified form) both in the 1940s by the Roosevelt and Truman administrations, and in other ways by the Reagan and Bush senior administrations as well, the thinking that lead to the decision to invade Iraq in March 2003 so as to replace despotism with democracy would seem to enjoy the benediction of almost a century of enlightened leadership associated with Wilson's initial concepts. Accordingly, when President Bush justified the invasion of Iraq by making claims about how dramatic the advent of democratic government could be, not only to the peoples of the Middle East but in fact to the entire structure of world organization, we may see him emerge as the most Wilsonian president in the history of American foreign policy—in fact, as a man better able to marshal American power and use it decisively to these liberal ends than even Woodrow Wilson himself.

Over the years, different aspects of Wilsonianism have been emphasized by different American presidents. Nevertheless, the centerpiece of what it means to be a liberal in the classic sense has traditionally been the belief that democratic states are more pacific and cooperative than their authoritarian counterparts, that therefore trust and reciprocity may well come to typify exchanges among them, and that as a result, ultimately there is not only moral virtue to such systems of government, but a critical practical utility in terms of attaining world peace that derives from their spread as well. Free trade, multilateralism, and American leadership all have importance in their own right in a Wilsonian order, but none carries the weight of a community of liberal democratic governments, restrained by the rule of law and resting on the consent of the governed, citizens who may freely organize and choose those who effectively rule through periodic elections.[26]

As a consequence, when President Bush justified the invasion of Iraq by making similar claims about how dramatic the advent of democratic government could be, not only to the peoples of the Middle East but in fact to the entire structure of world organization, it would seem that his Wilsonian credentials were quite in order. In 1917, Wilson hoped to "make the world safe for democracy;" Bush in speeches that have remained consistently liberal since June 2002 reaffirmed the commitment. Given this pedigree, how can we possibly dispute the claim that the Iraq War, like the Bush Doctrine itself, is in the tradition of American grand liberal strategy?

To some extent the arguments for continuity in the making of American foreign policy are convincing. Any solid analysis of Washington's ambitions for world order in the immediate aftermath of World War II will show a will to extend the reach of American power as far as it could prudently reach, and this essentially on the basis of Wilsonian presumptions.[27]

Yet to leave the impression that the Bush Doctrine is nothing but an updated form of Wilsonianism is to ignore the dynamic new framework for policy the administration was presenting, an ideology for imperialist purposes that must be grasped in its own right. In the 1990s, liberal internationalist thinking changed in fundamental ways that reflected in good measure changes in America's relative power position in world affairs. To fail to acknowledge the importance of these alterations is not simply to fail to understand the Bush Doctrine accurately but, as critically, to make it seem more traditionally based than is actually the case.

The Bush Doctrine was not a necessary development of Wilsonian thinking, the inevitable expression of American nationalism after 9/11 that its defenders often make it out to be. Indeed, without understanding the new concepts born of liberal internationalist work in the 1990s, the doctrine's self-assurance is well-nigh unintelligible. What is called for is an examination of the doctrine's intellectual presuppositions that sets it in its time, not in some past before the end of the Cold War, but in terms of what might be called *neoliberal* internationalist thinking as it developed after the fall of the Berlin Wall in 1989.

Beginning in the late 1980s and continuing through the following decade, liberal internationalist thinking managed to convert itself into an imperialist doctrine, a call bolder and more coherent in vision, wider in scope, and more determined in the power it sought to bring to bear than anything we might compare it to in the preceding history of the Wilsonian tradition. America had won the Cold War because it was liberal, and now, in conjunction with its equally liberal partners in the European Union gathered for the most part under its leadership in NATO, Washington could and should banish for once and for all tyrannical governments from the planet. Liberal internationalist thinking in the 1990s thus put behind it the counsels of prudence and restraint that previously had been part and parcel of its worldview in favor of a more expansive doctrine that recognized no limits to its embrace. Not so much historical amnesia over the tragic outcome of past experiences like Vietnam, but a new burst of historic confidence after the Cold War, explains the certainty with which the liberal internationalist message was promoted after 2001.

It is thus quite misleading to say as the neoconservative Robert Kagan did that "the striking thing about [the NSS] is that…[it] was hardly a novel concept, the Bush administration's new strategy was little more than a restatement of American policies, many going back half a century."

America did not change on September 11. It only became more itself…it is reasonable to assume that we have only just entered a long era of American hegemony…. But the only stable and successful international order Americans can imagine is one that has the United States at is center. Nor can Americans conceive of an international order that is not defended by power and specifically by American power. If this is arrogance, at least it is not a new arrogance.[28]

We should beware of such a seemingly common-sense approach. By reaching back across the generations to link the Bush Doctrine to past tradition, Kagan appeals to our patriotism. At the same time, he averts criticism of a policy he and his colleagues did so very much to author, shifting the responsibility from the shoulders of the neoconservatives to the course of American history.

While acknowledging both continuity with past foreign policy orientations and with deep-set features of American political culture, I would nonetheless like to stress the *singularity* of the Bush Doctrine and its *break* with the past. What we need to appreciate is how breathtakingly radical the American bid for world supremacy was as it appeared in the Bush Doctrine. Neither the scope nor the robustness of the quest for global domination can be at all adequately accounted for by past precedent or undercurrents of public opinion resting on nationalist or religious suppositions. Instead the doctrine conveys a tone of megalomania, a condition that we might argue is out of keeping with many strains of the American tradition, including earlier formulations of liberal internationalism. "America did not change on September 11. It only became more itself," declares Kagan. This assertion cannot pass the muster of historical evidence.

To be sure, apostles of empire like Robert Kagan knew how to tap in to public sentiment and to exploit undercurrents of American national thinking, all the while cloaking their ambitions with pious references to historical precedent. But to seize the full magnitude of what the Bush Doctrine portended—the conquest of Iraq, the domination of the entire Middle East, with the ability to exercise a "benevolent hegemony" over all of international affairs thereafter—we must see it in its own right, not reduce it to past antecedents or underlying sentiments. To do this requires looking not so much to the past history or to undercurrents of American culture so much as to developments in liberal thinking in the 1990s and to neoconservative dreams of American supremacy.

Enter the Neoliberals

Those who maintain that the neoconservatives did not author the Bush Doctrine alone are surely correct. They generally fail, however, to point to the indispensable co-authors of this extraordinary framework for liberal imperialism, people I will call the neo-Wilsonians, or neoliberals, for the most part academics of the center and center-left who during the 1990s had developed a set of ideas that, as much as anything the neoconservatives did, came to give the doctrine its intellectual panache.

If the neoconservatives' major contribution was to that dimension of the Bush Doctrine I called in the preceding chapter "the pillar of power," the contribution of the neoliberals was to its "pillar of purpose." Theirs was the notion defended empirically, theoretically, and philosophically that the promotion of democracy abroad was not only feasible, but that it would serve American security concerns. Hence, they were indispensable for what most observers agree was the defining mark of the doctrine, its optimism about changing the structure of domestic politics in the Middle East so as to usher in a new era of international peace.

On this score, the neoconservatives had little to offer. Prior to the Reagan years, most neoconservatives had been possessed of a strong streak of pessimism about the human condition, a sentiment that led them toward the theoretical tradition of realism in thinking about world affairs. The idea that a happy day of universal peace thanks to the internationalization of democratic government under the auspices of the American military was likely to take form simply was not likely to be theirs. Some of the old guard, like Irving Kristol or Jeane Kirkpatrick, refused to sign on at all to the belief that America's security needs could be served by fostering democracy abroad.

The neoconservatives who did back democracy promotion were certainly not of one mind. Like Richard Perle or Norman Podhoretz, some were willing to speak in these terms, but without terribly much conviction. Paul Wolfowitz and Charles Krauthammer, for their part, were selective in calling for democracy promotion, aware that some situations were far more favorable than others to democratizing regime change. So it was left to William Kristol and Robert Kagan, among the leading lights of the neoconservative movement, backed by a host of more minor writers like Joshua Muravchik and Max Boot, unreservedly to make the case that the advance of liberty abroad protected liberty at home.[29]

Left to their own devices, however, Kristol, Kagan, and company simply could not mount a powerful enough argument for democracy promotion abroad as an element of national security to give the Bush Doctrine the solid grounding it needed. Not only was just a minority of neoconservatives persuaded that the best defense of liberty at home was the expansion of liberty abroad, but *not a single member of this community, with the exception of*

Francis Fukuyama, ever contributed any original idea whatsoever with respect to this critical proposition. Certainly Leo Strauss cannot be invoked in defense of their intellectual standing in this respect. While Strauss was a believer in reason and freedom, and subscribed to a universalist notion of human rights, he was skeptical of all utopianisms, and persuaded that the Enlightenment idea of individual and social perfectibility had been at the root of much human evil. As a result, those neoconservatives for whom democracy promotion was an important matter, had to borrow the concepts that underlay such a pro-gram from the neo-Wilsonians, who in due course found that their work was being used to justify liberal imperialism on a global scale.

To arrange such a loan was not at all difficult. For during the 1990s (a term of convenience for a period that stretches from the late 1980s until 2001), working on their own, these generally nonpartisan or center-left intellectuals, most of them working at leading universities in the American academy, had managed to devise an argument for liberal imperialism that far outclassed in intellectual terms anything the neoconservatives were able to produce. So rather than reinvent the wheel, why not simply appropriate it?

Some neoliberal internationalists opposed the war. Others were surprised to find their ideas used to sanction regime change in Iraq. The liberal hawks who did support the Bush Doctrine, and as a result the Iraq War, were seldom Republicans. But it was in these neoliberal ranks, most certainly *not* with the neoconservatives, that we find the people who actually did the difficult recon-ceptualizing of the liberal internationalist argument so as to make its appeal so effective after 2001. In their hands, the propositions were established with the authority of the social sciences and the blessings of political philosophy that the spread of democracy was synonymous with the spread of peace, and that the appeal of democracy was well-nigh universal. Here were the men and women who gave an intellectual depth to the Bush Doctrine that to many made its logic so seductive. Here were the true authors of the most distinc-tive hallmark of the Bush Doctrine, its signature feature, the assurance that democracy abroad was a meaningful mission and that once accomplished it would mean security at home.

Here, too, is a principal reason for the lack of a serious anti-war move-ment in this country. Most of the neoliberals were Democrats. From Mad-eleine Albright to Hillary Clinton (to mention only these two), and under the auspices of the Progressive Policy Institute of the Democratic Party, those who might have opposed the Bush Doctrine instead became infused with a belief system that effectively made them support the idea of progressive imperialist wars. Their opposition to the Bush administration did not center on its goals but on its methods. They denounced the mismanagement of the Iraq invasion in a bid to take power themselves so that they could better achieve the same mission. What the leadership was slow to criticize in 2003 and thereafter, was the purpose of the war itself. In a word, the leading Democrats of the time were as convinced that America should make a bid for international supremacy as the Republicans. Where they differed, and the distinctions were minor, was on certain of the means to be used.

The active collaboration of neoliberals and Democrats in the Iraq War needs to be underscored. Stephen Holmes, one of the most acute observers of intellectual thought around the war, asked in the *Nation* on November 14, 2005, "How is the left to regain its moral bearings in a world where the right has brazenly stolen progressive ideas (human rights, liberation, democracy, relief of suffering) and marched the country into a bloody calamity under a false flag of liberty?" But the problem is that Holmes presumes that the left's ideas were "brazenly stolen" by the right, when in fact they were quite often gladly offered up for use by whoever could make use of them politically. The major regret was often that they hadn't been used aggressively enough by the Democrats.[31]

As a result, the liberal international community that works to further human rights and democratic government the world around is today in crisis. In the future, it may be successful in persuading countries to act together to stop acts of genocide and mass starvation, and it may be correct that democracies will remain each other's best supports in world affairs. But given the ambitions politically and intellectually this community once had, it is in a parlous state. Too many of its members have engaged themselves as agents of American imperialism for the spirit of their undertaking before 2003 ever to be regained. When Holmes asks how the left may "regain its moral bearings" the answer may well be that it cannot, except on the margins, as David Rieff has put it "offering a bed for the night."[32]

To conclude. Most certainly many of the terms of the Bush Doctrine have their antecedents in the American foreign policy tradition, just as much of its tone is in touch with religious and nationalist sentiments in this country. But what any accurate account of the doctrine should rather stress is change, not continuity, its boldness and singularity, its break with the past, its ideas that only were born in the 1990s, its relationship to a world situation that was radically new after 1991, and its authorship by a radical elite in this country, an elite that was not at all necessarily representative of its deep cultural moorings or its established political traditions. With the end of the Cold War and victory in the Gulf War, a new era of American greatness was born and with it a new set of ideas capable of presiding over this country's expanded capacities and enlarged ambitions. Just as the character of American power was without precedent, so too would be the doctrine that defined the nation's purpose in such a setting.

Seen from this perspective, the Bush Doctrine represented the convergence of neoconservative and neoliberal thinking for the genesis of what was essentially a new framework for American policy, something we must understand in its own terms, not by appealing to precedents or undercurrents so much as grasping the thing in itself. The neoconservatives were well aware of what they were doing. That leftist and nonpartisan neo-Wilsonians often could not see the wolf in sheep's clothing came from the unfortunate fact that they had offered their garments to him and he was glad to assume the disguise. With a perfect accent, a complete vocabulary, and excellent syntax, the wolf was growling in their language after all. Or to return to the title of this book, if a first pact with the Devil had been entered into by the neoconservatives in their bid for the United States to dominate world events, a second pact was concluded when the neoliberals took the apple offered them by the serpent and brought to the cause of world dominion their ideas on the rightness and efficacy of market democracy for all peoples.

The following chapter discusses the evolution of liberal internationalist thinking from the founding of the republic to the 1990s. Its purpose is to establish a sense not only of historical continuity but more especially of profound change. The argument that a break, a discontinuity, typifies the 1990s and thus that the Bush Doctrine needs to be considered as a framework for policy in its own right, is sure to be controversial, but the evidence that justifies making this claim is abundantly clear, as Chapters 4 through 7 will maintain.

To the extent this book's argument is persuasive, it may help to loosen the hold of neoconservative assurance in the extent of American power and of the neoliberal sense of self-righteousness that together have caused such harm. Even if the problem ultimately is one of a will to power that Americans in Washington share with humanity at large, this manifestation of an age-old problem has its specific personality, its unique identity that must be understood in its own terms as the United States set out to make a bid for world supremacy and in the process betrayed the American promise.

CHAPTER 3

Liberal Democratic Internationalism
Its Pre-Classical, Classic, and Hegemonic Stages

[After Afghanistan] Iraq was the most feasible next place to strike the blow.... We could set in motion a process that could undermine and ultimately remove reactionary regimes elsewhere in the Middle East, thereby eliminating the principal breeding ground for terrorism.... This was, then, in every sense a grand strategy...a plan for transforming the entire Muslim Middle East: for bringing it, once and for all, into the modern world. There'd been nothing like this in boldness, sweep, and vision since Americans took it upon themselves, more than half a century ago, to democratize Germany and Japan, thus setting in motion processes that stopped short of only a few places on earth, one of which was the Muslim Middle East.

John Lewis Gaddis, *Surprise, Security,*
and the American Experience

Trying to eliminate Saddam, extending the ground war into an occupation of Iraq, would have violated our basic guideline about not...engaging in "mission creep," and would have incurred incalculable human and political cost. We would have been forced to occupy Baghdad and, in effect, rule Iraq. The coalition would instantly have collapsed, the Arabs deserting it in anger and other allies pulling out as well. Under those circumstances there was no viable "exit strategy" we could see. Going in and occupying Iraq...would have destroyed

*the precedent of international response to aggression that we hoped
to establish. Had we gone the invasion route, the United States could
conceivably still be occupying power in a bitterly hostile land. It would
have been a dramatically different and perhaps barren outcome.*

George Bush and Brent Scowcroft, *A World Transformed*

As we saw in the preceding chapters, the Iraq War flowed like the mighty
Mississippi out of the Bush Doctrine, a statement of American grand strategy
developed during 2002 in a series of addresses that culminated in the publication of the National Security Strategy (NSS) of September 2002. The doctrine's
essential terms were that the United States had military and ideological preeminence in world affairs; that it would act unilaterally and preemptively if
it felt threatened by another state's challenge to the world order dominated
by market democracies that America guaranteed; and that once victorious in
battle it would see that the people of the defeated state were allowed to live
under a liberal democratic political order and participate in an open international economic order in such a manner that they would become responsible
members of the American Peace.

In a word, the Bush Doctrine was a grand imperial strategy of a sort never
before seen in the history of U.S. foreign policy. In its separate parts, such a
grandiose design did indeed have had its antecedents, but as a formal whole,
and in practice, it had no parallel. For a unipolar world, a unipolar message.
Its principal authors understood the Bush Doctrine in such large, historical
terms, and they were not mistaken.

To debate the logic of the Iraq War without addressing the character of
the Bush Doctrine risks misperceiving the motives behind the conflict and
so to engage us in meaningful, but ultimately secondary, concerns that may
well miss the broader picture. By contrast, to legitimize the Bush Doctrine by
making it the natural expression of American patriotism after 9/11 is to write
partisan history. It is a way to justify the Iraq War by placing a red, white, and
blue mantle on it when in fact the doctrine needs to be appreciated as a strategy unique in its daring, constructed for the United States by a small group of
individuals who had been thinking in such terms only since the early 1990s. In
sum, there are two ways to misjudge the historic wager of the Bush Doctrine.
One misses the forest for the trees, as in the hands of those who would treat the
Iraq invasion as though it were unconnected to a far more portentous strategic

design in Washington. The other is to minimize the extraordinary singularity of this forest, as in the hands of those who relate the doctrine, and so the war, to the grand tradition of American foreign policy, dismissing efforts to question its abrupt departure from convention.

The present chapter begins the development of the argument that whatever roots the Bush Doctrine undeniably had in the annals of American cultural life and the conduct of its foreign policy, it nonetheless represented a historic transformation in these beliefs and traditions. Thus, to call the degree of penetration of foreign ways the doctrine foretold "imperialism" risks understating the scope of what was envisioned. Empires have usually been content to leave their subject peoples to their own devices, honoring their own gods, if they will but pledge allegiance to the imperial authority. The Bush administration, however, sought far, far more than lip service to American leadership. Its goal was to reach out with a scope and a depth into the ways of foreign peoples that simply had no precedent in American foreign policy, indeed few in the annals of modern history, even if the occupations of Japan and Germany after World War II do suggest some analogies. While it is a certainty that the Iraq War emerged from the logic of the Bush Doctrine, it is far harder to make the case that this doctrine emerged from some inevitable tide of American history. It took a new distribution of world power, an active imagination, and an unprecedented degree of hubris to give birth to a doctrine with such a gargantuan appetite.

The Bush Doctrine and the American Foreign Policy Tradition

In the "war of ideas" that partisans of the invasion of Iraq have invited us to participate in, one of the major battlegrounds is that of the history of American foreign policy. As we saw in the preceding chapters, the most common spin to put on the Bush Doctrine is to relate it to precedents in American history, or to undercurrents in American national or religious discourse, implying thereby the *bona fides* of the Iraq War. The ambition is to blend the doctrine in to the greater narrative of American history and culture, so endowing it with a patriotic glow and removing from the shoulders of those who put together this extraordinary framework for American foreign policy the responsibility they should in fact bear for the consequences of their scheme for world supremacy.

In place of these accounts of history, I propose instead to recount the history of the idea of democracy promotion abroad in order to demonstrate the singular importance of the 1990s to the gestation of the doctrine. It was only then, flush with triumph in the Cold War, that a full-fledged ideology of liberal imperialism was born in the bosom of neoliberals and neoconservatives alike. Without rejecting completely the correspondences between the thinking of this period and past precedent or deeper cultural sentiments—that would be an impossible undertaking—I will advance the case that to understand the Bush Doctrine it is critical to grasp the reasoning of these two schools of thought as they developed between roughly 1986 and 2001, the immediate post-Cold War years I sum up as the 1990s.

A first battleground on which to launch an offensive against the war of ideas that would have us support the invasion of March 2003 is the terrain of history. Because comparisons between the effort to democratize Iraq and the record of American accomplishments with other countries are problematic, supporters of the Bush Doctrine have also sought to legitimize it by arguing that its *lettres de noblesse* lie in the annals of history. Before entering into my own historical narrative, it may be instructive to review perhaps the most sophisticated argument that has yet appeared linking the Iraq War to the course of American foreign policy so as to justify it, found in the work of John Lewis Gaddis.

The Case of John Lewis Gaddis

A number of American academics have stepped forth to legitimize the invasion of Iraq by presenting arguments that place it within the mainstream of the American foreign policy tradition. Among the first of them, and perhaps to date the best known, is the senior Yale University historian of American foreign policy, John Lewis Gaddis. During the Clinton years, Andrew Bacevich reports, Gaddis deplored "an absence of grand design" in Washington. The only consistent pattern he could identify was "one of responding to crises. There's a kind of incrementalism and ad-hocism to things."[1]

With the arrival of the Bush team in 2001, Gaddis could take heart. His hope for a grand strategy was quickly to bear fruit. In early 2004, Gaddis published a short history putting the Bush administration's Middle East policy into the context of nearly two centuries of American foreign policy. Dedicating his book to his "Yale Grand Strategy Students," Gaddis ennobled Bush's foreign policy by calling it an outstanding example of "grand strategy" and linking it to three others in American history.[2]

The first grand strategy was authored, we are told, by John Quincy Adams (when he was secretary of state) and was followed later in the nineteenth century by Presidents James Polk and William McKinley. It combined "preemption" and "unilateralism" with the goal of achieving containment and hemispheric "hegemony." The second grand strategy, one practiced in the twentieth century, was authored by Woodrow Wilson (although much more successfully practiced by Franklin D. Roosevelt). In contrast to the first tradition, the second combined "restraint" with "multilateralism" and the decision to promote democratic government for others. What the two grand strategies had in common was that both aimed at achieving hegemony, the first at a continental level, the second globally. In case these two traditions were not enough to make the case establishing the *bona fides* of Bush's invasion of Iraq, Gaddis threw in for good measure Thomas Jefferson's notion of the "empire of liberty," in which imperialism and freedom are fruitfully linked.

As Gaddis saw it, each of these grand strategies contributed features to the "war on terror" as the Bush White House grafted the democracy promotion of Wilson onto the unilateral preemption of Adams in a contemporary determination to reshape the Muslim Middle East by combining empire with liberty. The result was that "the Bush administration, whether intentionally or not, has been drawing upon a set of traditions...embedded within our national consciousness." Its end result was the almost instinctive conviction, expressed for some two centuries and again quite properly today, "that for the United States *safety comes from enlarging, rather than from contracting, its sphere of responsibility.*"[3]

Gaddis' breathtaking ambition was to anoint the Iraq War with the sacred oil of virtually the entire American foreign policy tradition. Posturing as Clio, muse of history, Gaddis offered such blessings as the academy can bestow on an undertaking whose logic in fact was more original in the annals of American history than he recognized. In any case, the lessons to be studied were not only those to be drawn from the occupations of Germany and Japan, which, as we shall see in Chapter 5, are not at all analogous to the situation in Iraq. Among a book of many surprises when it comes to its interpretation of the historical record was Gaddis' omission of the neoconservatives, a group of his partisan colleagues whose credentials for talking in terms of grand strategy were as sterling as any he might have identified. Gaddis would apparently have American history itself, a spirit "embedded in our national consciousness," responsible alone, without human intervention, for the immaculate conception of the Bush Doctrine.

What would we say of parallel efforts, for example, to place the Vietnam War within the logic of American foreign policy—which it unfortunately can be—then sanctified it for this reason and no other? Yet, uplifted by his synthesis of two centuries of American foreign policy that led to the invasion of

March 2003, Gaddis actually saw President Bush transformed from Hal, the profligate youth, to Henry V, the great English king. The Iraq War offered the opportunity to "repeat the Afghan Agincourt along the banks of the Tigris and Euphrates."[4]

Pace Gaddis, what the Bush administration achieved by blending the various foreign policy traditions into one—if indeed that was what took place—was not so much to receive the benediction of history, but rather its curse: the creation of an insidiously appealing, but deeply flawed, new tradition that blended a disregard for the limits on America's power with a self-righteous conviction that what it was doing was in the best interests of everyone on the globe—the peoples of the Middle East, of the United States, indeed of "world peace" itself. The great achievement of Gaddis's book was not, as he might hope, to legitimize this misbegotten policy, but instead to offer us a telling instance of the kind of flawed reasoning that led to such a debacle in the first place.

Accordingly, like liberals since Wilson's time, Gaddis has no doubt but that what is good for America is also good for others; and like many liberals (although not all, as the example of FDR illustrates), he has the congenital weakness of failing to understand the limits on American power. Gaddis expresses his faith clearly enough in the last pages of his book when he reports how he agrees wholeheartedly with Lincoln that the United States "is the last best hope of earth." Our enemies hate us "because they agreed with Lincoln. We are, therefore, like the Twin Towers, an irresistible target for those few whose aspiration is to kill hope." Hence, "we have to be ready to fight" for what America represents. To what end? To that "of removing the causes of terrorism and tyranny altogether."[5]

Surely this is not simply an impossible goal, but one dangerous so unreservedly to embrace. In the service of his mission, Gaddis gives a highly partisan spin to his account of the past. Consider his willful selectivity of choices for historical analysis. Gaddis looks at history that he imagines supports his view, not that which might trouble it—occupation policy of Japan and Germany after 1945, which worked spectacularly well, however irrelevantly to the Iraq experience, rather than at the more appropriate comparison of Vietnam, which most certainly did not achieve its ends. Moreover, he is so busy looking backward at history that he fails to look at the obstacles on every side today. Might it not have been preferable for us to have been presented with at least some analysis of Middle East politics (on which he has virtually nothing to say) rather than to see invoked selective interpretations of past grand strategies so as to favor the invasion of March 2003?

Gaddis's blinders seemed to be incurably in place. Writing in *Foreign Affairs* in 2005, a year after his book appeared, he remained true to form, speaking of the Middle East not in terms of its own history, but as we might now fear in terms of History with a capital H. "And what of the region's insulation from the wave of democratization that has swept the globe?" he asks. "Democratization has indeed been delayed in the Arab world.... To conclude that it can never take hold there, however, is to neglect the direction in which the historical winds have been blowing. And the best grand strategies, like the most efficient navigators, keep the winds behind them." Gaddis assured his readers that the Vietnam War was far worse than that in Iraq—he did this long before a final accounting could be made of the latter conflict, when there was every reason to think the cost could come to be much, much higher—and that he retained confidence in the "silent majority" of Iraqis to use elections responsibly so that ultimately the hope of Operation Iraqi Freedom might be realized.[6]

My guess for an explanation to this astonishing account of American and world history is that, for Gaddis, patriotic emotion trumped reason. Gaddis describes his encounters with his students, who report to him sentiments such as, "I love this country. I love this place. I love what we're doing here tonight [presumably in his Yale Grand Strategy Seminar]. I love it so much that I'm prepared to defend our right to do it, which is why I'm joining the Marines." Such sentiment allows Gaddis to close his book with yet another poignant exchange, when a student asks "in the dark and fearful days that followed September 11th: 'Would it be OK now for us to be patriotic?'" In the melodramatic final words of his book, Gaddis replies, "Yes, I think it would."[7]

Reconsidering the Historical Record

In order to engage in the war of ideas, we must lock horns with the war party's reading of the pattern of U.S. foreign policy that official Washington and its academic supporters are handing out. Let us then take up the story of American liberal internationalism as the proponents of the war in effect invite us to do, but not to applaud as good patriots would this ill-fated incursion into the Middle East so much as to appreciate both the originality and the foolhardiness of the Bush administration's call for the Iraq War. Let us see the bright line that should distinguish this invasion from what was mainstream liberal internationalism prior to the 1990s.

As a doctrine, liberal internationalism has evolved over time, each stage building on that which went before, but each having as well its own identity to be understood in its own terms. I posit five stages in the evolution of this ideology: *pre-classical* (from the Revolution to the Spanish American War), *classic* (the presidency of Woodrow Wilson), *hegemonic* (from the defeat of Germany to the collapse of the Soviet Union), *imperialist* (academic theory of the 1990s through the formulation of the Bush Doctrine in 2002), and *fundamentalist* (since 2002). My key argument will be that a break occurs between the hegemonic and imperialist phases of liberal international thinking, so that the liberalism of the Bush Doctrine was considerably different from formulations of this school's worldview only fifteen years earlier.

Because the liberal tradition up to the 1980s can be interpreted to counsel restraint at least as easily as war, and because liberalism changed in tandem with its times in the 1990s so as to lose virtually all of its cautious nature—then the study of the history of American foreign policy does indeed help us understand the logic of the Iraq War. But it does not thereby legitimize the conflict. What it allows us to do instead is to see the Bush Doctrine as more novel and more daring than most accounts allow. I thus accept the historical record as a ground to be studied but contest the viewpoint holding that through this process we will be reconciled with the invasion of March 19, 2003 as the faithful expression of an American foreign policy tradition in place since the occupations of Germany and Japan if not much earlier.

Pre-Classical Liberal Internationalism

What I call "pre-classical liberal internationalism" may be found in the 1770s in the first stirrings of the American Revolution—perhaps most vividly in the anti-monarchist tracts of Thomas Paine with their faith in universal self-government under the inspiration of the example of the American Revolution. ("The cause of America is in great measure the cause of all mankind," he wrote in the opening page of *Common Sense*.) Paine was not alone. Virtually all the founders repeatedly expressed sentiments that with government resting on the consent of the governed, the United States would be a model for other peoples, a beacon to the ages.

As President George Washington stated in his First Inaugural Address, "the preservation of the sacred fire of liberty, and the destiny of the republican mode of government, are justly considered as *deeply*, and perhaps as *finally*, staked on the experiment entrusted to the hands of the American people." More, in the part of the draft of this address that he chose not to include, the first president speculated on the example of America: "I rejoice in a belief that intellectual light will spring up in the dark corners of the earth; that freedom of inquiry will produce liberality of conduct; that mankind will reverse the absurd position that the many were made for the few, and that they will not continue slaves in one part of the globe when they can become freemen in another."[8]

As early as the 1790s, the character of American liberal internationalism became embroiled in world affairs with the wars surrounding the French Revolution. That revolution itself, Americans like Thomas Jefferson liked to think, found its inspiration in the example of 1776. Once events in France turned more bloody and dictatorial however—with the radicalization of the Revolution in 1792, the execution of Louis XVI in January 1793, followed by war between France and Great Britain, then the Reign of Terror, finally with the emergence of Napoleon as dictator—the mood decisively changed. From the first, Alexander Hamilton had favored the balanced constitutionalism of the British system as the best safeguard against the tyranny of government, whereas Jefferson continued for a time to applaud the sons of the French Revolution as better able to spread the blessings of freedom in Europe. In due course, Jefferson too was obliged to recognize that Napoleon's rise to power represented a perversion of the revolutionary process.

Whatever their disagreements, what Hamilton and Jefferson could both agree on was that the outcome of war in Europe would select what today we might call a dominant "regime type" that would have power in international affairs. The course of the struggle was therefore a legitimate national security concern for the United States. On either side of the debate—whether Americans favored the French or rooted for the British—the argument was likely to turn on which country would be more favorable to liberty on a constitutional basis.[9]

President Washington wisely counseled neutrality in the face of these faraway struggles. In what might be called the "Washington Doctrine," the Farewell Address issued in September 1796, the president called upon Americans to avoid the notion that the new nation might have "permanent inveterate antipathies against particular Nations and passionate attachments for others" and "to steer clear of permanent Alliances." Although his advice was followed for more than a century thereafter, the low profile that the United States adopted on the world stage did not mask its abiding sympathy for the spread of republican government abroad.

So we find Americans saluting the independence of Latin America, welcomed for a variety of reasons including commercial and security interests with the Monroe Doctrine of 1823, but in part because it appeared to signal another retreat of monarchical rule. Again the "springtime of nations" in 1848 that momentarily expressed the decline of imperial rule in Central Europe was warmly greeted in the United States, especially with the celebrations surrounding the visit of the Hungarian liberal Louis Kossuth. Americans also endorsed the variety of constitutional reform movements that arose from the mid-nineteenth to the early twentieth centuries in countries as different as Japan, Turkey, China, and Russia.

The belief in all these moments was that foreigners were taking inspiration from America. In this spirit, for example, President Lincoln expressed the conviction that America could have meaning for all of human history, so that preserving the Union was "the last, best hope of earth."

Yet for all its sympathy with liberal reform worldwide, pre-classical American liberal internationalism can be marked off from later periods by its lack of ideological sophistication and by its reluctance (if not its adamant refusal in the minds of those like President John Quincy Adams) to call for the use of American military might to secure the expansion of governments based on the consent of the governed. The result was that the pre-classical liberal doctrine was both provincial—its conceptualizing what might be gained for the United States should democracy take root abroad was thin compared to later thinking—and insular—America would work by force of example rather than force of arms to further the liberal cause worldwide.

The Spanish-American War in 1898 marks the transition out of pre-classical liberal internationalism into its classic phase. Now Washington would use force for the sake of other peoples, especially for those cruelly oppressed by Spanish rule in Cuba but also in the Philippines. And it could draw up for the first time a balance sheet that showed foreign possessions worth the effort in terms of what they might bring the United States. Still, the gains for America that control over the Philippines and Puerto Rico would provide were relatively modest (a boost in international prestige, better access to the China market based on a secure port in Manila, and a port in San Juan that might support an eventual Isthmus Canal). All this had to be weighed against the chance (as the anti-imperialists pointed out) that America would be drawn into faraway conflicts in the Pacific where it had no business being.

In light of later debates, the stakes were low. The taking of the Philippines and Puerto Rico marked an end point to American imperialism. At the turn of the twentieth century, when imperialist rivalries were partitioning Africa and threatening the political integrity of the Ottoman Empire and China, the United States played a cautious role in world affairs, its concerns for the future of democratic government more a domestic than an international issue.

Classic Liberal Internationalism

What I would call the "classical" stage of American liberal internationalism had to await the presidency of Woodrow Wilson (1913–1921). The genius of Woodrow Wilson was his ability to combine what had been implicit features of U.S. foreign policy into a relatively clearly expounded blueprint for world affairs, its centerpiece being the call for this country *to support the expansion of democratic governments abroad as a way of strengthening American national security.* Scarcely a week into his presidency Wilson announced his extraordinary "non-recognition doctrine" with respect to Latin America (and more particularly with regard to Mexico, which was then in the throes of a momentous revolution):

> We hold…that just government rests always upon the consent of the governed and that there can be no freedom without order based upon law and upon the public conscience and approval. We shall look to make these principles the basis of mutual intercourse, respect, and helpfulness between our sister republics and ourselves. We shall lend our influence of every kind to the realization of these principles in fact and practice, knowing that disorder, personal intrigue and defiance of constitutional rights weaken and discredit government…. We can have no sympathy with those who seek to seize the power of government to advance their own personal interest or ambition. We are friends of peace but we know that there can be no lasting peace in such circumstances.[10]

In this spirit of Republican anti-authoritarianism, Wilson endorsed the Mexican Revolution but intervened against military leaders who would usurp power, in order to see that it was kept on a constitutional, and consequently a democratic, track. "My passion is for the submerged 85 percent of the people of that Republic who are now struggling toward liberty," declared the president in 1914. "I challenge you to cite me an instance in all the history of the world where liberty was handed down from above. Liberty always is attained by the forces working below, underneath, by the great movement of the people." At the same time, the president insisted that these powerful popular forces organize themselves for peace and stability in a constitutional manner, fearful that otherwise anarchy followed by another dictatorship might be the bitter fruit of this hard-fought uprising.

Wherever he promoted democratic government abroad, Wilson had in mind American national security. Mexico had a 2,000 mile frontier with the United States and a population in the millions—moreover, it might eventually fall prey to a great power hostile to American interests. Stability in the

Caribbean and Central America guaranteed the Panama Canal—a commercial and strategic lifeline of the first importance to this country in the early twentieth century. To be sure, the framework for constitutional democratic government that Wilson held out to the Latin Americans was in their interest as well to adopt. But the president was essentially thinking in terms of American security when he advocated promoting democracy abroad. Here was the hallmark of "classical" liberal internationalism, a position far more intellectually mature than the liberal thinking that preceded Wilson's time.

In 1914, Nicaragua became an American protectorate and in 1916, Wilson intervened forcibly in the Dominican Republic to forestall action by that country's foreign creditors but also to democratize the land. His purpose was to bring better government to the Caribbean and Central America and at the same time to ward off powerful interlopers who might fish in the troubled waters of this region (through extending loans that could not be repaid, which would then warrant their intervention) to expand their influence to the detriment of serious American security concerns in the Gulf of Mexico and Panama. The democratization of Central America and the Caribbean would thereby serve a double purpose—to protect American strategic interests while by the same token promoting the well-being of these Latin peoples.

It is well worth noting, in light of current liberal thinking that democracy can plant roots with relative ease virtually anywhere in the world, that Wilson's efforts in these two countries were utter failures. What America left behind for the Nicaraguans and the Dominicans was not the blessings of liberty but the curse of the Somoza and the Trujillo families respectively. Racial cleavages, an agrarian economy, and an authoritarian political culture combined to dictate a defeat as speedy as it was complete of Wilson's hope for the region's democratization. Cynics may argue that Wilson got what he most wanted: stable governments friendly to Washington in the region. But the cynics are wrong. The president sincerely believed that American security best lay not in authoritarian governments friendly to the United States because they were dependencies, but in democratic peoples able to cooperate with their northern neighbor in a common enterprise of prosperity and peace based on the strength of democratic self-government.

Latin America was not the only, much less the primary, region that Wilson hoped to see democratized. In March 1917, the president welcomed the first phase of the Russian Revolution, which swept the czar from power, although he expressed his concern at the Bolshevik Revolution later in the year as a potentially dangerous development for Russia and world order. He was right.

By 1921 it was clear that Lenin's government would have no truck with "bourgeois" democratic practices, that instead the "dictatorship of the proletariat" would organize itself in Moscow and spread its ways through the Third International to all parts of the globe. To nationalist movements looking for a way to organize modern effective governments, Lenin offered an answer seemingly as cogent as Wilson's, for Marxism-Leninism, too, promised freedom and justice, prosperity and peace.

Wilson's greatest bid to spread democratic government came with his call for national self-determination for the peoples liberated from imperial rule by the Great War. With the collapse of the Austro-Hungarian, Russian, and Ottoman Empires the moment finally seemed at hand to make a reality of the promise of 1848 and promote the expansion of the nation state at the expense of imperial orders. In the hope that these power vacuums would be filled with democratic states, Wilson worked on the practical question of national borderlines, the rights of minority populations within the new countries, the character of the new governments themselves, and the problems of regional stability in an area turned over to nationalist forces now that these great empires lay in ruins. He worried that the Russian Revolution would turn against democracy. He believed that the kaiser's abdication could lead to the consolidation of democratic government in Germany and on this basis to Franco-German reconciliation, which he saw as the key to peace in Europe. His purpose was to bring a stable peace to Europe based on the expansion of democracy there and in the process to create a system of collective security among these democracies, which would redound to America's benefit. Here at Versailles was the fullest expression of the classic phase of liberal democratic internationalism.[11]

There is no need here to go into detail with the fruits of Wilson's efforts. Except in Czechoslovakia, where still today he holds a place of honor, Wilson's hopes came to naught. The failure of the Senate to ratify U.S. entry into the League of Nations (in many ways an outcome of Wilson's faulty handling of the matter), the Depression, the expanding appeal of communism in Europe, and the rise of fascism (and more especially Nazism), all combined to weaken liberal democracy's appeal in Europe. Meanwhile in the Middle East, the mandate system of the League provided for the disposal to European powers of peoples once promised their independence at the end of the war, Palestine and Iraq being awarded to Great Britain (which already held Egypt), while France gained control of Syria and Lebanon.[12] World War I had sowed the whirlwinds of history. With the Spanish Civil War as the prelude to a greater war, bringing together as it did the dangers of Bolshevism, fascism, and the fears of the Great Depression, the prospects for liberal democracy looked bleak by the late 1930s.

Nevertheless, what Wilson left behind was a blueprint, invaluable for those who followed him, as to how America should envision international order in an era of nationalism where the rival appeals of communism and fascism threatened to eclipse liberal democracy for all time. In the face of these totalitarian menaces (neither one of which Wilson, who died in 1924 after a long illness, lived long enough to appreciate as the dangers they were to become), the United States had found a way to promote democracy locally while appealing to democratic countries to unite internationally. Through open economic systems and multilateral institutions designed to coordinate their interests, the liberal democratic world might make itself a more formidable bloc in world affairs to counter threats to each country individually. What all of this presumed, however, was not simply U.S. participation, but Washington's leadership. In its classic period, liberal internationalism as an ideology had been born even if it was decades later before it became a powerful instrument of world policy.

The reason for Wilson's enduring appeal reflected not only American interests and power but also the growing need for peoples everywhere in the twentieth century to refashion state-society relations in ways that provided new definitions of citizenship and state organization so as to allow for the mass political participation of an increasingly nationalistic populace. Nationalism may be defined as an ideologically formulated sense of union among a people, giving rise to the call for a state to rule over a specific territory in a way made legitimate by some concept of popular sovereignty. A people's feeling of nationalism may be based on common kinship and ethnicity created by a common religion, language, territory, or shared history—factors that alone or together establish the boundaries of the group. What makes nationalism distinctively modern is not these feelings of solidarity so much as the demand for a state based on popular sovereignty. Liberal internationalism aimed to give a particular type of institutional form to these nationalist demands in the form of constitutional democratic government.

In the nineteenth and twentieth centuries (and still today) nationalism was a solvent of authoritarian and imperial rule. Its force underlay World War I, the collapse of the Austro-Hungarian, Ottoman, and Russian Empires thereafter, the fascist slogans of World War II, the wave of decolonization in Africa and Asia that followed this struggle, and the disintegration of the Soviet Empire and the Soviet Union itself beginning in the late 1980s. The overriding question that confronted nationalism was what to put in the place of that which it had destroyed. In a word, what did "popular sovereignty" mean in practice? What did citizenship mean in terms of rights and responsibilities? How was the state to be structured? What kind of party system would link the government to the people?

As the preceding discussion suggested, during the interwar years, the Wilsonian blueprint was matched by two others: those of communism and fascism. Communism appealed to the poor and had as its main power backer the Soviet Union. Fascism appealed to old order of church, property, and royalty, afraid of the communist challenge and contemptuous of what it saw as the weakness of liberal democracy. In its extremist form as Nazism, fascism came to power in Germany. For its part, liberal democracy appealed to the middle class, marginalized ethnicities, and those everywhere who feared overly powerful government. The great powers that stood for this form of state were Great Britain and the United States. In the Spanish Civil War that broke out in 1936, it began to seem that the least likely of these forms of government to survive would be liberal democracy.

The greatness of Wilson lay in his understanding that channeling the force of nationalism into liberal democratic governments that would respect their citizens as well as their neighbors was the best solution reason could establish as to how domestic and international order might be created in a way consonant with human dignity and American national security. Although his ideas did not win the peace that followed 1918, they were resurrected to altogether better results after the victory of 1945. For thanks to Wilson, liberal internationalism had now become enough of an ideology—a coherent set of ideas covering a wide array of social questions that could mobilize the support of many interests and specify political institutional forms to be taken—that it could survive to offer an alternative to the totalitarian movements of the 1930s. Classic liberal internationalism was set to enter its hegemonic phase.

Liberal International Hegemonism

Despite the terrible reversals to liberal democratic hopes in the interwar years, the Wilsonian dream survived to reemerge in more robust (because realistic) form as a blueprint for world order after World War II. Franklin Roosevelt's notion of the United Nations refined Wilson's version of the League by making it clear that the institution was no embryo of world government. FDR's Bretton Woods system gave far more form to an open international economy than Wilson had ever imagined. FDR's notion that the occupations of Germany and Japan be dedicated to the democratization of these two militaristic peoples embodied the age-old liberal belief that democratic government could profoundly influence the domestic and external behavior of those who enjoyed it. And the president's call to the European powers to liberate their colonial empires, and to Moscow to permit the peoples of Central Europe to organize freely their own governments after the war, revealed his conviction that democracy might take root in lands where it had never been practiced. As importantly, President Roosevelt understood how indispensable American leadership was to the success of this bold vision.

Nor was FDR's (or subsequently President Harry Truman's) liberal faith misplaced. The Cold War was eventually won by the United States largely because of the way it had organized the market democracies of Western Europe and Japan to resist communist power and thanks to the appeal of these ideas to many of the peoples of Europe under Soviet control.[13]

Essentially, what had occurred by 1947 was the emergence of an American two-track strategy. Containment—the primary track—assumed that world affairs followed a policy script that treated world affairs as following the law of the jungle. The Soviet Union was an adversary of the most basic kind. However, alongside containment the world of market democracies organized themselves by another mode of interaction, one of cooperation and interdependence based on increasingly integrated economies and more deeply rooted democratic governments that participated together in a wide variety of international organizations—what we would now call globalization. From this perspective, the conclusion of the Cold War represented not so much the triumph of one country over another (the United States over the Soviet Union) as the victory of one form of social, economic, and state and interstate system over another (open market capitalism and liberal democracy over communism and central planning).

I would call the period from 1944 to 2000 the years of liberal internationalist hegemonism. With Wilson, a classical liberal framework had been engendered intellectually, but it sank no roots in the international relations of its time. With Franklin Roosevelt and Harry Truman, by contrast, liberal values became ideologically more systematized and expansive, giving rise to important intergovernmental institutions and these in turn to much more concrete interests. In its hegemonic phase, liberal internationalism frankly depended on the exercise of American primacy over the world of market democracies. This hegemonism was imbued with the spirit of multilateralism, although ultimately it was Washington that saw that the world of market democracies was richly endowed with international economic organizations such as the World Bank and the General Agreement on Tariffs and Trade (today the World Trade Organization), with military alliances of which the North Atlantic Treaty Organization was by all odds the most critical, and with initiatives such as the Marshall Plan that aimed to undergird democratic governments and economic integration in Western Europe.[14]

Despite its growing self-confidence, liberal internationalism remained a "track" in Washington's foreign policy, a line of approach that worked in support of the containment of communism, a hope for a better tomorrow in a world that otherwise obeyed the law of the jungle. Hegemonic liberalism thus had a degree of restraint to it, however much it looked forward to a day when its message would spread farther afield. It understood that at best democracy promotion could be *a* central concern in American foreign policy, not *the* priority consideration it was to become in a later stage.

Both multilateralism, whereby Washington sought allied support, and containment, whereby Washington looked for ways short of war with Moscow to create a stable world system, reflected an American appreciation that, however great its power position most certainly was, Washington's ability to move world events nonetheless remained limited. In these circumstances, hegemony—substantial as the word may sound—presupposed that the United States would work incrementally with the world as it was.

As a consequence, restraint in expecting that other countries would easily become democratic was another attribute of the hegemonic period. The threat of communism coming to power in Southern Europe, for example, was widely appreciated by liberal internationalists. Italy had the wherewithal to be a democracy, but in Greece, as in Spain and Portugal, Washington saw how unlikely it was any third force between the extreme right and left could hold power and threw in its lot with authoritarian government. "He may be an s.o.b., but he's our s.o.b.," Roosevelt had said of Somoza in Nicaragua, and the judgment was later used to cover a variety of other circumstances. The United States had a limited amount of power at its disposal and the democratization process was a terrifically difficult initiative to undertake.

Where the prospects for democratic consolidation were evident, the Marshall Plan promised support. Where the prospects of democratic government were less bright, as in the Eastern Mediterranean, the Truman Doctrine promised support to non-communist government nonetheless. As a consequence, in countries critical to American security such as China, Turkey, and

Iran, authoritarian governments were accepted for what they were—necessary expedients in an imperfect world where American power was quite obviously not up to any mission of liberalizing regime change. "Realistic" or "selective" liberal internationalism was the only practical way to proceed.

The hegemonic stage of liberalism marked a significant advance beyond the classic period by virtue of its ability to create local and international structures in line with its ideological expectations. But it needs to be underscored in light of how this ideology was to evolve following the Cold War that Washington expected to cooperate most closely with its democratic partners while moving gingerly where its authoritarian allies were concerned. Liberalism's choicest model might be that of the European community, where authoritarian countries like Spain, Portugal and Greece were by the 1970s democratized thanks to the example of their northern neighbors, who offered to include them in what today is called the European Union conditional on their full-scale liberalization. Elsewhere, confidence in the transition to democracy was more muted. In a word, liberal internationalist thinking in its hegemonic phase recognized at once the great power at America's disposal but also its constraints. In light of what was to come, this stage today appears not only to have been a cautious, restrained, and prudent form of liberal internationalism, but one that was enormously effective as well.

Categorizing the period from the 1940s through the 1980s as one dominated by a hegemonic brand of liberal internationalism risks oversimplifying reality, of course, so at least two reservations are called for at this point. First, we should remember that some administrations were not at all liberal in their thinking about world affairs. Neither Lyndon Johnson (1963–1969), Richard Nixon (1969–1974), nor Gerald Ford (1974–1977) supported the promotion of human rights and democratic governments in American foreign policy making. Apparent exceptions such as the Helsinki Process, which quickly constituted a major liberal initiative toward loosening Soviet control over Central Europe, were not at all seen as having such a promise by Henry Kissinger when he agreed to these terms.[15]

A second reservation on any generalization about the importance of democracy promotion is that those presidents whose administrations fall within the hegemonic period expressed their loyalty to the democratic creed in world affairs in markedly different ways. For President Dwight Eisenhower (1953–1961), the focus was on the "captive nations" of Eastern Europe that needed to be restored to democratic life by having the boot of Soviet control lifted from them. Elsewhere Eisenhower's appeals were more muted, while in Iran and Guatemala, he gave the green light to the CIA to topple constitutional governments that could fairly claim to be democratizing their countries (the overthrow of Mohammad Mossadegh in 1953, that of Jacobo Arbenz in 1954). The centerpiece of liberal internationalism for President John Kennedy (1961–1963) was the Alliance for Progress, an effort to promote democratic government throughout the hemisphere as a way of warding off the possibility that the Cuban Revolution might be repeated. By joining a call for land reform to state restructuring, Washington was engaged in an unprecedented initiative toward Latin America. And for President Jimmy Carter (1977–1981), the way to democracy ran through his "human rights crusade," which he conducted against regimes favorable to the United States as well as against those that were hostile, and which he naively believed to be far less political than it actually was. Each of these administrations had its liberal democratic features, but each was distinctive in the way they were pursued.

During the hegemonic era of liberal internationalism, two phases stand out as especially important—its opening in the 1940s with a blueprint for world order authored in Washington by Democrats, and its conclusion in the 1980s on terms authored by Republicans that meant victory in the Cold War for the United States. Here are the liberal bookends of the contest with communism, its opening heralded by the extraordinary range of measures Washington backed to arrange for cooperation among the market democracies, its conclusion marked by the presidency of Ronald Reagan, who made liberal internationalism not only respectable in Republican circles but imaginable as part of the "new thinking" of Mikhail Gorbachev as well.

Neoconservative partisans of the Bush Doctrine profess a special affinity for the presidency of Ronald Reagan, whom they see as authoring their model for combining values with power in the pursuit of a better world. Because the Reagan years are so often invoked by the liberal imperialists who organized the Iraq War, it is critical to review the lessons of his administration to see his relevance to current policy.

Prior to the administration of George W. Bush, no presidency since Wilson's time had been more liberal in world affairs than Reagan's. True, there is a significant problem in awarding him this title given his suspicion of multilateral institutions like the United Nations. One could explain this, perhaps, as a well-founded distrust of international organizations not dominated by democratic states—Wilson himself had at first thought to restrict membership in the League of Nations to democratic countries

alone—for in every other way Reagan was an exemplar of liberal internationalism. NATO, then, would be his multilateral organization of preference, not the UN.

As one would expect from a Wilsonian, Reagan propounded the conviction that Washington had a leadership role in world affairs in good measure
because of its moral example; he repeatedly asserted that only democratic governments could be considered legitimate and be trusted friends of the United
States. He argued that a world order run by democratic states would be more
prosperous and peaceful than any other. He designed anti-statist economic
policies to reduce the strength of government relative to civil society. He unreservedly endorsed international open markets. Finally, Reagan indicated a
willingness to use force for the defense of freedom worldwide.

Reagan's decisions to put pressure on the Soviet Union through an accel-
erated American arms buildup, and through "freedom fighters" attacking
communist governments in Nicaragua and Afghanistan, undoubtedly played
their part in ending the Cold War by making Moscow increasingly aware of
its economic and technological weakness relative to the United States. However, Reagan and his closest aides, Secretary of State George Schultz and Secretary of Defense Caspar Weinberger, were capable of negotiating an end to
the Cold War in ways that were successful in influencing Soviet leader Mikhail
Gorbachev by proclaiming the virtues of market democracy and inviting the
Soviet Union to reform in liberal terms.

A critical aspect of the peaceful collapse of the Soviet empire and Soviet
Union between 1989 and 1991 was that liberal thinking was successful appealing to Gorbachev's sense of the direction reform in his country needed to go.
He heard variants of the liberal argument from within the Soviet party itself
(where reform groups began to form as early as Nikita Khrushchev's effort
in 1956 to de-Stalinize the country), from the so-called "Eurocommunists"
(especially in Italy), from reform communists within the Soviet bloc (especially in Czechoslovakia), from socialist democrats like Olaf Palme, Willy
Brandt, and Elliot Trudeau, as well as from more conservative democratic
leaders he came to respect, particularly Margaret Thatcher. But there is no
reason to discount the influence Reagan and his very persuasive Secretary of
State George Shultz had with their own ideas for "constructive engagement"—
the effort to get authoritarian regimes to democratize in their own interest.
Reagan and Schultz contributed to Gorbachev's "new thinking," that is, not so
much because of their military preparedness but because they combined these
initiatives with the conviction that only open markets and more democratic

government were in the long run capable of restoring the fortunes of the Soviet Union and so its place in the world.[16]

Because the Cold War was in a good measure an ideological contest between liberal democracy and Marxism-Leninism—rival blueprints of the state and of state-society relations, each with a claim to be the model for all the peoples of the earth—then a possible end for it was the intellectual collapse of one of the two systems of thought and organization. The essence of Gorbachev's New Thinking came to be an ideological capitulation to liberal democracy, although it misperceived itself to be a viable version of reform communism. *Perestroika* with *glasnost*—that is, economic and political liberalization combined—need not have been the Soviet choice, as the Chinese decision to have the former without the latter indicates. For Gorbachev to associate the two together must be considered due in some substantial measure to his acquaintance with liberal doctrine.[17]

As a liberal internationalist who backed democracy promotion abroad and military expansion at home, Reagan played something of an intermediary role between what would later be liberal imperialism and what was at the time of his presidency liberal hegemonism. Like the later imperialists, he had a well-nigh religious conviction that democracy was the answer to humanity's problems and a willingness, at least rhetorically, to use force to back up his beliefs. However, like the hegemonists, Reagan was in practice cautious and restrained, waiting for history to takes its course, as he and Secretary Shultz often put it, convinced as they were that communism was fated to collapse in short order without an overly aggressive strike from the West.[18]

The restraint characteristic of the hegemonic period of liberal internationalists remained dominant in the White House during the presidency of George H. W. Bush (1989–1993). Bush was well known for saying he did not have "the vision thing" and announced that he would not "dance on the Berlin Wall"—that is, he would follow in the spirit that Wilson announced in 1918 of having "peace without victory" and so not complicate the plight of a Soviet leadership in crisis. He also reassured Chinese leaders in the summer of 1989 that the Tiananmen appeals for democracy—even when invoked with the statue of the "Goddess of Liberty" deliberately modeled on the Statue of Liberty—had no support from his administration. In short, he would not use this historic moment of Soviet or Chinese vulnerability to push aggressively for the spread of democratic government.

As the quote that serves as an epigraph for this chapter indicates, the senior President Bush was restrained after the Gulf War as well. "Our prompt withdrawal helped cement our position with our Arab allies, who now trusted us far more than they ever had. We had come to their assistance in their time of need, asked nothing for ourselves, and left when the job was done." The apparent failure to push his advantage in 1991 set this president apart from the rising tide of liberal imperialists born of the end of the Cold War, including, as we have seen in the preceding chapters, top Pentagon officials during his own administration who were highly critical of his decision not to enter Baghdad so as to bring about democratizing regime change there and who came to occupy important posts in Washington with the inauguration of George W. Bush in January 2001.[19]

Nevertheless, Bush emerges as a "selective" supporter of democracy abroad whose primary emissary to this end was Secretary of State James Baker. After his extraordinary accomplishment of securing a reunified Germany as a democratic member of NATO, the great question by late 1991 became "whither Russia?" In his efforts to help guide political events after the fall of the Iron Curtain and the end of the Soviet Union itself, Baker reiterated five principles governing American policy toward this vast region: minority rights be considered sacrosanct; human rights be respected; borders were inviolable; changes were to come through peaceful means; and the Helsinki Final Act and the Charter of Paris confirming these norms and practices were to guide conduct. In his words:

> The opportunities are historic. We have the chance to anchor Russia, Ukraine, and other republics firmly into the Euro-Atlantic community and the democratic commonwealth of nations. We have the chance to bring democracy to lands that have little knowledge of it, an achievement that can transcend centuries of history.... This historic watershed, the collapse of communist power in Bolshevism's birthplace, marks the challenge that history has dealt us: to see the end of the Soviet empire turned into a beginning for democracy and economic freedom across the former Soviet empire.[20]

Although Bill Clinton campaigned for the presidency in 1992 on the basis of pushing a human rights agenda with respect to China and Haiti more strongly than President George H. W. Bush had done, once in the White House (1993–2001) he became more prudent. For a moment, the slogan of the new administration was that containment would be replaced by the "enlargement" of the sphere of market democracies in the world. But particularly after the reversal of American fortunes in Somalia in October 1993, Clinton pulled back from ambitions he had earlier expressed to restore democratic order to Haiti and to intervene more forcefully in the Balkans so as to end Serbian outrages there. Eventually, the president did act, but only after the African-American community twisted his arm with respect to Haiti in 1994, and after events in the first part of 1995 convinced him that peace was possible in the Balkans (leading to the Dayton Accords of that year).

The policies of Slobodan Milosevic in Kosovo finally produced a NATO air attack on Serbia in 1999, but again with a restraint that indicated Clinton's reluctance to put much stock in democracy promotion in the Balkans. His encounters with China, where Clinton at first linked trade and investment rights with that country to human rights reform, quickly ended in failure. Clinton argued thereafter that economic prosperity could be expected to lead to democratic reform in that country, hence the way to Chinese democratization would be through its membership in the World Trade Organization.[21]

Clinton's restraint enraged the neoconservative imperialists. Lawrence Kaplan and William Kristol denounced his "evident discomfort with the use of American power" maintaining that he "dithered" and was "feckless." Kristol and Robert Kagan concluded that Clinton had "not been up to the larger task of preparing and inspiring the nation to embrace the role of global leadership...[he was] disinclined to sacrifice blood and treasure in the name of overseas commitments. His Pentagon officials talk more about exit strategies than about national objectives. His administration has promised global leadership on the cheap refusing to seek the levels of defense spending needed to meet the broad goals it claims to want to achieve in the world." In 1999, the neoconservative David Wurmser published a book about Saddam Hussein (with an introduction by Richard Perle) called *Tyranny's Ally*—where the "ally" was none other than Bill Clinton himself.[22]

The restraint characteristic of the Clinton years was clear on Iraq as well, where, as in so many other matters, the president followed the example of his Republican predecessor. Despite strong pressure from neoconservatives to act against Saddam, especially after they were organized in the Project for a New American Century in 1997, Clinton basically continued the policies of Bush senior—an economic embargo, protection of the Kurdish community in the north, and air attacks on Iraqi military installations that challenged Anglo-American over-fly rights established after the Gulf War of 1991. His critics were correct: lacking a plan for what to do with Iraq if the United States conquered it—unable, that is, to conceive of the expansion of American security thanks to Iraq's democratization with the élan that the administration of George W. Bush was able to muster only a few years later—Clinton temporized.

My point here is not a full history investigating the characteristics of the hegemonic period, nor to investigate the Cold War years and their immediate aftermath in great depth, but rather to set off the period of the 1990s from that which proceeded it. Still, it is worth noting that, ironically enough, despite being from opposed parties, Jimmy Carter and Ronald Reagan were more dedicated to democracy promotion abroad than either George H. W. Bush or Bill Clinton. Yet what marked all of these administrations was a decided reluctance to push too hard on the promotion of human rights and democratic government in countries and regions where such thinking seemed likely to suck the United States into endless problems without solution. Where democratization could happen with relative ease—in Poland, the Czech Republic, Slovakia, Slovenia, or Hungary, for example, after the fall of the Iron Curtain—it might be reinforced by inviting these lands into NATO and the European Union. Washington would salute the coming of democratic government to South Africa, Chile, and South Korea as well. So, too, the first genuinely democratic election in Mexico's history in 2000 could be greeted as a welcome new beginning. Elsewhere prudence dictated reserve.

The bottom line then, if one can summarize a general mood during such a variegated period, is a sense of measured restraint in American foreign policy, expressed in a recognition that however great its power might be, Washington was nonetheless limited in the impact it could have on world affairs. The result was to act multilaterally whenever possible (especially with NATO but also in the UN), to be cautious in trying to push domestic reform in countries where the prospects for democracy seemed dim, and to count as trumps the economic attraction of the democratic world and its example of freedom rather than to rely on military force to expand human rights and democratic government around the globe. Such was the essence of liberal hegemonism.

The Emergence of Liberal Imperialism

In order to make the case that the Bush Doctrine is distinctive enough to be called bold and original, capable of representing a fundamental sea change in American foreign policy, it is critical to demonstrate that change came about in the liberal creed beginning with the end of the Cold War, which inaugurated America's status as the world's sole superpower. This change was of such a dimension that a new stage of liberal thought may be said to have emerged, one with a new set of instructions as to how the United States well might act on the world stage.

I call this fourth historical stage of thinking "imperialist." Its tenets laid claim to ideological domination of the world, proclaiming that it had a tried and proven institutional framework (coming in a wide variety of forms, to be sure) capable of providing freedom, justice, prosperity, and peace to its adherents. Its tenets asserted as well that any other form of government lacked the legitimacy, efficiency, and essential trustworthiness that democratic states enjoyed. Non-democratic states should be pressured to liberalize, and if they actually present a danger to what under Madeleine Albright came to be known as the "Community of Democracies," they might be attacked and transformed into democracies thereafter so as to render them positive players on the world stage.

In a word, there was only one road to salvation. The most decisive aspect of liberal ideological discourse that made it imperialist, however, was that it grew more and more comfortable backing up its claims to legitimacy with a call to arms not simply in self-defense but especially in order to promote liberal values and institutions over peoples who did not share them. Liberal internationalism was now calling itself "scientific," and like so many other crusading "sciences" before it—be it that of fascist racism or of communist dialectical materialism—it found the ability to use violence for the sake of "progress" in a world it sought to remake to its heart's desire.

Liberal internationalist imperialist thought began to mature in intellectual circles by the late 1980s and continued to develop until 2001, a period of some fifteen years. I refer to this thinking as typical of the 1990s so as to establish its coherence as a worldview well before it emerged in the corridors of power in Washington in 2001. As we have seen, the administrations of Bush senior, and more especially Clinton, endorsed democracy promotion, but with a restraint and an emphasis on multilateralism and economic development that made any such policies quite cautious. While liberal internationalist thought in both its neoconservative and neoliberal varieties was becoming more aggressively self-confident in think tanks, universities, and nongovernmental organizations throughout these years, neither of these two presidencies gave an overly warm embrace to such reasoning in terms of rethinking the direction of public policy.

In reaction, many liberal internationalists—be they neoliberals or neoconservatives—were disappointed. Here was a moment when the United States possessed unparalleled power, but it did so little. Haiti, Rwanda, the Balkans—why would Washington not act? During the Cold War, liberal internationalists objected to Washington's support for client authoritarian regimes around the globe, but they understood on occasion the tactical necessity for such relations. With the Cold War over, these authoritarian regimes no longer served the national interest. Without external support, they had grown weaker as they no longer served the purposes of either Moscow or Washington. Now was the time to act against them both for the sake of their subject populations and for the long-run interest of the democratic world itself.

Ideologically, the 1990s was an intoxicating moment. Liberal internationalists were understandably quick to claim credit for the victory over Soviet communism. To be sure, American military determination had played a role, but without the organization of fellow democracies in NATO—the most successful long-term, voluntary multilateral defense organization in world history—how well would the West have fared in the contest with Moscow? Nor was the military dimension the only reason for success. Open, integrated economic markets had played their part as well. Put differently, liberals were persuaded that the United States had won the Cold War not so much because of *the degree* of power it had amassed but because of *the style* of its power: its insistence on international economic openness and integration, its loyalty to liberal values and democratic government and multilateral organizations that in the final analysis were all products of Wilsonian thinking.

The tendency for liberal activism to increase was encouraged by the power vacuums that opened in various countries once subject to Soviet control. First Central Europe, then Russia, began to cast around for new ways of organizing state-society relations. At the same time "fraternal" communist parties the world around were in danger of collapse. The result was an increased demand in Latin America and South and East Asia for liberal democracy to explain itself in terms of local challenges.

The reason should be evident: the collapse of Soviet communism was the end not simply of the Soviet state but of a model for political organization the world around. What, then, would take its place? Responses such as George Soros's Open Society Institute, Freedom House, Amnesty International, and Human Rights Watch grew enormously in influence in these years, complemented by a range of democratization efforts undertaken by other nongovernmental organizations, think tanks, university centers, independent journalists, and scholars. These actors in turn were sometimes funded (although in many cases these organizations refused government resources) by governmental organizations like the Agency for International Development and the National Endowment for Democracy not only in the United States but also in the European Union.

If liberals sensed opportunity in Central and Eastern Europe, they confronted emergencies in other parts of the world. A military coup ended the first democratic government Haiti had ever known in 1991. Cambodia fell into a murderous civil war. Domestic strife underlay a terrible famine in Somalia by 1992. The genocide against the Rwandan Tutsi in 1994 became involved with regional animosities, meaning that some five million people had been killed in Central Africa, especially in the Democratic Republic of the Congo, within a decade. The suffering in Sudan reached genocidal proportions. In the Balkans, Serbs were persecuting Croatians, Bosnians, and Kosovars. Famine stalked North Korea. In all these instances and many more, humanitarian intervention, perhaps based on armed might, seemed the only way to avert catastrophe. Given that the democratic world no longer faced a security threat of any real importance, why would one hesitate to respond to such urgent needs?

So we arrive at what one leading liberal imperialist, Michael Ignatieff, endorsed as "the nonnegotiable demands of human rights" for the entire world community.[23] As such language suggests, as the decade progressed liberal imperialism became increasingly ahistorical and apolitical—all that seemingly mattered was that its demands be met. A sense that dramatic conversions could be expected from the benighted, failing which a forced conversion—what then-UN Secretary-General Kofi Annan once labeled "induced consent"—should be undertaken, gained a hold of a good part of the liberal internationalist community.[24]

Here is the beginning of liberal "intoxication," a mood that expressed itself for some in fundamentalist liberal internationalist thinking that emerged after 9/11. The intoxication drew from the perennial wellspring of liberal secular humanism that goes back to the days in which the slave trade was ended and, in the United States, abolitionism was born, based in good measure, without doubt, on the traditional fervor of traditional American Christianity, now expressed in secular terms by the nationalist triumphalism that neo-Wilsonians, like neoconservatives, felt with the collapse of the Soviet Union.[25]

Although the rational secularism of most of the American human rights community has its religious progenitors, the history of Marxism-Leninism as an ideology demonstrates as well that deep moral fervor unconnected to concepts of the Almighty may have a powerful hold on the human mind. Indeed, it is worth wondering if many true-believing, Soviet communists would have behaved any differently from liberal American imperialists in the 1990s had Moscow won the Cold War. Under the guise of advancing the cause of "proletarian internationalism" would they not eventually have sponsored the establishment of communist governments the world around had it been Washington that capitulated in 1989? Would Moscow not similarly have insisted that what served its national interests also served those of the oppressed who awaited freedom and justice from the hands of their exploiters so that its imperialism was too was "benevolent"? Communism had always been a secular crusading religion with its imperialist impulses. It now appeared that liberal internationalist ideology was capable of the selfsame intoxication.

Nevertheless, it is not enough to say that liberal internationalism entered an imperialist phase simply by virtue of reflecting on the course of the Cold War and by responding to the political vacuums opening up with the demise of communist governments and movements in various parts of the world. Stronger stuff was called for. Liberalism needed to engender new concepts appropriate for the time for it to be capable of being intellectually imperialist.

Let me establish the provenance of liberal internationalist thought as it moved beyond hegemonism to imperialism by virtue of three essential concepts spun out by liberal intellectuals between the late 1980s and the turn of the millennium. These concepts marked pointed departures from past ways liberals conceptualized the world. They made claims to being theoretically original, empirically verified, and philosophically imperative. Taken together they represented a new day, one in which America's standing as the only superpower would be complemented by an imperialist ideology that sanctified its historical elevation, a nationalist creed for empire worthy of a people that enjoyed such an exalted status.

The most important of these new concepts was called *democratic peace theory*. It asserted that were the democratic world to expand the ambit of those who were structured as it was, peace would be more assured and American national security correspondingly enhanced. Consequently, it was desirable both morally and practically that other peoples democratize their governments.

A second concept claimed that democracy was a "universal value" such that any people could be introduced to this form of state-society relations so long as local obstacles to this seemingly natural vocation of humankind were removed. Previously, talk of a "transition from authoritarian to democratic government" had seemed a difficult undertaking. Now a revisionist current set in. Great men with great ideas could make history. A democratic transition from authoritarian or totalitarian rule seemed a less daunting mission to undertake.

The third concept maintained that the terms of international sovereignty consecrated by international law and precedent should be waived in certain instances. Previously, international law and custom held that a state was legitimate and immune from attack unless it acted as a belligerent itself, so long as it exercised effective control over the population it claimed to rule. However, liberal jurists in the late 1980s began to argue that a state could be stripped of its legal (and so moral) immunity from invasion if it systematically engaged in serious human rights abuses against its population or was determined to have, or be trying to amass, weapons of mass destruction.

The appearance of these three concepts in highly articulated form in the 1990s was original to liberal internationalist thinking. Given their logic, "rogue states" could legitimately be attacked for the sake of the people they oppressed; the people themselves would rally to their liberation by rather easily democratizing once the tyrants were removed; and the result would be increased security for the democratic states that had launched the assault as the "zone of democratic peace" would be extended. In a word, "the end of history" might be within reach, its promise was peace, and the instrument that would bring it into being was American power exercised against the world's tyrants.

These ideas amounted to a witches' brew so far as their policy implications were concerned. Obviously they reflected continuity with the past. Without the experience of the Cold War, which had created and proved the worth of international liberal institutions and practices, such ideas could not have been born. They most certainly were not formed out of whole cloth after the collapse of the Soviet Union. Yet at the same time, such thinking had not existed in other than embryonic form prior to the 1990s. It was their combination during this period that allowed the Bush Doctrine to take on the fatal character that it did in 2002.

By insisting on the importance of this "new thinking," we can see that the doctrine is much more than a mildly updated form of Wilsonianism or otherwise faithful to American culture and tradition. Apologists looking to legitimize the war by invoking the American way, refer to Reagan, FDR, and Wilson, Germany and Japan, whatever is at hand to make their case. But their evidence is simplistic if for no other reason than they glide over counterexamples (like Vietnam), make false analogies (as with Germany and Japan), and fail altogether to consider the powerful new thinking that liberal internationalists brought forth in the 1990s. The fact that this style of thought was not born of neoconservatives but of neoliberals is an important point to emphasize as well, for it suggests the extent to which the Democratic Party, as well as the Republican, fell under the control of the incubus of liberal imperialist thinking.

In the chapters to follow, I propose to turn in more detail to the 1990s so as to find there—much more than in earlier expressions of Wilsonianism—the fatal reasoning that led so many liberal internationalists to evolve into neo-liberal imperialists and so to become war hawks, in the process contributing to the calamity of war in the Middle East and to the betrayal of the American promise once held high by this very same school.

CHAPTER 4

Liberal Imperialism I
Democratic Peace Theory

Of all the causes which conspire to blind
Man's erring judgment, and misguide the mind,
What the weak head with strongest bias rules,
Is pride, the never-failing vice of fools.

A little learning is a dangerous thing;
Drink deep, or taste not the Pierian spring;
There shallow draughts intoxicate the brain,
And drinking largely sobers us again.

Alexander Pope, *An Essay on Criticism*

Analyses of the Bush Doctrine often link it to established traditions in the making of American foreign policy. As we have seen, while most historians would surely agree that the doctrine is most reminiscent of the thinking of Woodrow Wilson, some invoke the Reagan presidency, others refer back to the administrations of Truman or Theodore Roosevelt, while still others return to thinking under presidents Lincoln or John Quincy Adams to find the roots of the policy announced in 2002. Yet another line of explanation is to link the doctrine to long-standing religious or nationalist sentiment that makes a fighting faith such as the Bush administration hoped to encourage a part of what it means to be American.

No doubt these historical antecedents and underlying cultural convictions have explanatory power. Yet we should beware of two pitfalls in looking to the past to explain the present. First, in many respects the thinking behind the Bush Doctrine was born in the 1990s, not in some earlier era. America's position in the world had changed and the dominant thinking that guided its perspective on world order had as well. The uniqueness of its stance on world affairs needs underscoring. It is fair to a point to say that the doctrine is in the Wilsonian tradition, but to see it as no more than that, as if it were the natural, modern embodiment of a tradition nearly a century old, beggars the imagination. Second, the effort to establish the doctrine's lineage by looking to past precedent is frequently a form of argumentative manipulation, part of the war of ideas conducted against the American public, a spin to make us think that the patriotic credentials of the Iraq War are in order for an undertaking very much in line with the American spirit. In fact, it is quite possible to be in touch with American cultural forces and foreign policy traditions and yet to be highly critical of the Bush Doctrine.

Liberal Internationalism Triumphant: The 1990s

Let us therefore consider the major influences on the Bush Doctrine as arising thanks to dramatic changes in Wilsonian thinking in a period which for convenience we'll call the 1990s (in effect, 1986—2001). In retrospect, it seems virtually preordained that liberal internationalist thinking would evolve in a more militantly aggressive direction in the 1990s. Here was the ideology that had done so much to organize the winning side in the struggle with Soviet communism. With victory attained, it confronted a radically changed world where the collapse of communist governments previously ruling over hundreds of millions of people called forth demands to engender new forms of state-society relations that corresponded to the liberal democratic blueprint. Authoritarian single party states were to be replaced by competitive party democracies, freedom of the press, rights for minorities, and the introduction of market economic relations into a context previously dominated by managed production and trade—all this to be accomplished overnight by peoples mobilized through strong nationalist feelings to make demands for a better life. Simultaneously, the nightmare scenarios of nuclear conflict gave way to talks of disarmament and mutual understandings among people. The House of Europe might expand from the Pyrenees to the Urals, and all this under the flag of freedom. Above it all, America stood supreme.

For liberal internationalists in the 1990s, the fall of the Berlin Wall was understandably seen as one of the great events in world history. It signaled the end of a terrible period of ideological struggle with the deaths of tens of millions of people, a period that stretched from the nationalist nightmare of World War I through the unspeakable horrors of the fight against fascism now finally to the collapse of Soviet communism. The victor in this long-term war of secular faiths was liberal democracy, a creed coming for the first time now to a full sense of its doctrinal importance and possibilities. Rivals might appear to the reigning ideology, but whether it was Islamic fundamentalism of the Taliban or the Ayatollah Khomeini, or the "Asian values" of Lee Kuan Yew, the legendary leader of Singapore, or the call for "African solutions for African problems," the challengers to the predominance of democracy's appeal were easily dismissed as possessed of vain concepts altogether lacking in serious intellectual weight. If Marxism-Leninism, which styled itself "the theory of theories" and had been the ruling political conceptual framework for a quarter of humanity, had collapsed in its contest with liberal democratic internationalism, how seriously could one take such conceptually thin challenges as "Asian values" or "African solutions" or Islamic government as blueprints for domestic and international order in the twenty-first century?

Liberal democracy had the most sterling of qualities to recommend it to the new world born of the collapse of Soviet communism. Fruit of Enlightenment thought in the eighteenth century (but with roots that went even further back to the Renaissance and the Reformation), nurtured in practice by the slow evolution of the institutions of democratic government over a period of at least two centuries, tested in battle by a fascist foe in World War II, only to be confronted by communism thereafter and to win this contest too, liberal democracy's triumph was by any historical measure an extraordinary feat.

Despite the terrible challenges of the second half of the twentieth century, under liberalism's auspices a good part of the world had emerged as rich, free, and stable. The European Union had come into existence and expanded, the North Atlantic Treaty Organization had proved its mettle in protecting the peace, international trade among advanced industrial democracies had handily surpassed all records of the past. In a word, levels of prosperity, freedom, justice, and peace were being reached within the club of free market democracies of a sort that had no precedent whatsoever.

Given such a record, could it be that the 1990s were an historical watershed, an epoch that marked a sea change between the long period of human existence marked by the struggle for survival and a new age of liberty? Could it be that it was America's mission as the undisputed superpower at a moment of history pregnant with change to carry forward this noble task?

The exhilarating mood of progress was highest among those who welcomed the demise of communist rule in Central and Eastern Europe, but how could it fail to be contagious in other parts of the world as well? In places as different as Latin America, sub-Saharan Africa, India, and China the conviction was growing that somehow the market democracies led by the United States had a blueprint for success that other peoples could copy without losing their individuality. Economic prosperity, honest government, individual and group rights in civil society (including those for ethnic and religious minorities and for women), peace among neighbors to replace the threat of nuclear annihilation—such was the implicit promise. If China and Russia could be brought into the orbit of the democratic community, a new world order would surely soon appear. Hobbes's state of nature—the recurrent metaphor of the realist school of thought, dominant among international relations specialists—would be replaced by what the liberals hoped to be Kant's promise of perpetual peace.

To be sure, challenges to the spread of freedom, justice, and peace persisted in regions of the world torn by anarchy, poverty and disease (much of sub-Saharan Africa), single-party government (China, North Korea, and Cuba most especially), religious obscurantism (the question of whither Islam), economic mismanagement on the part of states heavily indebted to the international system (Southeast Asia) or deep social tensions with a history of military rule (Latin America and Pakistan). In addition, there were the problems of the proliferation of weapons of mass destruction, access to energy resources, and the question of environmental degradation and pandemic diseases, all of which called for sustained multilateral cooperation.

Indeed, vigilance still needed to be exercised in the democratic countries themselves. Economic justice was under assault in some market democracies where the rise of globalization threatened to reduce the middle class and impoverish the working class in favor of a small elite of international businessmen. Rights for women and minorities needed to be consolidated and expanded.

Yet these difficulties had to be seen in context of rapid, radical success. While this was no moment to reduce vigilance over the health of democracy at home, it might be anticipated that the collapse of communism both as an ideology and as a leading form of state power would so shake up world politics that a new day for the expansion of market democracy would follow.

After the horrors of the twentieth century in which liberal internationalists had fought first with fascists, then with communists, it was time to take stock of what had been accomplished and organize to secure the benefits of victory for future generations.

Such arguments were all the more persuasive given the turmoil that continued to bedevil human relations. Haiti, Somalia, Cambodia, Rwanda, the Democratic Republic of the Congo, Sudan, Croatia, Bosnia, Kosovo, North Korea, Iraq, Syria, Iran. Here were humanitarian nightmares of the first order, to which should be added the fear of nuclear, biological, and chemical weapons in the hands of irresponsible states, which the international community needed to mobilize to handle. The Cold War was over, but it remained to win the peace thereafter. As the liberal internationalist Samantha Power put it in her Pulitzer prize-winning book published in 2002:

> Despite broad public consensus that genocide should "never again" be allowed, and a good deal of triumphalism about the ascent of liberal democratic values, the last decade of the twentieth century was one of the most deadly in the grimmest century on record. Rwandan Hutus in 1994 could freely, joyfully, and systematically slaughter 8,000 Tutsi a day for 100 days without any foreign interference. Genocide occurred after the Cold War; after the growth of the human rights groups; after the advent of technology that allowed for instant communication; after the erection of the Holocaust Museum on the Mall in Washington, D.C.
>
> ...What is most shocking about America's reaction to Turkey's killing of the Armenians, the Holocaust, Pol Pot's reign of terror, Iraq's slaughter of the Kurds, Bosnian Serbs' mass murder of Muslims, and the Hutu elimination of Tutsi is not that the United States refused to deploy U.S. ground forces to combat the atrocities.... What is most shocking is that U.S. policymakers did almost nothing to deter the crime.... Indeed, on occasion the United States directly or indirectly aided those committing genocide.[1]

For the liberal internationalist community, the challenges ahead divided into several sorts. One was to consolidate democratic transitions in regions where popular forces were already moving in that direction—Poland, the Czech Republic, and South Korea, for instance, perhaps Mexico, Brazil, South Africa, and Turkey. A second was to convert leading states with some prospects for liberalization to democracy—Russia and China especially. A third was to rescue populations-at-risk from state-sponsored terror or social anarchy—the Balkans, parts of sub-Saharan Africa, and Iraq, for example—and to stop the proliferation of weapons of mass destruction as with North Korea and Iran.

Many shoulders lent themselves to the tasks at hand for with the fall of the Berlin Wall there was a bipartisan tone to the liberal mood in the United States. If concern over human rights and democracy promotion had traditionally been largely a matter of center-left political thinking in the European Union and the United States, conservatives had come to play a critical part. The presidency of Ronald Reagan had brought to the fore a group of Republicans who wanted a clear moral message in American foreign policy, and organizations like Freedom House, the American Enterprise Institute, or sections of the National Endowment for Democracy replied to their concerns as did a growing constituency of Christian activists. Neither the administration of George H. W. Bush nor that of Bill Clinton corresponded to the hopes of many of these liberal internationalists, be they of the left or of the right. Nor did it appear likely when George W. Bush became president that he would turn in a liberal direction either. Still, the thinking, organizing, and activism went forward during the 1990s as lobbyists, non-governmental organizations (NGOs) and think tanks, university centers, and individual writers of note, reflected on the world around them and the way their ideas could be turned into policy.

In a world now far removed from the 1990s by the attack of 9/11 and the invasion of Iraq, we must not forget the exhilaration of the 1990s, a brief moment when history seemed to be moving in a progressive direction thanks in good measure to American efforts. For liberal internationalists, the task was to consolidate this forward movement.

Liberal Internationalism Evolves Into a New Stage

Liberal internationalism has never been an organized movement with a formal institutional structure, recognized leaders, and clear party affiliation that led its advocates into political office on an agenda of promoting democratic reform abroad. Prior to the 1990s, it is difficult even to use the word "ideology," in the sense of a highly structured, coherent doctrine of political choice with a sense of history, past, present, and future, to denote it. Working with other countries that had open economies and democratic governments was obviously good for the United States, but just why this was the case still lacked authoritative theoretical, rather than rhetorical, affirmation.

With the end of the Cold War this was to change. The neoconservatives, and others more to the center or left who might be called neo-Wilsonians or neoliberals, saw an open window of opportunity to push for a better and more stable world order. They did not hesitate to move their agenda forward.

The first chapters of this book reviewed at some length the thinking of the neoconservative movement. In contrast to them, the intellectuals who in the 1990s became what I call *neoliberals* looked back not to the Reagan years so much as to Democratic precedents. They saw in President John Kennedy's Alliance for Progress or President Jimmy Carter's human rights crusade encouraging examples of democracy promotion in the period after the occupations of Japan and Germany, the watershed undertaking of liberal democracy also inspired by Democratic leaders. Unlike the neoconservatives, many Wilsonians had been willing to work for détente with the Soviet Union, understood defeat in Vietnam to suggest the limits of American power, and were suspicious of the efforts by President Reagan to achieve military superiority through a "star wars" anti-ballistic defense system. During the twelve years of Republican administrations, 1981–1993, they tended to work in universities, foundations, and think tanks, and they expressed their activism through NGOs that proliferated in the 1990s to promote human rights and democratic government worldwide.

Left liberals before the 1990s were also unlike neoconservatives in their ambivalence about the use of American power. Following Vietnam, they had a generally allergic reaction to the use of American military force, for whatever the rhetoric of its application during the Cold War, armed intervention seemed more likely to end up reinforcing authoritarianism, rather than backing progressive governments abroad. But with the Cold War over, the utility of authoritarian allies seemed questionable. Would it not be more positive for American interests to see such clients replaced with liberal friends? The aim would not be the affirmation of American supremacy such as the neoconservatives looked forward to, however, but the strengthening of a Community of Democracies.

Despite their differences, there was an increasing ability in the 1990s for those who favored human rights and democracy promotion, be they right-wing neoconservatives or left-leaning neoliberals, to work for a common cause. Of course tensions persisted. But as a high-profile, September 1993 letter to President Clinton on the subject of Bosnia demonstrated, these two groups could link arms and call for action, not only in the Balkans but wherever genocidal threats emerged.

Signed by many international leaders headed by Margaret Thatcher, and including among the Americans such disparate personalities as George Soros, Karl Popper, Susan Sontag, Albert Wohlstetter, Richard Perle, Henry Siegman, and Paul Wolfowitz (to list but a few), the letter opened: "In Bosnia the situation goes from bad to worse. The people there are in despair about their future. They are victims of brutal aggression. But they are also the victims of the failure of the democracies to act." Citing Saddam Hussein's invasion of Kuwait as a precedent, the signatories declared:

> If we do not act immediately and decisively, history will record that in the last decade of this century the democracies failed to heed its most unforgiving lesson: that unopposed aggression will be enlarged and repeated, that a failure of will by the democracies will strengthen and encourage those who gain territory and rule by force.... Against a dictator who will yield only to superior force, the West can threaten most ferociously in the hope that threats alone will be enough to stop aggression.... But if the West doesn't use force at all, or if it uses it symbolically rather than substantially to reduce Milosevic's power, or if it uses force to coerce Bosnia capitulation, the message received will only bring American and Western resolve into contempt.[2]

As these words indicated, with the end of the Cold War the mood among Wilsonians had changed. They had become far more aggressive about promoting human rights and democratic government in areas of the world where tyrannical regimes remained in power. But much more than simply a change in mood was occurring.

To become capable of seizing the times of the post-Cold War era, mainstream liberal internationalism needed to revise its doctrine so as to be relevant to a new era. Such an undertaking soon came to mean leaving behind the relative restraint of liberal hegemonism, which had typified the Cold War. What was called for was a more action-oriented ideology capable of expressing the new self-confidence of liberals everywhere and of engaging state power on their behalf. In a word, liberalism as a doctrine had to mature from *hegemonism* to *imperialism* in the sense that concrete ideas were required to be put forward as to how the world was to be changed.

The wish was mother to the deed. In short order, centrist and left liberals were to be found arguing for a more forward, engaged, and demanding foreign policy for democracy promotion than their predecessors had dared to imagine. In the process, a new stage of Wilsonian thinking was born, one that now quite definitely was a political ideology come of age in that it linked people together with an understanding of history to forward a political program based on triumph in the Cold War. Containment was dead; now on the agenda was what the Clinton administration referred to as the "enlargement" of the community of democratic peoples. Liberal internationalism, which had been the "second track" of American policy during the contest with the Soviet Union, now became the sole track that made sense.

To be sure, when push came to shove and the Wilsonians heard the clarion call of the neoconservatives to rouse themselves to action under the banner of making the world safe for democracy by democratizing the world after the attack of 9/11, many of them would refuse the call to arms. For most who opposed the coming war with Iraq, the Bush administration's unilateralism was simply unacceptable. We should recall that it was a major tenet of Wilsonianism that the United States would work with like-minded countries through international organizations for the common good. The result would be not only increased legitimacy for the use of armed force, but also burden sharing in dangerous undertakings. Unilateralism of the sort endorsed by the neoconservatives thus flew in the face of the long-term Wilsonian effort to work for a collective security system, pooling as much sovereignty as was possible. In early 2003, when it became apparent that Washington would not work through the United Nations, indeed that it would spurn its NATO allies and mock the pretensions of the European Union, these Wilsonians parted company with the neoconservatives and those left liberal hawks who supported the march to war. Many others, however, joined the war party, having been convinced by the logic of the neoconservative position that once American leadership had proved its worth, unilateralism would show itself to be the high road to multilateralism, for others would quickly support Washington's mission, realizing it was for the common good.

Whether they opposed the coming of the invasion of Iraq or not, the critical point to grasp is that neo-Wilsonians as a group had, wittingly or not, made sophisticated arguments during the 1990s as to why imperialism in the name of democratic regime change could be a legitimate undertaking for the United States. Combining democratic peace theory—the notion that democracies do not fight each other—with arguments as to the "universal appeal" of democracy, and adding to these concepts the argument that states that were gross violators of internationally recognized human rights were illegitimate and so might be attacked, neoliberals had created an increasingly explicit imperialist ideology that could be used by whoever would appropriate it. How long could it be, given the nature of the human condition, before a group aware of American supremacy on every chess board of world affairs looked for an ideology to expand this country's sway even farther? Whether they actively endorsed the Bush Doctrine (as many did) or whether they did not, the neo-Wilsonians had given birth to ideas that were the constituent elements of a new brand of American imperialism, a loaded gun put into the hand of whoever would pick it up.

If a single person first raised the flag for all to salute, it was the neocon-servative Francis Fukuyama in the summer of 1989 with an article in the *National Interest* that took the American intellectual community by storm. His essay argued that liberal democracy had finally emerged as the only viable blueprint for world governments and international relations in the aftermath of the defeat of communism and fascism.[3] As Fukuyama explained his mes-sage of 1989 three years later:

> I argued that a remarkable consensus concerning the legitimacy of liberal democracy as a system of government had emerged throughout the world over the past few years, as it conquered rival ideologies like hereditary monarchy, fascism, and most recently communism. More than that, however, I argued that liberal democracy may constitute the "end point of mankind's ideologi-cal evolution" and the "final form of human government," and as such con-stituted "the end of history." That is, while earlier forms of government were characterized by grave defects and irrationalities that led to their eventual collapse, liberal democracy was arguably free from such fundamental internal contradictions.[4]

Fukuyama warned that the triumph of bourgeois liberal democracy might create what Nietzsche had labeled "men without chests," self-centered individ-ualists who sought comfort, not challenge, in the world and so were incapable of moral struggle, heroism, and greatness. But he did recognize that while the advanced democratic world had left the Hobbesian struggle for survival that constituted the story of history and so was "post-historical," a good part of humanity remained "stuck in history" and that within this world "the old rules of power politics continue to apply." Fukuyama anticipated clashes between these two worlds, so the argument was implicit, to be made more explicit by others, that a crusade by the Kantian world against the Hobbesian state of nature could give a sense of purpose to the democrats of the post-historical world, rousing them from the torpor of their "post-historic," or "post-Hobbes-ian," lives by reaffirming their commitment to liberal democratic values.[5]

Fukuyama's ideas created a stir in good measure because they were in keep-ing with the times. Liberal internationalist democracy was re-conceptualizing itself, becoming more coherent as an ideology, seeing itself as having a dis-tinguished history and the possibility of an even more distinguished future. Like any ideology worth its salt, liberalism was engendering a general theory of history and its place therein; it was acquiring an important new measure of self-understanding, self-confidence, self-importance, and, most dangerously, self-righteousness. Most critically, neo-Wilsonianism had a purpose and a mission, for it understood that the historical moment in which it came to this consciousness was one that favored its rapid expansion.

In short, *liberal internationalism, whether in its neoconservative or neoliberal form, affirmed not simply its ideological primacy in world intellectual affairs, but still more basically the primacy of the ideological as the leading determinant of human destiny.* Prior to 1989, neither the primacy of liberal thought, nor the primacy of ideas in the making of history, would have been easily defensible propositions. Following 1989, each assertion drew its committed adherents. Fukuyama expressed the idea early and well, but we might almost say with Hegel (a thinker Fukuyama liked to reflect upon) that here was a concept that the times required be born. When, after 9/11, various neoconservative and neoliberal imperialists began speaking of a war of ideas, they were reflecting the convictions of their time. That these ideas reflected, in turn, a very material reality—the emergence of the United States as the world's lone superpower—and that these ideas might therefore have been considered an expression of American nationalism that could give rise to American imperialism, was not a consideration anyone at the time troubled to entertain, even if a familiarity with Hegel might have suggested just such a thought.

American universities were the initial seedbeds of many of the new liberal internationalist ideas, although important impetus appeared in work sponsored by private foundations like the Carnegie Endowment or George Soros's Open Society Institute, by the United Nations, and especially by the American government through the Agency for International Development and the National Endowment for Democracy. So, too, Amnesty International, Human Rights Watch, and Freedom House became household names in liberal circles worldwide.[6] Professional journals and conferences presided over often fierce debates that stimulated thought and disseminated ideas. Networks of collaborators materialized. Contacts with government officials, the mainstream press, and public opinion gained in intensity. The result was that in the course of the 1990s more was done to conceptualize a formal liberal internationalist ideology than had been accomplished in all its preceding history as a way of thinking. That it should be an expression of American nationalism and that it could become the justification of American imperialism in retrospect is only too clear.

Ideological mobilization requires something of the same organizational infrastructure as military preparedness. Long-term strategy needs to be laid out, tactical missions must be identified, chains of command established, teamwork and pride encouraged. Of course in intellectual endeavors organizational unity is far, far harder to establish than when a military is formed. But intellectual unity was achieved in loose form for the task of updating Wilsonianism to be in league with its times.

A book needs to appear on the matter of how the intellectual life in the United States proved fertile to the undertaking, but its focus will be clear. Doubtless it would point to the unprecedented cooperation that emerged among committed intellectuals working in universities, centers, and think tanks, and their impact on the publishing world of books and journals. Scholarship was paralleled by activism. Powerful NGOs proliferated, acting as they did in concert with government agencies here and in the EU, and with progressive foundations with subsidies to dispense. The result for liberal internationalists was that the 1990s was truly a golden age. In their excitement, they sensed that their historic moment was at hand.

Nor were these ideas restricted to a self-selected set of intellectual mandarins. We might think of the relationship between intellectuals and policy makers in terms of a conceptual food chain. Ideas are formulated, debated, and ultimately synthesized for public policy in the United States—beginning, for example, in periodicals like *International Organization, World Politics,* or *International Security* that are intended for a strictly academic audience. The most salient ideas are then taken up in "executive summary" form in periodicals like *Foreign Affairs* or *Foreign Policy.* So the intellectual elite produces material to be consumed by the policy elite. One might think of these several levels as having different actors: the scholar, the scholar-activist, the activist, and the policy maker in Washington. Here is the transition belt that links academic thinking of the 1990s to the later policy positions adopted by the Bush administration after 2001.[7]

The Three Concepts That Created the Ideology of Liberal Democratic Imperialism

What, then, were the leading ideas that permitted the emergence of an ideology of liberal internationalist imperialism? In a world as variegated and in flux as that of the American social sciences no effort to reflect the diversity of opinions expressed can hope to be fully adequate to the task. However, I believe that organizing the "new thinking" of neo-Wilsonianism into three conceptual groups that correspond to three separate disciplines within the American academy does justice to the collective movement that was underway and demonstrates quite clearly that liberal internationalism was a dynamic ideology capable of engendering an imperialist framework for understanding world events and for justifying direct military action to mold world affairs.

For three concepts, three different schools of academic experts stepped forth. The first innovation in Wilsonian thinking grew from liberal international relations specialists who promoted the view of democratic peace theory. Their essential claim was that a world order dominated by liberal democracies would by its very character necessarily be one of peace. By the same token, democratic peace theory implied that non-democratic states were inherently aggressive and would likely be hostile to the liberal world for the very freedom it enjoyed. This argument's theoretical contribution to imperialist policy was to suggest that should America successfully act to expand democracy abroad then the country's national security would be promoted. It is the main subject of this chapter.

The second set of innovations originated in comparative political studies. Here neo-Wilsonians diminished the importance of the preconditions an earlier generation of scholars had thought necessary for foreign peoples to democratize in favor of seeing democratic government as having a "universal appeal" greatly aided by sophisticated leadership of the sort that could be witnessed with Václav Havel, Kim Dae Jung, or Nelson Mandela. The theoretical contribution to imperialist policy was to increase the conviction that foreign peoples could rework their political and civil life in a democratic direction more easily than had earlier been appreciated. It is the subject of the chapter that follows.

The third set of new ideas came from liberal international jurists who redefined sovereignty so as eventually to open to military attack non-democratic states that were either gross human rights abusers or accumulating weapons of mass destruction. As will be seen in Chapter 6, these neo-Wilsonians in effect blessed the tanks that would lead the charge.

Taken together, three different schools of analysis, born essentially of a liberal internationalist American academic system largely identified with the political center-left, came to have a profound influence on how policy in Washington could be legitimately formulated. They were the deep intellectual underpinnings, the substance itself, of those aspects of the Bush Doctrine that promised a new world order once the dust of military battle had settled.

Analyzed separately, these three concepts may not seem particularly volatile intellectually. Combined, however, they become a veritable witches' brew, capable of working in syncretistic fashion to formulate a compelling imperialist

ideology. According to these formulations, the world's people were both desirous and capable of democratic government given the right leadership; states
that opposed changes toward liberalization could be pronounced illegitimate;
and outside forces that pushed for democratic governments where they did not
exist were enhancing their own security as a result.

None of these ideas had existed in more than embryonic form prior to the
1990s; all were conceptualized in a mature form ready for policy adoption by
the turn of the millennium. That their collective impact would be to sanction American imperialism would in due course become glaringly apparent as
together they provided the ideological rationale for the political pillar of the
Bush Doctrine and the expectation that first Iraq, then the "Broader Middle
East," could be brought into the club of democratic nations—a gain at once for
the peoples of this region and for world peace, as well as for American security.
Or so the theory implicitly asserted.

Propelled by their ideological innovations many neo-Wilsonians became
liberal hawks, ready to join their neoconservative counterparts in a call for
invading Iraq, indeed for going as far as their strength could take them. As
we shall see in Chapter 6, these intellectuals used their influence to pull the
Democratic Party in the same imperialist direction. Even where these liberals
held back from the war, their ideas could be used to validate the engagement.
Here was liberal internationalism's "betrayal of the America promise" invoked
in the title of this book, the notion that a doctrine originally founded as anti-
imperialist and pro-freedom and peace could in due order convert itself into
an imperialist ideology calling for war.

The First Concept of Liberal Democratic Imperialism: The Desirability of Expanding the "Zone of Democratic Peace"

If the well-being of the globe's peoples, international peace, and the foundations of American national security could all be significantly improved by the
expansion of democratic government and market economies worldwide—the
old Wilsonian promise—then it would seem to follow axiomatically that it
should be a priority concern of U.S. foreign policy to foster such developments
with all the means at its disposition. "Our interests and our values are one"
becomes the mantra. Such was a fundamental premise of the Bush Doctrine
and such was the decided conclusion of more than a decade of liberal academic
theoretical and empirical investigations formulated by international relations
experts preceding the attack of September 11, 2001. How these concepts were

formed in neoliberal circles, and what their conceptual underpinnings are, constitute essential elements of understanding how the United States came to be involved on the terms that it did in the invasion of Iraq in March 2003.

The roots of liberal internationalist confidence in the progress that the spread of democratic government would have for American national security go back at least to the presidency of Woodrow Wilson. However, far more sophisticated statements came to be heard in defense of such a proposition in the 1990s. For most American liberals, the new impulse to champion democracy as a form of hardheaded "national security liberalism" (and so escape the labels of being "idealistic," "moralistic," and "naïve" that they had always labored under before) saw its first important stirrings in 1983. That year, professor Michael Doyle published two essays in *Philosophy and Public Affairs* establishing on the basis of empirical and analytical analysis his finding that democratic peoples did not fight one another.

Here and in later publications, Doyle was careful to admit that the definition of a democratic government may be debatable (so that it might be argued democracies had fought one another, as in the American Civil War or in World War I), and that more mature democracies may be more pacific toward other democracies than those that are young. He also was clear to say that democracies are not necessarily pacific collectivities, that indeed they may be prone to wage quixotic crusades against authoritarian states. These allowances made, Doyle nonetheless stood by an important conclusion: for reasons peculiar to their values, interests, and institutions, democratic peoples were far less likely to engage in armed conflict with one another than any other form of governmental system.[8]

Doyle was not the first social scientist to speculate on the question of the existence of a "democratic peace," but his ideas went further and received more attention than others who had forayed into the field. His initial inspiration came from his study of Emmanuel Kant's *Perpetual Peace*, published in 1795. Here Kant held that what he called "republican" government, if it expanded worldwide, might create an era of "perpetual peace" thanks both to the peace-loving character of such governments based on the popular will and to their unprecedented capacity to cooperate together for the common good. Doyle transposed the argument to modern times, subjected it to empirical verification, and found that the evidence sustained Kant's beliefs.

Doyle's seminal argument launched a rapidly expanding and dynamic field of democratic peace theory in academic studies, which in due course meant a revival of liberalism in the academy among students of world affairs, and eventually the birth of neo-Wilsonianism. The new theory was born fighting. Prior to the late 1980s, the analysis of international affairs in the United States had been dominated by the so-called realist school of thought, which held that regime type (the kind of governmental organization a country possessed) was of little importance when it came to explaining a state's behavior in foreign affairs. What mattered was a government's relative power position in an anarchic international system equivalent to the state of nature, where the law of the jungle was ultimately what counted. As a consequence, for realists it was not of great import in understanding a state's conduct to know whether it was democratic or authoritarian. Not Kant but Hobbes was the author of the texts to be studied. Realism, then, was the opponent the liberals of the 1990s set out to slay.

For liberals, "regime type mattered," "democracies were different." Thinking such as Doyle's, which insisted that democratic governments behaved more peacefully compared to other states in their mutual interactions, necessarily put into question realism's place as the reigning paradigm for the study of world events. Perhaps the leading question of international relations according to realism—"Why War?"—could now be displaced by one favored by liberals—"How Peace?" If the paradigm shift occurred, and liberals were committed to this undertaking, then realism would be deposed in favor of Wilsonianism in the academy. The next step was to set a new agenda for public policy thereafter, focusing new attention on how the United States might expand the prospects for democratic government worldwide for the sake of promoting peace.

Not coincidentally, this fierce debate intersected with the end of the Cold War. As it became increasingly possible to argue that it was not so much the United States that had scored a victory over the Soviet Union as it was "liberal internationalism" that had defeated "proletarian internationalism," the debate at the scholarly level became still more intense. If this were true—and liberals insisted adamantly that it was—then the consequences for the future of American foreign policy were clear: *international peace depended on the consolidation of the victory over communism by the expansion of democratic government around the globe.* The implications of such a doctrinal innovation should be plain to see, even if Doyle had explicitly warned against the imperialist temptation.

The reader will be spared the details of the academic arguments that broke out, first as realists tried to defend their paradigm against the liberal assault, then as liberals struggled among themselves for pride of place in articulating their doctrine. The battle became more intense yet as those academics struggling to be close to those in power in Washington jockeyed for position. No one has done an empirical study of how the character of university professorships, or journal topics, or articles in leading newspapers, or grants awarded by foundations, evolved over the 1990s. I have no doubt but that any such investigation would indicate a prodigious expansion in the public exposition of neo-Wilsonian concepts. Original in thought, comprehensive in argument, long-term and policy relevant in implication, this ideology—homegrown American—had finally arrived.

The undisputed place of American power in the world was now complemented by an ideology that saw itself as the champion of this historical development and the guide as to how Washington might consolidate and extend its leadership position in world affairs. Liberalism presented itself as the embodiment of American nationalism. And it could present its concepts as established "scientifically." In the oft-quoted words of Jack Levy, "in general wars involving all or nearly all of the great powers, democratic states have never fought on opposite sides. This absence of war between democracies comes as close as anything we have to an empirical law in international relations."[9] And such a "law" might well have policy implications. Lincoln's adage that the United States was "the last, best hope of earth" might now take on historical flesh.

Put in summary form, democratic peace theory holds that just as leaders in a democracy come to power through negotiated compromises based on non-violence and enshrined in the rule of law, so in much the same way democratic states can resolve conflicts among themselves. The preference for nonviolent problem-solving approaches is enhanced by the transparency, predictability, and sense of accountability of constitutional democratic leaders at the domestic level that may spill over into their relations with leaders of other democracies.

Moreover, to the extent that democratic politics exist alongside open, capitalist economic institutions, the opportunity is present for integrating world markets and creating thereby interdependent economies, which in turn should contribute to peace among nations by giving each people a tangible stake in the well-being of others. As the rule of law basic to domestic democratic order and necessary for economic openness comes to be institutionalized in multilateral organizations, a collective security system might be consolidated capable of maintaining the peace. With the confluence of these three organizing forces—political democracy, open market economies, participation in multilateral organization—liberal democracies should be ready and able to cooperate in networks of mutual reciprocity in handling problems that arise among them short of outright war.

It should come as no surprise that the round of economic globalization ignited in the latter part of the twentieth century was conceptualized by neo-Wilsonians as the practical, as well as the intellectual, handmaiden of the expansion of democratic government in liberal internationalist circles in the 1990s. During the Clinton years, for example, the buzzword came to be that American foreign policy was centered on protecting and promoting "market democracies" the world around. As President Clinton himself argued with respect to China in making a case to support its membership in the World Trade Organization, for example, increased international economic openness would lead to integration that would be at once a force for peace and for the rule of law and hence for democratization.

Democratic peace theory thus had a dimension of international economic thinking intrinsic to its argument. Openness stimulates economic growth that in turn creates a middle class and an increasingly complex division of labor, we are told, both of which have an affinity with democratic government. Moreover, international integration increases the stakes that countries have in each other's well-being so that a "win/win" attitude edges out the "you win/I lose" competitive fears of an earlier time when economies were predominately national in organization. In addition, cooperation across national boundaries will increase the need for multilateral organizations, which in turn will contribute to the growth of international law and patterns of cooperation for conflict resolution and mutual interest. Finally, by "depoliticizing" the economic realm through privatization, deregulation, and openness, the protectionist and mercantilist forces that can lead to competitive imperialist pressures would be dampened.

Consider the spectacular confirmation of theory offered by the European Union. Here was a fratricidal region second to none, which in recent history had endured wars that took tens of millions of lives. Yet in less than fifty years, from the late 1940s to the early 1990s, the world was witness to an extraordinary development: war among Western Europeans had become unthinkable. With the collapse of communism to the East, the entire continent might be spared nuclear conflagration. The reasons were easy enough to identify. Germany had quickly emerged from the war as a consolidated democracy; the Common Market had integrated economic relations among its member states in a deep and dramatic fashion; a process of "shared sovereignty" had engendered a complex web of multilateral institutions providing the member states the ability to harmonize their interests; and the menace of the Red Army had given a sense of common values, interests, and urgency to the enterprise. With the end of communism, Eastern Europe might follow suit (as the expansion of both NATO and the EU anticipated). A historical transformation of the first order in world affairs had occurred before our eyes and this thanks to liberal internationalist practices.

Three Tenors of Democratic Peace Theory: Russett, Moravcsik, and Rawls

The American academy never sleeps. The sense of mission and ambition among its Wilsonian members, most of them in the process of metamorphosing into neoliberals, offers a telling example. During the 1990s, empiricists among international relations experts validated the existence of a democratic peace, theorists thereupon elevated liberal internationalism to the status of being a "science," and philosophers could speculate positively on the implications of these findings for world peace.

To illustrate how democratic peace theory came to have the intellectual preeminence it enjoyed, let us consider three leading exponents of the matter: Bruce Russett, an empiricist at Yale; Andrew Moravcsik, a theorist now at Princeton; and John Rawls, a philosopher at Harvard. Aided by many other academics, in the late 1990s this triumvirate (although not necessarily self-consciously acting in unison) established a complex, sophisticated, and politically powerful perspective on the superiority and importance of democratic governments for world peace that was indispensable to the intellectual appeal of the Bush Doctrine in the period after 9/11.

The Empiricists: The Case of Bruce Russett and John Oneal

The job of empirically validating the existence of a peace among democracies was a hard fought battle. Critics of the effort advanced all manner of logical, historical, and empirical arguments to dash the credibility of such a portentous claim.

But in *Triangulating Peace: Democracy, Interdependence, and International Organizations,* an important book that came out in 2001 building on investigations largely conducted in the 1990s, senior Yale international relations professor Bruce Russett and University of Alabama professor of international studies John Oneal seemed to close the debate. With a historically long-term, multi-set range of variables, the authors demonstrated to the satisfaction of most liberal internationalists that Jack Levy was right in 1988: the proposition that democracies do not fight one another is the strongest empirical finding students of international relations have yet made about the conduct of states in the world system.

That the empirical grounding of the democratic peace will continue to be contested should be self-evident. Yet in the mind of most observers, Russett and Oneal had provided statistical evidence as conclusive as any reasonable person could require to confirm the hypothesis that democracies do not go to war with one another, indeed that the more mature they are in their liberal framework, the more cooperative they become as well. When to their democratic character our authors added a country's proclivity toward international economic open-ness (hence its willingness to be economically interdependent with other liberal economies) and such peoples' membership in multilateral organizations, their robust statistical findings became even more powerfully persuasive. Something new was afoot in world affairs: a Kantian "virtuous circle" was being born wherein free market democracies might be related to each other in peace. The age-old problem of world affairs, "Why War?", might finally be becoming obsolete as we finally came to understand "how peace" could be achieved—through the expansion of free market democracies around the globe.[10]

What are we to make of liberal democratic peace theory as the basis of public policy? Its clear implication is that as more and more governments democratize, peace will replace war in the international system. Therefore, it is in the interest not only of peoples who are already democratic, but of humanity in general, that this form of the state be generalized.

Russett and Oneal provided to such an argument the benediction of "science." "We have tested Kant's theses using social scientific methods, something that only recently became possible.... It is now possible, 205 years after Kant published *Perpetual Peace,* to evaluate his theory scientifically."

> History, specifically the years 1885–1992, can be used as a laboratory to assess the peacefulness of democratic, interdependent states linked by IGOs [international governmental organizations]. Our research is also made possible because voluminous information about this historical period has become available in a form necessary for statistical analysis. In addition, the statistical procedure, software, and computing capacity necessary for analyzing this massive amount of information have been developed. Our data would be useless were it not for the technological revolution that has made computers so prodigious and so cheap.[11]

After evaluating Kant's argument "scientifically," our authors make bold to conclude, "our findings and their implications for the future should encourage us to do what we can today to ensure that the Kantian peace is strengthened where it now operates and spread to areas still gripped by real-politik." Never do they suggest that "the three Kantian elements"—democratic government, open markets, and membership in multilateral institutions—are in fact dependent on, and serve the interests of, American power. Maintaining the virtue of their liberal assumptions, they would have Russia and China incorporated into an apparently acephalous democratic community. So they close their chapter with the confident observation, "the unipolar character of our world is inevitably transitory. It does provide, however, the opportunity to create a more peaceful world, one based not so much on military force as on the principles of democracy, interdependence, and international cooperation. Kant would say it is a moral imperative."[12]

A moral imperative? Apparently unaware that others might see their "moral imperative" as no more than an expression of self-righteous American nationalism and a goad to American imperialism, Russett and Oneal would put American foreign policy at the service of maintaining a "Kantian" system. Could anyone but a nationalist American (or Tony Blair) be fooled by such a conceit and fail to sense the danger of such utopian reasoning?

International Relations Theory: The Case of Andrew Moravcsik

With all due respect to the work of Russett and Oneal, the mandarins of the social sciences in the American Academy are not empiricists but theorists. They are the ones who engender the concepts of understanding the empirical "facts" that are argued over as we seek to perceive more clearly the dynamics of historical interaction. Anyone familiar with theory in the social sciences knows how beguiling ambitious frameworks for understanding may be, especially when they are at once grand in scope and simple in design. Marxism has its insights—as well as its blind spots—thanks to its reliance on dialectical materialism. Realism works in terms of the balance of power. Liberalism could now step proudly forward possessed of its own "scientific" confirmation, democratic peace theory.

In the social sciences, we may posit three essential conditions for a theory to be worthy of calling itself a "paradigm" as democratic peace theory does: internal conceptual congruence, unified external boundaries, explanatory reach. If it is also open to empirical verification, it may even qualify to be called a "science."

First, the concepts that make up the theory must be found to be *internally congruent with one another and empirically confirmed*. Thus, with democratic peace theory, we should be able to demonstrate that open economic systems are less likely to go to war with each other than closed economic systems, which will be more warlike. We should likewise find that democratic governments are less likely to go to war with one another than non-democratic governments, which will also in general be more bellicose. Finally, we should demonstrate empirically that when countries combine having both open economies with democratic states, then it is more likely yet, because of reciprocally reinforcing processes between economic and political factors creating a spillover into international organizations, that such peoples—those who live in market democracies—will stay at peace with one another as compared to their non-market, non-democratic counterparts, who will be found to be more warlike. What we have, then, are three empirically validated, congruent concepts that may be combined into a mega-concept: democratic market peoples engaged in multilateral organizations do not go to war with one another. Rigorous empirical findings allow democratic peace theory to be born.

Second, to have a theory, we must establish that our variables—in this case market democracies working through multilateral institutions—establish a *unified and comprehensive framework* for the theoretical analysis of a range of serious world issues—in this case the most important questions of world affairs, the origin of war and peace. The *self-sufficiency* of the variables manipulated by the theory means that it has boundaries, borders, limits. The theory is able *to generate internally* answers to whatever questions it addresses.

Whatever the dangers of a theory closing in on itself this way (and as we shall see they are considerable), democratic peace theory seemingly fulfills all these requirements. Concepts are empirically validated each by itself, then as a coherent interlocking set. The concepts are adequate in and of themselves to explain the logic of a significant aspect of history—the logic of war and peace. Internal congruence and external borders are established. A social science theory is at the point of being born.

Yet a third trial exists. A rising theory must take on the explanations offered by already-established paradigms of explanation and show its strength. Thus, if thanks to democratic peace theory we can separate the world into a Kantian zone and a Hobbesian zone—a "pacific union" of civilized interaction and a barbaric "state of nature"—then we transcend the categories of realist analysis for which such distinctions do not hold, given that realism posits the entire international system as essentially Hobbesian. Liberalism can "understand" realism, but realism cannot repay the compliment, meaning that the former makes finer distinctions and has a broader theoretical reach. In a word, liberalism trumps realism by subsuming and transcending it as a theory of world affairs.

If we have accomplished this three-fold project—complex internal congruence, self-sufficient unity, and explanatory reach—then we become dominant thinkers in the social sciences, guardians of a theory that gains insights into the workings of history itself, perhaps counselors to those who wield state power. Accordingly, writing in 1997 in *International Organization*, a flagship periodical of the academic international affairs community, Princeton professor Andrew Moravcsik declared that the time had come to "reformulate liberal international relations theory in a nonideological and nonutopian form." His ambition was a lofty one, for it meant nothing less than trying to displace realism with liberalism as the dominant paradigm for the study of world affairs. That such a challenge should be made after the Cold War might come as no surprise. Still, the job needed to be done.[13]

The approach Moravcsik took in language difficult for the uninitiated to follow corresponds to my outline above for how democratic peace theory could claim the status of a scientific theory for itself. Although Moravcsik's primary focus was on the way state-society relations made for a distinctive kind of foreign policy in liberal statecraft, there is no reason his account cannot cover democratic peace theory as well. For a theory to be properly considered a "paradigm" for investigating how the world works, for it to be a mega-theory in other words, Moravcsik explained that first, it must "be general and parsimonious demonstrating that a limited number of microfoundational assumptions can link a broad range of previously unconnected theories and hypotheses." Second, a paradigm must "be rigorous and coherent, offering a clear definition of its own boundaries." Third, it must "demonstrate empirical accuracy vis-à-vis other theories." Fourth, it must "demonstrate multicausal consistency," which turns out to mean that "liberal theory is analytically prior to both realism and institutionalism because it defines the conditions under which their assumptions hold."

Writing a few years later and referring to the work of Imre Lakatos, Moravcsik phrased the same definition more pithily: "A scientific research program…contains a hard core of inviolable assumptions, a positive heuristic, and a resulting 'protective belt' of 'auxiliary hypotheses'." Because liberalism satisfied all these conditions, Moravcsik anointed it as the dominant paradigm for the study of world affairs.[14]

Moravcsik was not solely, or even primarily, interested in democratic peace theory, but in liberalism as an even vaster scheme for understanding the conduct of certain states. Still, he could argue that the theory that held primacy for the study of world affairs was liberal internationalism. Deservedly perhaps, such an exaggerated claim led to this "science's" undoing, much as Marxism's claim to be "a theory of theories" proved to be self-defeating intellectual overreach. For given the level of mystery that continues to surround the human condition, any claim for dominance by a social science paradigm will invariably prove dangerous since the theory itself will necessarily contain blind spots, be it Marxist or realist, constructivist or feminist. At the very moment, then, that Moravcsik was announcing the liberal internationalism was becoming "nonutopian and nonideological" it was, ironically enough, becoming both utopian and ideological, a cause for concern for what it meant for American foreign policy.

By virtue of social science's insistence that a theory have internal consistency, borders, and superiority over rival explanatory systems, paradigms cannot correct their misperceptions. They are closed to insights from without. Their self-sufficiency is their undoing. For the sad fact is that no single paradigm can account for the total logic of world affairs (or even the affairs of a single human heart). And while the attempts to generate verifiable propositions into human behavior may indeed yield insights—no one should doubt but that liberal internationalism has its cogent lessons to teach on the logic of international relations—the effort to create a dominant paradigm inevitably leads to important failures in understanding induced by the demands for rigor of the theory itself.

Liberal Philosophy and the Democratic Peace: The Case of John Rawls

If theory trumps empiricism, then philosophy represents the highest summit theory can hope to achieve. Not surprisingly, given the tenor of the times, John Rawls, America's preeminent liberal political philosopher of the 1990s, was also bitten by the democratic peace argument, making out of it the possibility for a neo-Kantian "Society of Peoples" able to live on the planet without war, in what he termed a "lasting peace."

In *The Law of Peoples* published in 1999, Rawls addressed the possibility in the world such as we know it of a "realistic utopia." His ambition was to specify why we should put our faith in liberal political orders for reasons of both morality and practicality. Given the extent to which he referred to democratic peace theory, there can be no doubt but that liberal internationalist empirical and theoretical social science findings deeply informed Rawl's philosophic conclusion.[15]

In *The Law of Peoples,* Rawls considers liberal societies to be indisputably the highest form of organized political life our kind has achieved. He also recommends that liberal peoples cooperate with—not conflict with—what he calls "decent hierarchical" regimes. His hope is presumably that over time democratic ways might become more generalized thus drawing into their ranks decent hierarchical states that will liberalize, yet he is clear that they should be treated as members in good standing of the world community provided that their conduct remains sober.

But Rawls also recognizes a third form of regime, the "outlaw state," for which he has other recommendations. Outlaw states remain resolutely in the realm of the state of nature, obeying the laws of movement specified by Hobbes. They are brutal, treacherous, and aggressive. He concludes that, "all people are safer and more secure if such states change, or are forced to change, their ways."[16]

What implicitly emerges from Rawls' argument, then, is a form of "just war." For the sake of its own preservation, the Kantian world should expect trouble from the barbarians, and when aggression occurs, its mission should be to convert them to liberal ways. The danger is also an opportunity, however, for it establishes the possibility of finally achieving a "realistic utopia."

In the final lines of his book, Rawls comes to a conclusion that should surprise no reader of this book: that liberal imperialism is justifiable. The passages are well worth noting given the importance of their author.

> The idea of realistic utopia reconciles us to our social world by showing us that a reasonably just constitutional democracy existing as a member of a reasonably just Society of Peoples is possible.... This alone, quite apart from our success or our failure, suffices to banish the dangers of resignation and cynicism. By showing how the social world may realize the features of a realistic utopia, political philosophy provides a long term goal of political endeavor and in working toward it gives meaning to what we can do today.
>
> In this monograph on the Law of Peoples, I have tried to extend these ideas in order to set out guidelines for a liberal society's foreign policy in a reasonably just Society of Peoples. If a reasonably just Society of Peoples, whose members subordinate their power to reasonable aims is not possible, and human beings are largely amoral, if not incurably cynical and self-centered, one might ask, with Kant, whether it is worthwhile for human beings to live on the earth.[17]

From Neoliberal Democratic Peace Theory to Neoconservative Imperialist Practice

The movement from the theory of the democratic peace to the practice of the democratizing war should be rather easy to grasp at this point if the cumulative impact of empirical, theoretical, and philosophical discourse is appreciated. If democracies are by their nature peaceful and cooperative with one another, if authoritarian states are by their nature warlike, then to prepare for perpetual peace one might be well advised to consider democratizing war, especially if the historical moment favors the liberal democracies. Neoliberal democratic peace theory becomes then a claim to cultural superiority and an encouragement to belligerent behavior—an update of race theory, to put not too kind a comparison to it—backed up by a quasi- (or pseudo-) scientific legitimacy thanks to the efforts of the American academy.[18] The result is a "just war" argument that could be used to legitimize the kind of attack that United States launched on Iraq in March 2003.

To be sure, the neoliberal proponents of democratic peace theory may well object that their findings did not give the United States a hunting license to take on any country it chose for reform. Michael Doyle had been explicit in the 1980s that quixotic crusades could be counterproductive if foreign peoples lacked the presumed characteristics that could lead them to democracy or if American power were too limited to make the emergence of democratic government likely.

Many who endorsed democratic peace theory would agree. For example, although Bruce Russett was able in 1993 to wax eloquent on the promise of the democratic peace for pacifying world affairs, he nonetheless cautioned:

> External military intervention, even against the most odious dictators, is a dangerous way to try to produce a "democratic world order." Sometimes, with a cautious cost-benefit analysis and with the certainty of substantial and legitimate internal support, it may be worthwhile.... Even so, any time an outside power supplants any existing government the problem of legitimacy is paramount.... At the very least intervention should not be unilateral. It must be approved, publicly and willingly, by some substantial international body like the UN.... Peacekeeping operations to help provide the conditions for free elections, monitor those elections, and advice on the building of democratic institutions are usually far more promising than is military intervention.[19]

Such warnings notwithstanding, the neoliberals had made what was to them a convincing case that world peace, and American security, would be vastly better served were democratic governments to proliferate around the globe. While Russett recognized in the early 1990s that implementing the liberal promise might be dangerous, by the turn of the century he had apparently mellowed, and other neo-Wilsonians would emerge, as we shall see in the next chapter of this book on comparative political analysis, to make the task seem less daunting. As they did so, the beacon that Russett and Oneal had lit, along with a cohort of liberal internationalists contributing to democratic peace theory in its empirical, theoretical, and philosophical modes, burned all the brighter. Indeed, so brightly did it burn that we could call it the sacred fire of the Bush Doctrine itself.

What neoliberals had done was to give intellectual depth to the otherwise empirically and theoretically unbuttressed argument current in neoconservative circles since the 1940s. That totalitarian systems were inherently evil, while liberal democracies were essentially good, was a fundamental assertion for this school of thought. Now neoconservative feelings had confirmation from the neoliberals.

Hence, given the "advances" made conceputally by neoliberals, there was nothing new about Natan Sharansky's distinction, influential in neoconservative circles, between what he called "free" and "fear" societies. The former, the world of the liberal democracies, were inclined toward peace with each other. The latter, the world of authoritarian and totalitarian regimes, were inclined toward war—especially toward liberal democracies whose ways so threatened the claims to legitimacy despots liked to make. To take up the cudgels in the name of democracy, then, was not only justifiable self-defense, it was also filled with the promise of a golden age of peace if its mission of converting foreign peoples into democracies was satisfactorily accomplished.

We know that President Bush was most impressed with Sharansky's writings and had a copy of his book *The Case for Democracy* distributed throughout his foreign policy circle as recommended reading. In Sharansky's hands, democratic peace theory became nothing less than what international relations specialists would immediately recognize as a doctrine of "just war":

> Now we can see why nondemocratic regimes imperil the security of the world. They stay in power by controlling their populations. This control invariably requires an increasing amount of repression. To justify this repression and maintain internal stability, external enemies must be manufactured. *The result is that while the mechanics of democracy make democracies inherently peaceful, the mechanics of tyranny make nondemocracies inherently belligerent.* Indeed, in order to avoid collapsing from within, fear societies must maintain a perpetual state of conflict.[20]

Only a short step separated statements of this kind from President Bush's assertion that terror could be staunched best by regime change in the Middle

East. "The world has a clear interest in the spread of democratic values, because stable and free nations do not breed ideologies of murder," he declared to the American Enterprise Institute on February 26, 2003. "They encourage the peaceful pursuit of a better life." Or in his State of the Union Address of January 31, 2006, "Dictatorships shelter terrorists, and feed resentment and radicalism, and seek weapons of mass destruction. Democracies replace resentment with hope, respect the rights of their citizens and their neighbors, and join the fight against terror."

The policy consequence of democratic peace theory thus at once promised a golden age of peace should this form of government dominate the international system and warned of conflict with non-democratic regimes as these tyrannical systems turned their efforts toward war. President Bush repeatedly made the case for war for the sake of peace, as in an address at the National Defense University on March 8, 2005:

> Our strategy to keep the peace in the longer term is to help change the conditions that give rise to extremism and terror, especially in the Broader Middle East. Parts of that region have been caught for generations in a cycle of tyranny and despair and radicalism. When a dictatorship controls the political life of a country, responsible opposition cannot develop and dissent is driven underground and toward the extreme. And to draw attention away from their social and economic failures, dictators place blame on other countries and other races, and stir the hatred that leads to violence. This status quo of despotism and anger cannot be ignored or appeased, kept in a box or bought off, because we have witnessed how the violence in that region can reach easily across borders and oceans. The entire world has an urgent interest in the progress, and hope, and freedom in the Broader Middle East....
>
> It should be clear that the advance of democracy leads to peace because governments that respect the rights of their people also respect the rights of their neighbors. It should be clear that the best antidote to radicalism and terror is the tolerant hope kindled in free societies. And our duty is now clear. For the sake of our long-term security, all free nations must stand with the forces of democracy and justice that have begun to transform the Middle East.

Thanks to neoliberal democratic peace theory, the president's assertion had strong intellectual undergirding. Not so much neoconservative arguments, which had little more than rhetorical substance to it, but neoliberal ideology, with all its empirical, theoretical, and philosophical paraphernalia, became the intellectual substance of the pillar of purpose advanced by the Bush Doctrine.

Here is the reason neolibs who opposed the Iraq War (in the very few cases in which they did so) had no solid ground to stand on theoretically speaking when their own vision of the world was appropriated by Washington. Was it not standard fare in the 1990s for these liberals to divide the world into the saved (the fellowship of liberal democracies), those that might be saved (Russia, China, Turkey, and Mexico, for example), and the damned (those possessed of ideologies that rejected the advent of liberal democratic ways)? How could there be any negotiation with this last set of states, when instead we must insist on their essential untrustworthiness and hence call for regime change? Wasn't the only permanent solution to the danger of rogue states grossly abusing the human rights of their citizens or threatening their neighbors with weapons of mass destruction, regime change and democratization? So the "moral clarity" advanced by neoconservatives against moral relativists could easily conclude on the basis of evidence accumulated by the neo-Wilsonians: to protect the peace, wage war.

Not surprisingly, the template for policy offered by democratic peace theory was used repeatedly (and in theoretical terms, accurately) by official Washington. So in speech after speech, as in the National Security Strategy of the United States published in September 2002, President Bush divided the world's countries into three principal categories. First were our democratic allies—Canada, Australia and New Zealand, Japan and South Korea, the members of the European Union, Israel, Taiwan, South Africa, and most of Latin America. With them any idea of military conflict was banished as simply unthinkable and instead their continued support of our leadership was deemed obvious (even if they sometimes are free riders and refuse to acknowledge the benefits of American power). Our interests and values were very close, and historical experience had taught us the overriding importance of cooperation. This was the "free world," more recently called "the civilized world," a region some intellectuals even had the temerity to call "post historic."

The second circle of countries the president recognized were those we hoped to work with, especially Russia and China. Turkey and Mexico figured next in this ranking, along with Brazil. President Bush typically acknowledged that they were not yet democracies but welcomed such liberalizing trends he saw as indications that peaceful, indeed cooperative, relations with them were to be anticipated.

A third circle of countries was more problematic. Sometimes, as with Uzbekistan, they were simply ignored, for however internally repressive they might be, they were cooperating with the "global war on terror." However, by their very nature, authoritarian (and all the more totalitarian) states were capable of being "rogue" or "backlash" states in world affairs or in harboring movements that upset global peace. The president typically indicated military action against such states and movements was possible because of the threat of terrorism or of nuclear proliferation and laid their shortcomings to their lack of democratic government and the violence they practiced toward their own populations. The "axis of evil"—Iraq, Iran, and North Korea—was just such a collection of states, one whose numbers might be expanded at will.

From a policy point of view, the wonder of the ideology was that its concepts were so flexible that the president could decide which country was a democracy, which was not. Dealing harshly with apparent democracies such as Venezuela under Hugo Chavez or Palestine under Hamas might seem to be more difficult, but the concept of "illiberal democracy" conveniently existed so that these sham democracies too could be seen as international pariahs with whom no substantive agreements were likely.[21]

The bottom line, then, was that the promise of democratic peace theory emerged as essential to the promise and the practice of the Bush Doctrine. By virtue of a democracy crusade, Washington reserved to itself the right to separate the goats from the sheep in world affairs, and to act in relationship to each in a way that legitimized whatever conduct the United States chose to pursue. To repeat President Bush's most famous declaration, contained in his Second Inaugural Address of January 2005:

> We are led by events and common sense to one conclusion: The survival of liberty in our land increasingly depends on the success of liberty in other lands. The best hope for peace in our world is the expansion of freedom in all the world.... So it is the policy of the United States to seek and support the growth of democratic movements and institutions in every nation and culture with the ultimate goal of ending tyranny in our world.

The expectations set by the assurance of democratic peace theory amount to a form of utopianism, one born in the left of center academy, purveyed forward to Washington by a cadre of scholar-activists, and finally appropriated with a vengeance after 9/11 thanks to the attentions of the neoconservatives. On our side stand the elect. On the other side, stand those who cannot be trusted. In between lie the few—their identity as outlaw barbarians or as civilized peoples varies as their relationship with Washington varies—hoping that the world's sovereign will give them their *lettres de noblesse,* or fearing that such recognition as they have received will in due course be retracted.

The general mood was summed up by Secretary Condoleezza Rice's repeated evocation of "the freedom divide," which in turn recalls President Lincoln's statement in 1858 that the United States "cannot endure permanently half slave and half free." In the event, a great civil war settled the matter internally for the United States. The same prospect now frankly confronted this country in world affairs in its effort to promote what the Bush administration repeatedly called the "single sustainable model for national success: freedom, democracy, and free enterprise."

The intellectual advantage of the neoconservatives in a situation such as this was that they were not constrained by the attempt to make a scientific theory of their worldview. They were proudly realists *and* liberals, aware of the need for American power for a variety of self-interested reasons besides democracy promotion, *and yet* of the desirability of moral purpose. If they were not as complex in their thinking as the neoliberals, they were politically far sharper.

The Bush administration thus could combine a realist appreciation of the need for leadership born of neoconservative thinking with neo-Wilsonian democratic peace theory. Here was the new voice of American nationalism, speaking in distinctly imperialist terms. As Rice put it in her testimony before the Senate Foreign Relations Committee deliberating her appointment as secretary of state on January 18, 2005: "One of history's clearest lessons is that America is safer, and the world is more secure, whenever and wherever freedom prevails. It is neither an accident nor a coincidence that the greatest threats of the last century emerged from totalitarian movements.... The challenges we face today are not less daunting." Yet Rice was able to cut through the neoliberal reservations about American unilateralism by a brilliant, yet apparently self-evident, reformulation of multilateralism that made it an instrument of American leadership.

> First, we will unite the community of democracies in building an international system that is based on our shared values and the rule of law. Second, we will strengthen the community of democracies to fight the threats to our common security and alleviate the hopelessness that feeds terror. And third, we will spread freedom and democracy throughout the globe.

The extraordinary result was that neo-Wilsonian democratic peace theory had laid the groundwork both for launching an imperialist war defending the Kantian system by expanding its boundaries against Hobbes's state of nature. Given its blinders on the character of leadership, neoliberals were unable to criticize a hegemon that talked of its benevolent intentions when in fact its pursuit of power was as old as human history.

A doctrine of peace had become one of war. A doctrine of national self-determination had become one of imperialism. The promise of solidarity among democracies had bred disunity. The viability of the "zone of peace" was endangered by a leadership whose character could not be seen for what it was thanks to intellectual blinders of the very intellectuals who had given rise to such a "scientific" understanding of world affairs. American nationalism had become a form of internationalism that had no limits on its ambition.

The irony—or the scandal—of this story has a reasoning whose logic is complicated, but once examined painfully obvious to behold. The liberal promise for freedom and peace had been betrayed by its own hand into a nationalist war-making creed. Once this form of reasoning had taken hold in simplified form of the elites of the two major political parties, America's destiny as an imperial power could be sealed.

The Case of Larry Diamond

How did democratic peace theory move from the ivory tower to policy makers? To go from theory to practice requires a transmission belt of ideas, the best vehicle for which are those who might be called the "scholar-activists." While some of these liberals were neoconservative, far more of them were neo-Wilsonian, that is, liberal hawks affiliated with the Democratic Party or independent in their political leanings. So the deadly intellectual virus was transmitted.

Consider the case of Larry Diamond, a prominent neoliberal scholar-activist working since the late 1980s to study the dynamics of the transition to democracy so as to aid the process. Diamond, who is a Democrat, is headquartered as a scholar at the Hoover Institution, a conservative research institute usually identified with the Republican Party on the campus of Stanford University. But as an activist he is surely better known in Washington, DC. In the nation's capital, Diamond works with the National Endowment for Democracy, a government-funded agency that sponsors democracy promotion in countries where the State Department thinks this advisable and that funds the *Journal of Democracy*, which Diamond co-edits. He is also considered a "guru" of the Agency for International Development, whose mandate is to promote democracy with a $500 million annual budget. And he is a signatory member of the Progressive Policy Institute of the Democratic Party, which calls for "tough internationalism" and places democracy promotion for the Middle East at the top of its foreign policy agenda.

Given his scholar-activist credentials, no wonder Diamond signed on after the fall of Baghdad to help the Iraqi Provisional Coalition Government navigate the transition from Saddam's despotism to democratic order. With Diamond we find an excellent example of the kind of link between the thinking of the neoliberals and the neoconservatives that lead to the appropriation of democratic peace theory by those who formulated the Bush Doctrine. We can also see in his story the reason so many in the Democratic Party were unable to oppose effectively the Iraq War when it occurred.

Take, for example, Diamond's 1994 paean to democratic peace theory, which could read as a prelude to the Bush Doctrine:

> Democratic countries do not go to war with one another. Democracies do not sponsor terrorism against one another. They do not build weapons of mass destruction to use on one another or threaten each other with. Democratic countries are more reliable, open, and enduring trading partners.... They are more environmentally responsible.... They are better bets to honor international treaties.... Precisely because they respect within their own borders competition, civil liberties, property rights, and the rule of law, democracies are the only reliable foundation on which a new world order of international security and prosperity can be built.[22]

Diamond was certain he had found the panacea to the world's ills. In a report to the Carnegie Commission on Preventing Deadly Conflict, completed in 1995, he entitled his first chapter "Why Promote Democracy?" and then gave a list of the most salient issues that he assured his readers might well be solved if democratic governments expanded. Subdivision of problems to be so managed included no less than Russia, China, Islamic fundamentalism, political terrorism, and ethnic conflict. As we might expect by now, neoliberal democratic peace theory provided Diamond a firm sense of intellectual confidence, one that neoconservatives could embrace without hesitation.

> [P]romoting democracy is vital to our national security—not just to serve our values and ideals, but to defend against serious, possibly devastating, threats to our safety and well-being. That the defense democracy provides is preventive, and therefore subtle and at one remove, makes the case harder to establish but also more compelling.[23]

Writing again in 2001, Diamond once more sounded the democratic peace theory trumpet, proposing that if the United States looked, as he thought it should, for "an overarching mission and purpose, there is no more appealing and compelling goal than the promotion of liberal democracy." Sounding as if he were in a warm up for what would soon be called the Bush Doctrine, Diamond wrote:

> In short, never in world history has there been a more fertile and propitious moment for wedding the founding principles of America to its global strategy and power. It is now possible to imagine a world in which all the major component states will be liberal democracies. It is now time to declare this our goal as a country, and to turn our resources, our energy, our imagination, and our moral and political leadership in the world to that end.[24]

The bottom line, then, is that in hands like Diamond's, liberal democratic peace theory became a self-conscious warrant for imperialist war-making. Those peoples who lived in other consolidated democracies might fail to see the extent to which they were protected by the world system centered in Washington; they might even have the cheek to feel menaced by the American determination to dominate global politics. But disrespect is the common lot of imperial powers—to be feared, even despised by the very people they protect. Here are Nietzsche's "men without chests" free riding on American vision, courage, and power. What our democratic allies should understand is that by promoting market relations and democratic government worldwide, the United States is promoting their interests too. By definition, America stands for freedom and the wars it wages are for peace. Once the democratic peace theory is internalized its logic becomes Orwellian: war means peace—one cannot logically define reality differently. The example of Diamond shows how easily a message whose origins lie in rather complex intellectual manipulations can be communicated to the general public for the sake of promoting a "progressive" war.

The Achilles' Heel of Democratic Peace Theory

Given its empirical validation, its theoretical rigor, and its philosophic edge, what could possibly be wrong with democratic peace theory? The answer lies in a mistake in its theoretical formulation that then corrupts both its empirical and its philosophic dimensions.

The mistake is to suppose that liberal theory, as "theory" was defined above, has a watertight ability to explain the democratic peace. It does not. Without an appreciation of the role of hegemonic leadership in creating the zone of democratic peace, consolidating its workings, and protecting it from its enemies within and without, the history, character, and destiny of the "Society of Peoples" in world affairs cannot be adequately appreciated. Just as the hegemon—the United States—was indispensable for the "Community of Democracies" to come in to being, so might deficiencies in its leadership lead to its unraveling.

This elementary point is indispensable to understanding how liberal hawks may have come to a gross misperception of the character of American power after 9/11. Why was such an appreciation lacking? In a word, the blind spot appeared because the liberal internationalists had no robust theory of the character of international political leadership, except for a simplistically misleading trust in market democratic states. And they had no such theory for a very good reason. Their theory prohibited them from having one.

We may recall that one of the prerequisites for a conceptual approach to be sophisticated enough to be called a "theory" as it is laid out by Moravcsik (and he is right on this score) is that its internal conceptual scheme must be able to count for the essential dynamics of the process it claims to explain. The problem for liberal theory, however, is that *hegemonic leadership as a complex role is not a conceptual variable that this approach to the study of world affairs can claim as its own.* Instead, such a political role in the international system falls under the explanatory variables of realism, the school of thought that liberalism hopes to supersede.

It is realism, not liberalism, that debates why states act as they do in terms of power dispositions and underlying dynamics of human nature. In its provincial pride, liberal theory as it came to maturity turned its back on such matters. Or better, to the extent it conceptualizes the question it simplistically sees authoritarian or totalitarian governments as irremediably "evil" and liberal democracies as inherently "good." How then could the United States, with all the medals on its chest, be motivated by other than good intentions if it acted in the name of democracy as it launched an attack on a country with a leader as sordid as Saddam Hussein? If in some back recess of their minds the neo-Wilsonians might have admitted that the possibility existed that the United States was an expansionist imperial power with motives as old as recorded history, they were prevented by the strictures of subscribing to their "scientific" theory from articulating the criticism. To have done so would have been to have stepped out of the logic of their paradigm of thinking.

In short, the role of a Prime Mover (in this instance, quite obviously the United States) in creating, sustaining, defending, expanding, and consolidating the zone of democratic zone of peace is not a consideration serious liberal theory can admit. To those of us who know something about history, or who are possessed of simple common sense, for liberalism to be staked to such a position may seem preposterous. But there you have it.

Instead of seeing the indispensable role of great power leadership for the Community of Democracies, liberal internationalists preferred to talk as if some kind of internal magnetism offered by the character of being market democracies alone explained their pacific character toward one another. By failing to recognize the critical importance of a Leviathan, liberal theory cannot discuss the possible dangers to which the great power that presides over the destiny of the Community of Democracies is prey. Suppose the Prime Mover for some reason (a financial disaster, say) implodes? Suppose, rather, it asks the other members of the community to embark with it upon a perilous mission that fails (the current invasion of Iraq, for instance)? Suppose a rival emerges from outside the community (China, with the temptations it can offer to members of the liberal club to defect, for example)? Suppose a single great power within the community is joined by another and disputes its title to leadership (should China democratize, for example)? Any of these developments is rather easy to imagine. All of them are fraught with the gravest of consequences for the unity of the "zone of democratic peace." None of them is a subject liberal theory can entertain because, to repeat, they all fall outside the perimeter of issues it can address and stay true to its pretensions to intellectual rigor. Yet any or all of these dangers may surface. What the hegemon gives, the hegemon may take away. And if that happens, liberal theory remains silent.

The trouble liberal theory has identifying the characteristics of state power that it might have learned from realism means that it places the "zone of democratic peace" in a state of grace that is an altogether more exalted position with respect to the dynamic of history than it deserves. Yes, the United States is a liberal democracy, child of the Enlightenment, a country whose interests to some extent correspond to values that history attests are indeed noble. But for all that, the United States remains a country directed by people whose ambitions may be somewhat less than always the most elevated. Washington is peopled by self-interested special interest groups, after all, and as a state the United States has never been above riding roughshod over other peoples in the name of national security.

The idea that the United States has been granted some kind of historical dispensation to act out of the necessary genius of its character for the betterment of all humanity is a notion that common sense would repudiate. The problem, however, is that people high on the elixir of liberal democratic peace theory might actually believe that American foreign policy, if conducted in the name of democracy promotion, was deserving of unrestricted loyalty.

In a word, we most surely have not arrived at "the end of History," as Fukuyama told us in 1989 we had. And the enemy of peace and freedom may not be only those living in the barbaric world of history. The unexpected surprise is that even those of us who are post-historic, Kantian, concerned about our "pacific union" with those in the "civilized" world who are like-minded, may be among those who behave in a rogue manner. We ourselves may be capable of brutal, self-aggrandizing behavior. And all this in the name of expanding the "zone of democratic peace." It is arrogant folly indeed to believe that somehow we have come to embody virtue, every act of government being one that leads to freedom and peace. We are "post-historic"?

Here is the price liberal internationalist theory has paid by wedding itself to multilateralism as a sufficient dynamic for collective action of the Community of Democracies in world affairs. By virtue of its inability to recognize theoretically the importance of American leadership in world affairs and the dangers it might run with consequences for liberalism worldwide if Washington ran amok, the theory could not see crises on the horizon that were the product of a liberal democratic state acting in a way faithful to the terms of liberal internationalist imperialism.

It is irrelevant for liberals to reply, as they are likely to do, that there is a "force multiplier" to multilateral action that makes it more effective, so that unilateral leadership is not needed. Perhaps in some circumstances they are correct. Or they may assert that eventually America's relative power will decline, so that the Community of Democracies needs to find ways to handle common interests in a mutually acceptable manner. Again, why object? But the deepest reasons for liberals to fail to analyze the character of American leadership of such a community is that the purity of their claims to having a theory worthy of the title scientific does not permit Washington such a role. For theory to be theory, it must be watertight. Hence leadership is not a concept to be analyzed.

Let us state as a law of social science theories that they always and everywhere have their blind spots. However insightful they may well be on specific questions, the social sciences are not yet scientific enough to provide single-theory explanations for major questions bedeviling the human condition. In 1844, the young Marx had the hubris to declare in his *Economic and Philosophical Manuscripts*, "communism is the riddle of history solved *and knows itself to be that solution*" (emphasis in the original). During the 1990s, liberalism became prey to much the same ill. The ultimate irony comes when Moravcsik announces that thanks to his insights he "reformulates liberal international relations theory in a nonideological and nonutopian form appropriate to empirical social sciences." What his essay actually accomplishes is precisely the opposite. He makes liberalism ideological and utopian to a degree it had never before reached.

So, when Moravcsik discusses how states within the liberal community interact in a section of his essay called "interdependence and the international system," no mention at all is made of a Prime Mover. His omission is no oversight. It follows from the definition of what a theory is itself that to admit the notion of a hegemon as indispensable for the zone of democratic peace, and as holding in its hands (for better or for worse) the fate of the Community of Democracies, would ruin the purity of liberalism's internal cohesion and external boundaries and so its claim to scientific status. In a word, Moravcsik is obliged by his own thinking not to analyze the role of leadership given that this is a variable whose logic has already been well explained by the rival paradigm of realism. To say that this presents a problem for liberalism's ability to understand international politics is to be kind about our wording.

The blind spot democratic peace theory generated was its inability to see the need for, or the danger of, visionary hegemonic leadership by a single state of the Community of Democracies if the zone of peace is to survive in the world such as it is. Perhaps at some time in the very distant future, this community will prove able to pool sovereignties such that effective collective action can be taken in high-risk circumstances. But for today and for the foreseeable future, to ignore the importance of strategic vision held by the United States is to be theoretically sophisticated and practically foolish.

As I have indicated, empiricists bow before theorists in the social sciences. Hence, the problem in liberal theory necessarily came to corrupt the liberal empirical investigation of Russett and Oneal. One of the most striking features of their book—the work that along with others I consider to be the best produced by democratic peace theorists—is that the United States' will and ability to lead a confederation of market democracy is totally ignored as an explanatory element in the successful record they present of democracies not waging war upon one another. Astonishingly enough, Emmanuel Kant is their focus, not Wilson, Washington, or the United States, all of which come in for no serious attention whatsoever.

At one point, Russett and Oneal do evaluate the evidence that hegemony increases or reduces violence in world affairs, but quite properly, given their theoretical allegiances, they do so to distinguish liberalism from realism, not to blend the two. At another point, they speculate on the need for a hegemonic power to ensure that peace be preserved, yet explicitly rejected it as a "false hope." One result of their approach, for example, is that they do not make the success of the European Union dependent either on American insistence or on Soviet threats. An immaculate conception apparently occurred, free from either the hegemonic inducements of Washington or the hegemonic menace of Moscow. In a breathtaking ahistorical leap of faith, Russett and Oneal follow theory's imperative and make the zone of democratic peace depend on a "virtuous circle" of the "Kantian triangle": democracy, open markets, and multi-lateralism. Not for them to sully such a sunny world with talk of Hegemons, Prime Movers, or Leviathans. Not for them to mention the United States.[25]

Yet surely any serious review of the historical record since 1945 must quickly reveal that American leadership was indispensable for free market democracies to win the Cold War. Washington formed the Community of Democracies, defined its purpose, provided collective economic and security goods, gave it vision and determination. Inconvenient though the fact may be, without a paramount political force to hold together, discipline, and direct the democratic community, its life span was, and is, likely to be, as Hobbes would have predicted, short, nasty, and brutish. And what the hegemon gave, it may take away by poor leadership. But given the closed, self-sufficient character of liberal theory as it came to be in the 1990s, if facts disturbed the theory, too bad for the facts.

The problem that bedevils Rawls likewise flows from the theoretical and empirical base he builds upon. To be sure, liberal democracies are the children of the Enlightenment, one of the glories of world history. Yet they are not, for all this, spared the stain of original sin; they are not immune from egoism and arrogance, the temptations of power that haunt human destiny across the ages. Rawls concedes no such point. The Society of Peoples, which he assumes already to be coming in to existence, has as its primary concern its internal coordination for the common good. What he does not discuss, presumably because he has shut his eyes to such matters thanks to liberal theory, is that such a society—the Community of Democracies—will perforce need leadership. Had he done so, Rawls might have perceived that this leadership in our age of continued human frailty will come in all likelihood from a single state, and that this state might be possessed of a range of ambitions, one of which, the will to power, outranks in attraction all others that the story of our kind can recount. The blessings of liberal democracy, in short, cannot eradicate our lower ambitions. However much we may salute Kant, let us beware the Hobbes within us all.

To be sure, Rawls died before the invasion of Iraq and there may be reason aplenty to doubt he would have supported this war. I do not know whether Russett or Moravcsik supported the war, but I do know that Larry Diamond, surprisingly enough, claims to have opposed it.[26] Yet all these neo-Wilsonians, or neo-Kantians, were presumably well aware that ideas may have consequences. They had quite obviously loaded an ideological pistol with their assertion that "we" were superior, standing only for peace and the common good, whereas "they" were fallen, indeed that "outlaw states" in the domain of Hobbes's state of nature should be seen as inherently dangerous and might be attacked.

What is striking in the study of these thinkers is their excitement with the practical implications of the theoretical argument they were making. Russett and Oneal write of a "moral imperative" that should inform American foreign policy thanks to their empirical findings. Moravcsik is convinced he has made liberal theory "nonutopian and nonideological" and so has fathered a scientific paradigm. Diamond asserts that American foreign policy should look for "an overarching mission and purpose," and concludes, "there is no more appealing and compelling goal than the promotion of liberal democracy." When it comes to Rawls, one senses as well in his final words, quoted above and coming close to the end of his life, his deeply felt sentiment that for a liberal, life can finally find meaning in the pursuit of a universal democratizing mission.

Democratic peace theory of the 1990s had made all these thoughts and emotions possible. Without in all probability having voted for George W. Bush or contributed to the writing of the doctrine that bore his name, these neoliberals had made an essential contribution to a framework for foreign policy that had no obvious precedent in the country's history.

Elevated by theoretical analysis to being a "science," confirmed by strict empirical standards of the quantitative method, espoused by a leading political philosopher, democratic peace theory meant America was ready for empire.

CHAPTER 5

Liberal Imperialism II
Democracy as a Universal Value

The [high government official speaking of Iraq] said that guys like me were "in what we call the reality-based community," which he defined as people who "believe that solutions emerge from your judicious study of discernible reality.... That's not the way the world really works anymore," he continued. "We're an empire now, and when we act we create our own reality. And while you're studying that reality—judiciously, as you will—we'll act again, creating other new realities, which you can study too, and that's how things will sort out. We're history's actors...and you, all of you, will be left to just study what we do.

Ron Suskind, *New York Times*, October 17, 2004

Now faith is the substance of things hoped for, the evidence of things not seen.

Hebrews 11:1

Quite by itself, as we have seen in the preceding chapter, democratic peace theory was enough to turn what I have called "liberal hegemonism" in world affairs into "liberal imperialism." By promising a vastly improved international order if the leading peoples of the globe were governed by democratic values, habits, and institutions, neoliberal internationalists in the 1990s specified a goal to be achieved that could serve expansionist interests in Washington. For the most part these neo-Wilsonians, or neoliberals, were conscious of the policy implications of their research, which they felt had reached the status of a scientific conclusion, even if some of them were initially careful to reject the notion that an armed crusade was likely to be an effective way to expand the zone of peace.

An obvious intellectual problem remained. It was one thing to believe that the world would be a better place were all its people governed democratically. It was quite another thing to hold that such a development was likely to occur easily or quickly. And it was yet another thing again to hold that the historical agents to bring about rapid democratization were not domestic actors who called for "revolution from above" or "revolution from below," but instead foreigners who in the name of an armed humanitarian intervention could bring about "revolution from outside."

In short, democratic peace theory most certainly contributed mightily to the emergence of liberal internationalist imperialist thinking—who can doubt it for a second—but in and of itself, it was not fully adequate to the ideological task of justifying something of the magnitude of the Bush Doctrine and the Iraq War. We should therefore understand the reluctance of some of this theory's proponents to push for too robust an expansion of the American dominion. The liberal international relations experts who contributed so importantly to the ideology often lacked the conceptual apparatus necessary to tie an argument about the character of states in world affairs once they were democratic to the very different question of how they became democratic in the first place. In a word, more work remained for the liberal internationalist academy to perform.

Difficulties In Promoting the Transition From Authoritarian to Democratic Government

The academic domain in which the reconceptualization of the transition to democracy would proceed is called *comparative political analysis*. Traditionally, this field of study has been area specific, requiring of its students immersion in the language and culture of peoples defined by a relatively common historical experience. While the assumption of comparativists is that the human experience has its important commonalities, the working agenda of the field has been to break the greater story of our kind into more discrete cultural-historical units, each with its own singular dynamic arising out of its own unique experience and identity. The operational assumption was that the various peoples of the world were in many respects distinct enough that when change occurred it would be in terms of a logic inscribed in their character more likely than being the product of a universal process of change.

As a result, the field of comparative political analysis as conceived between around 1950 and 1985 might accept the harsh reality that not all the world was ready to be democratized, and so counsel restraint and patience in pushing for it to happen. The academic disciplines concentrating on "late-industrializers," "underdevelopment," or "the Third World," as most of Africa, Asia, and Latin America were variously referred to, agreed that "modernization," as the process of the transition from traditional authoritarian to a more effective form of government was typically called, would likely be no easy matter. Culture and society were densely woven historical realities that although certain to change, perhaps in revolutionary ways, were not necessarily fated to become democratic.

Yes, democracy works, this earlier generation might well affirm. Its solid foundations are both moral and practical. However, the obstacles to creating such a political system, as opposed to having the benefits of one already in place—the problems of democratization in an authoritarian context, whatever its type—are considerable. Established elites resist the diminution of their power; excluded sectors of the population rise up in long-repressed indignation at the old order; new ways of doing things invite rampant corruption; war with neighbors wanting to fish in troubled waters or fearful for their own stability is a frequent possibility.

Prior to the late 1980s, therefore, most comparativists worth their salt would have been skeptical that democracy could easily take root in cultures far different from the West. True, Japan and India had both become democracies, developments that showed the ability of this form of government to organize the political processes of non-Western peoples. But thanks to having an industrial base, a strong sense of national unity, and a fear of communism expanding in Asia, Japan had characteristics that lent themselves to this outcome with relative ease and had fallen under American occupation, whereas India had experienced generations of British rule where an institutional and ideological structure favorable to the eventual emergence of democratic government had been laid.

Elsewhere, prospects seemed noticeably dimmer. Consider the basic proposition of a democratic polity. Civil society is empowered to do much as it will at the same moment the state is limited by internal checks and balances and by its obligation to conform its behavior to the rule of law and the wishes of the governed. A limited state operating under a set of unfamiliar and incomplete rules need not be a weak or corrupt government, but it may well be both and often is. An empowered civil society may find consensus through negotiated compromise on the purpose of political power, but again it may well fall into civil war and it often does. In short, one should not be starry-eyed in recommending democratic governments to peoples who have never practiced it before.

If democratic transitions may be difficult undertakings, democratization at the point of a bayonet—what we might call "gunboat democracy"—may be especially difficult to institutionalize. Such an effort has trouble building on local forces and will almost surely excite a nationalist reaction against it. The success of gunboat democracy depends on the predominance of nationalist forces that are in general agreement with the proposition that such a conquest may favor their interests. Such was the reaction in important elements of the Japanese and German populations after World War II, and such the widespread feeling (outside force was not at all needed) in Poland, Hungary, and Czechoslovakia after the fall of the Berlin Wall, and in Slovenia as Yugoslavia imploded.

The result of these deliberations was that comparative political studies in the period before the 1990s stressed "preconditions" and "sequences" or "stages" in the development of a democratic polity. For example, so far as democratization was concerned, the *sequences* tended to have changes in the state precede those in civil society, which would then progressively be mobilized into a new political order. The *preconditions* for democratization would include such factors as the existence of a middle class, an ethic of tolerance for social diversity, a sense of national unity, some tradition of limited central government, and leaders possessed of a commitment to a democratic transition backed by movements that supported such efforts.

In summary, the field of comparative analysis prior to the late 1980s would give cold comfort to the idea that liberal imperialism, however well-meaning it might intend to be, could actually foster democracy in many parts of the world, including most especially in the Middle East.

"New Thinking" in Comparative Political Analysis

The job of the rising generation of comparativists of the 1990s (once again, I use this decade to cover a longer time period, from about 1986–2001) was to challenge the traditional paradigm of analysis with its reservations about the likelihood that democracy could come quickly or easily to parts of the world that had never known it. Its ambition was to speak of global transformations that swept all peoples before it, of the permeability of boundaries, of a universal appeal to democracy, in short, of a coming convergence of what it meant to be human.

For the neoliberal international relations experts we reviewed in the preceding chapter, the task had been to come up with a new concept—democratic peace theory—and to use it to challenge the claims of the realist tradition to an understanding of world affairs. Something of the same process was occurring at about the same time among the neolib comparativists. A new thinking was emerging stressing not only interdisciplinarity but cross-regional comparisons. The new thinking also focused with special intensity on the question of the democratic transition, that is, on how peoples without prior experience with democratic governments might come to have it as the authoritarian systems that had dominated them in earlier years crumbled at the end of the Cold War. To give a concrete example of a subject an earlier generation would not have tackled, Latin America and Central Europe might now be studied together in terms of their transitions to democracy.

The period of the 1990s thus tried to overcome the burden of sequences and preconditions in favor of a less complicated, altogether more rapid, inauguration of democratic ways. Increasingly comparativists sensed that with the end of the Cold War new historic winds were blowing, a window of possibility was open with the conviction growing that liberal democracy was the only way a people could provide stable and efficient government for themselves.

Such debates within the academy could potentially have important repercussions on American foreign policy. If the old guard were right, the United States should be careful about pushing change abroad. It should count Germany and Japan important historical exceptions to the rule that peoples change in their own ways and that efforts by outsiders to influence the process might do more harm than good. If the new guard were right, the United States should seize the opportunity it had to move history and so encourage democratic transitions abroad with all the means at its disposal.

The relevance of these disputes to the origins of the Bush Doctrine should be apparent. In the so-called war of ideas, the American academy was now in a position to unite democratic peace theory with the new thinking about the democratic transition. The essence of the political purpose of the doctrine would be born, even without Bush as president.

While neoliberal internationalists could point to the *desirability* of democracy expanding worldwide thanks to democratic peace theory, neolib comparativists could argue that it was actually *feasible* to expect such a development could occur. If these two elements of thinking could be successfully combined, the obvious outcome would be a powerful alloy that could lend serious intellectual weight to an imperialist enterprise of the kind the Bush Doctrine eventually came to embody.

In the American academy, experts seldom work in lockstep with one another. That said, conferences, foundations, publications and the like tend to create intellectual trends, forms of thinking that act synchronically with one another even if each field remains to an important extent a preserve unto itself. Accordingly, the rise of interdisciplinarity in the American social sciences in the 1990s proceeded apace with efforts to break down regional boundaries on comparative political analysis.

The result was increased communication between separate fields of study. Given their interests both in the structure of the international system and in the character of domestic political regimes, liberal scholars were especially good at bridging regional and disciplinary divides. They could bring different regions of the world into focus together in terms of common problems or relating them all to global forces. Accordingly, neo-Wilsonian comparativists turned to the work of democratic peace theorists just as their liberal international relations counterparts looked with interest on what regional experts were saying.

Surely it was no accident that the American victory in the Cold War coincided with a melding of international relations theory and comparative political studies. The call went out, subliminally if not consciously, to comparative political analysts (although other fields might be involved) to explain how a push from outside in terms of global forces (the term "American imperialism" was avoided, to be sure) could conceivably transform politics inside countries and regions long distant from democratic ways. By the 1990s, a group of international liberal comparativists was ready to answer the challenge.

Well before the end of the Cold War, changes beginning in the mid-1970s in Southern Europe (Spain, Portugal, and Greece) heralded a new age, one which saw the emergence of vigorous democracy movements and governments as the successors to right-wing military governments. Changes within the Catholic world as well indicated progressive developments might be expected in the Philippines and Latin America. Thanks in good measure to Mikhail Gorbachev's "new thinking," by 1989, with the fall of the Berlin Wall and the Iron Curtain, and by 1991, with the implosion of the Soviet Union itself, it was evident that the Cold War had ended with the triumph of liberal democracy over communist government. To an increasing number it seemed as if democratic governments and open markets were inevitable developments the world around. Countries as different as Poland, Czechoslovakia, Hungary, Slovenia, South Korea, South Africa, and Chile were moving quickly to transform themselves into free market democracies. In China and Russia the winds of change were evident too, as they were also in Mexico and Turkey. Charismatic leaders might be found of the stature of Kim Dae Jung in South Korea or Nelson Mandela in South Africa to lead their people forward aided by an international community increasingly mobilized to help the transition. Most importantly, perhaps, Washington no longer needed to cooperate with the despotic rulers it had once worked with in order to contain communism. Freedom House certified 41 countries out of 150 in the world as democratic in 1974; by 2002 that number had reached 121 out of 193, a rise from 27 percent to 63 percent.[1]

In the case of Iraq, for example, George Packer reported that the distinguished Iraqi-American democracy activist Kanan Mikaya had modeled his thinking about a future democratic regime in Baghdad by reflecting on the words of Václav Havel and Charter 77 in Czechoslovakia. Makiya described himself as being deeply influenced by the European Enlightenment and a universalist about human rights, not a relativist. Packer sums his attitude up as making him "an Arab dissident in the manner of Havel and Solzhenitsyn." Paul Berman paints much the same picture of Makiya.[2]

In such circumstances, the old concerns of comparative political analysis about the necessary prerequisites or sequences for democratization seemed negative attitudes, holdovers from an earlier era in the brave new day of seemingly limitless possibilities. Now a new paradigm could find support in the American Academy, one where new trends could be professionally rewarded. The mood was all the more elevated because traditionally the study of the political order of the peoples of Latin America, Eastern Europe, Africa, the Far East, and the Middle East had been variations on themes of authoritarian and totalitarian government. Liberal comparativists could now feel that their studies of the process of the democratic transition might lead to a better future for the peoples they studied. If the American government could be persuaded to participate in the endeavor, so much the better.

Rethinking the Democratic Transition

New thinking among what we can label neoliberal comparative political experts could bring fresh insight to intellectual categories of thinking at home. For the conversion of liberal restraint into optimism—and hence to contribute to the growing ability of this internationalist ideology to evolve from hegemonism to imperialism—liberal intellectuals in the 1990s had to find ways to make the democratization process easier to envision. A first step was to overthrow the idea of sequences in the development process; for instance, the idea that an authoritarian or a constitutionally limited, non-democratic state might be the necessary prelude to a democratic opening, or that a phase of rapid economic development might pave the way for democracy. Another conceptual innovation was to dispute the notion that any single factor, such as a level of economic development or ethic of social tolerance, was necessary as a precondition to liberalization. Because concern with sequences and preconditions had been staple elements of comparative discourse prior to the 1990s, dispensing with these categories of analysis as old-fashioned negativism could be seen as a major intellectual achievement.

Some agent of change still had to be identified, of course. The most critical element in the new thinking of liberal comparative politics in the 1990s was that it selected as the defining variable in the success of the democratic transition the character of political leadership. The ideas leaders brought to their reforming mission, the conflict management styles they adopted "to get to yes," their character as fathers of their people, founders of a new order—all these aspects of change seemed to acquire at this historical juncture an importance they had hitherto not possessed to the extent they might matter now.

Leadership studies: What could be more American? Where there's a will there's a way, the self-made man, the legends of American entrepreneurship (strong in the 1990s with the dot-com revolution and the record profits of American business)—these creedal elements of the story of America underlay the changes in intellectual circles. Even more important, one could point to the success of leaders like Kim Dae Jung, Nelson Mandela, Václav Havel, Pope John Paul II, and Lech Walesa, or to individuals of lesser world fame who had nonetheless skillfully managed (or were managing) what academics had thought unlikely—the quick and peaceful transition to democracy in Greece, Spain, Portugal, Chile, Hungary, Slovenia, South Korea, and elsewhere. Had the United States not been founded at a similar propitious moment, when the liberal ideas of the Enlightenment had allowed our Founding Fathers the vision not simply to rid the thirteen colonies of British rule but then to create representative democratic institutions for the American people thereafter?

Hence the appearance of a wave of books on democratic transitions that centered on the character of strong leadership with the right ideas. In some cases, curriculum innovations included entire new programs on such matters as leadership, decision making, styles of negotiation, and conflict resolution. In established fields, examples of the ways in which successful political entrepreneurs had worked were subject to the kind of analysis that could make the lesson of their efforts available to others. George Soros might be available for funding if all else failed (which given the governments promoting these efforts was unlikely to be the case). In all these instances, the bottom line was the growing conviction that committed leadership with the right ideas and proper backing, which could be international as well as local, might bring about democracy where previously such an enterprise might have seemed an impossible dream.

Consider as an example of an alteration in perception the work of what most American academics would agree to be the most distinguished social scientist working in the area of political change, Samuel Huntington. In 1968, Huntington had published an enormously influential book, *Political Order in Changing Societies*, one of whose major messages was that the "order" necessary in the political realm of countries emerging into modernity might have to be military so as to forestall the advent of communism. But in 1991, Huntington published another widely read book, *Third Wave: Democratization in the Late Twentieth Century*, in which the critical role of a democratizing elite now emerged as the single most important variable in an attempted transition to democracy. To be sure, Huntington argued here that there were deep-set cultural reasons to think that the Muslim world and China would stay immune to the appeal of the democratizing "third wave." Huntington never was a liberal imperialist, and in fact went out of his way to denounce any such ambitions. Nonetheless, his ability to concentrate most of his book on demonstrating how a democratizing leadership might successful reconfigure the political life of its country represented a sea change in his thinking that was indicative of an era.[3]

Others had already pushed much further than Huntington. In 1990, Giuseppe Di Palma had published a well-received book *To Craft Democracies: An Essay on Democratic Transitions* whose opening paragraph spoke for the hopes of this decade of liberal internationalist scholarship in the field of comparative politics:

> Far be it from me to advocate a new social science orthodoxy. Yet there is a rekindled public and scholarly interest in the prospects for democracy where democracy does not now exist. That attention and the renewed theoretical optimism among a number of scholars deserve a fair hearing. [I am writing] in defense of that optimism.

Chapter titles for Di Palma's work tellingly include "How Democracy Can Grow in Many Soils"; "Why Transferring Loyalties to Democracy May be Less Difficult than We Think"; "On How to Sell One's Craft"; and more ominously, "Democracy by Diffusion, Democracy by Trespassing."[4]

Reviewing the book in 1991, Princeton University professor Nancy Bermeo saluted Di Palma for being in the vanguard of a growing "consensus on the importance of leadership.… Dozens of scholars in the United States are publishing or preparing manuscripts which argue that elite choices were critical to the transformation or consolidation of particular regimes. Arguments that underline the importance of choice are intrinsically hopeful and they seem to be multiplying." Bermeo then went on to cite favorably upbeat one-liners from Di Palma concerning his suggestions as to "how to beat the odds against democracy" and "make the improbable possible." "Crafting can be decisive anywhere," she stated, and so she agreed with Di Palma that democracy imagined as "marketing" or a "game" opened welcome fresh ways of thinking outside the box, of going beyond the naysayers of an earlier generation with their list of "absolute obstacles" to liberalization. Now Bermeo, like Di Palma, would embrace the new spirit of the post-Cold War era and argue in favor of "possibilism."[5]

A related intellectual trend in the 1990s focused on the "social construction of reality," and could be found in a wide variety of academic fields from feminism to multiculturalism. In due course, this form of thinking appeared in domestic and international political analysis as well. "International politics are socially constructed," declared Alexander Wendt in perhaps the best-received of the "constructivist" texts of the times. "The structures of human association are determined primarily by shared ideas rather than material forces," Wendt argued, "identities and interests of purposive actors are constructed by these shared ideas rather than given by nature." While Wendt's focus on "the constitution of interest by ideas" dealt principally with world affairs, he made it clear that his approach could be used at the domestic level as well. And he understood, too, that his argument related him to the greater tradition of liberalism or "idealism."[6]

I would like to call the variety of arguments that "ideas matter," or that "social constructions" are malleable, a form of *voluntarism*, a notion increasingly powerful in the 1990s that political choice, dependent on individuals of exceptional leadership talents and possessed of a clear idea of what a democratizing mission was about, might be able to make history. Francis Fukuyama helpfully labels the way the transition to democracy was viewed before the late 1980s as being like "Marxism," indicating thereby that such a process would likely be slow and grow from the evolution of a society's social, economic, and cultural structure, whereas during the 1990s, a form of "Leninism" set in, indicating thereby the role that great ideas, great leaders, and political daring could play in making history.[7] Whether it was in courses on conflict resolution or negotiation management, on feminism or multiculturalism, a new emphasis was apparent in the academy on ideas, identity, and leadership, one pregnant so far as public policy on a wide range of issues was concerned with what Di Palma and Bermeo had so attractively labeled "possibilism."

The result, as these comparative theorists appreciated, was to make change, not continuity, more conceivable in a people's political life if the primary determinants could be the right set of ideas and the right set of leaders to introduce them. To be sure, leadership studies and institution building had long been recognized as important topics. The point is not that they were suddenly introduced in the 1990s, so much as that the study of other features of democratic transitions lost in relative standing. Because choice mattered, ideas mattered, so that constitution making became even more in vogue. Was a presidential system better than a parliamentary system?; a multiparty system better than a two-party?; a quick national election better than working incrementally with voting from the municipal to the provincial to the national level?; a strong federal system better than one that delegated only limited power to provincial authorities? In the political arena itself, how was the military best neutralized and the crimes of the old regime treated now that a new hierarchy of values was in place? Here were the questions to be asked so that choice could be effectively exercised. Political science asserted its mastery of the social sciences as political entrepreneurship was not simply analyzed but was connected to political philosophy so that the mission of democratization could be accomplished.

I do not mean to imply that leadership studies are unimportant to the study of history; they most certainly are. Nor do I mean to suggest that they only started so far as analyses of democratic transitions appeared during the 1990s. As influential books by Juan Linz and Alfred Stepan showed in the 1970s, and as the work cited by Huntington in 1968 demonstrated, leadership studies are integral to our efforts to understand political order, democratic or otherwise.[8] My point instead is to insist on the sharply growing *relative* importance of these analyses in the 1990s and on the progressive ends their authors meant to put them, as opposed to an earlier epoch when other aspects of political life drew more or greater attention, and when the role played by leadership was seen as harboring *problems* and not being so highly charged with "possibilism."

The intellectual reformulation of the democratization process served an obviously important practical agenda. What had previously seemed a difficult task to envision now became radically simplified. Whereas previously culture, history, and socioeconomic patterns weighed heavily on developments, now choice, volition, ideology, and leadership emerged as critical. How had thinking evolved that led to voluntarist conclusions such as Di Palma proposed in 1991, and how were these arguments turned toward a consensus as the decade proceeded?

If we return to the "fossil evidence" of writing in comparative politics in the 1980s, an indication of the metamorphosis from hegemonic pessimism to imperialist optimism may be found in the important four-volume series (also published in a single combined tome) edited by Guillermo O'Donnell, Philippe Schmitter, and Laurence Whitehead in 1986 under the general title *Transitions from Authoritarian Rule: Prospects for Democracy.* In the concluding volume, the editors announced their preference that such transitions be to democracy, yet confessed that "objective" factors such as earlier thinkers had invoked—level of economic development, character of ethnic divisions, cultural and historical political legacies—might block this outcome. Nevertheless, focusing on "political strategies" and introducing "indeterminacy" and "uncertainty" into the process of political change, they concluded that perhaps there was ground for cautious optimism that democracy could catch on worldwide. By balancing political groups, players, and general ideas and schemes of "political strategizing" against objective obstacles, democracy might indeed be a conceivable outcome.[9]

In this influential series, then, we perhaps can see the origins of the argument that men and ideology can be prime movers of political order at certain historical junctures, a speculative argument to be sure, one just breaking loose from an earlier conceptual paradigm of political change. Tentative though it still may have been in 1986, voluntarism or Leninism was coming to the fore.

The Case of Larry Diamond

An even better example of the change in thinking, because it can be plotted across a longer period, may be found in the work of Larry Diamond. In a series of respected edited books concerned with transitions to democracy dating back to the late 1980s, Diamond emerged as a leading analyst and advocate of emerging democratic governments worldwide. In his earlier work, Diamond and his co-authors applied the standard social science framework that stressed the weight of a variety of factors—including considerations of leadership and of institution building, to be sure—making the democratization process a difficult one because of the complicated set of influences that went into the undertaking. Nevertheless, the hope was there that at some point democratic government would spread into parts of the world then without it.

In the late 1980s, Diamond, Juan Linz, and Seymour Martin Lipset had edited a well-received four-volume set of books on democracy in developing countries. In the fourth book in the series published in 1989, the authors declared, "we wish to state quite clearly here our bias for democracy as a system of government." They then went on to consider possible alternative non-democratic regime types that might have normative support apart from democracy, yet while they conceded that some were perhaps better than others, all had serious flaws and none could hope to measure up to the promise of democratic life.[10]

In 1990, Diamond, Linz, and Lipset published a book based on their earlier series that tried to go above regional to international patterns of democratization. In a second edition of this book in 1995, the three editors reflected in a more partisan manner than before on "the global advance of democracy" which they attributed in part to "the demise of its historic ideological rivals. Fascism was destroyed as a vital force in World War II. The appeals of Marxism-Leninism withered with the harsh repressiveness, glaring economic failures, and loss of revolutionary idealism of existing Communist regimes…. Democracy became—partly by choice and political learning and partly by default—the only model of government in the world with any broad ideological legitimacy and appeal."[11]

Nevertheless, they continued, "By the early 1990s, this ideological hegemony was increasingly under challenge from two forceful and self confident alternatives." One was "fundamentalist advocates of the Islamic state," the other a form of "illiberal democracy" touted in the Far East by Lee Kuan Yew, former prime minister of Singapore, and Mahathir bin Mohamad, prime minister of Malaysia. In short, democratizers needed to engage in an ideological contest, for if the door was in many places open to progress, alternative modes of organization remained in competition.[12]

The work of Diamond and his associates therefore deserves to be considered as a self-conscious ideological offensive to spread the values and institutions of democratic government as far as possible. True, these writers did not call for the use of military force. But in their claims for universal ideological primacy for liberal democratic government and social relations, an assertion not simply of values but also of institutional organization was being advanced that could lend itself to ideological imperialism on a grand and global scale.

By 2003, with the Iraq War just started, once again it was Diamond who announced his allegiance to what he knew to be a different perspective, "one profoundly in defiance of established social science theories." In an essay entitled "Can the Whole World Become Democratic?" (his answer was that it could), Diamond asserted, "Even in countries lacking virtually all of the supposed 'conditions for democracy'," empirical evidence shows clearly that democracy was on the march for the important reason that "the understanding and valuing of democracy is widely shared across cultures."

> Two-thirds of Africans surveyed associate democracy with civil liberties, popular sovereignty, or electoral choice. About two-thirds of Africans surveyed (69 percent) also say democracy is "always preferable" to authoritarian rule. The same proportion rejects one-party rule and four in five reject military or one-man rule. Even many who are not satisfied with democracy believe it is the best form of government…. Latin Americans…are more ambivalent. But overall 57 percent still believe democracy is always preferable and only about 15 percent might prefer an authoritarian regime. In East Asia, only a quarter in Taiwan and Korea, about a fifth in Hong Kong and the Philippines, but less than a tenth in Thailand believe that democracy is not really suitable for their country. In all five of these systems, consistently strong majorities (usually upwards of two-thirds) reject authoritarian alternatives to democracy. So do strong majorities in the ten post-communist countries now negotiating membership in the European Union.[13]

In the course of his survey, Diamond noted Arab exceptionalism: "Only in the Middle East is democracy virtually absent. In fact, among the sixteen Arab countries, there is not a single democracy, and with the exception of Lebanon, there never has been." Nevertheless, Diamond reassured his readers, "Arab thinkers, scholars, and civil society activists are themselves challenging the democracy and freedom deficit that pervades the Arab world." Contributing to his confidence that this region of the world too might be ready for liberalization were polling surveys that showed that embracing Islam as a religion did not predispose Muslims to be less supportive of democratic government than anyone else.[14]

My own reading of the evidence of this polling is distinctly less sanguine than Diamond's. For instance, the African surveys on which he depends to make his case show that only 9 percent of Africans understand that elections are a core component of democracy, and their interest in securing such arrangements appears to depend almost solely on the belief that their economic condition will improve should such a regime be installed. To suggest that there is a long road indeed between the attitudes indicated by Diamond's data and the actual construction of consolidated democracies is to be kind about my phrasing. For who does not want more honest and effective government? Yet as we have seen, when the process of democratization begins to unroll, with the empowerment of civil society and new rules regarding the state, what at one time seemed so attractive may easily enough become a nightmare.[15]

The point, in any case, is not to suggest that Diamond's argument is misleading (although I think it quite obviously is) but rather to indicate the optimism he expressed that the winds of history were blowing in the progressive direction he favored. Again, a comparison of past scholarship working with survey data is illuminating for the intellectual sea change it indicates. When in a classic study from the 1960s, Gabriel Almond and Sidney Verba had analyzed public beliefs and attitudes to see how they prepared a people for democracy, their approach had been largely cultural. People trusted government officials or tolerated social diversity to varying degrees because of more deeply set patterns of creed and authority. The mood of their study, then, was to anchor beliefs in deeper cultural substructures and to imply continuity over change. To a generation of earlier scholars like Almond and Verba, the idea presented by Diamond that one could substitute "barometers of public opinion" for such culturally rich and sensitive analysis would have seemed intellectually irresponsible. But to the generation of the 1990s, one that had a democratizing mission to accomplish and felt the winds of history at their back, such objections to optimistically evaluating the likelihood of rapid change by earlier thought were simply swept away.[16]

Accordingly, in January 2006, Diamond could be found opening an essay entitled "Iraq and Democracy: The Lessons Learned," not with cautions against ever repeating such a venture, much less with self-criticism for his embrace of democracy as a "universal value" and democratic peace theory as the desired framework for American foreign policy, but instead with the bold statement, "Iraq is not yet lost." What followed was a list of suggestions from "dealing with the insurgents" to "pick the right [electoral] system" that testify to the steadfastness of his commitment to democracy's universal appeal.[17]

Voluntarism From Outside

Could local leaders working with the ideas of liberal democracy be enough to overcome deep-set historical resistance to progressive change? To make their case more persuasive, the neo-Wilsonian comparativists had an intellectual and practical ace up their sleeve: support from international forces would lend their backing to local democratization efforts. Globalization was not only economic but cultural and ideological. Hence groups like the Open Society Institute, Human Rights Watch, Transparency International, Amnesty International, Freedom House, and many others could make a difference, indeed in some instances, all the difference.

Accordingly, democracy could now be seen as a process borne by international, and not strictly domestic, political forces. The number of books and articles on this matter defy counting. A few titles convey their flavor: John Boli and George M. Thomas's edited volume, *Constructing World Culture: International Nongovernmental Organizations since 1875;* the second edition of Jack Donnelly's *Universal Human Rights in Theory and Practice;* and Elizabeth Borgwardt's *A New Deal for the World: America's Vision for Human Rights.*[18]

For a taste of the arguments, consider another book published by social scientists to general acclaim in 1999, Thomas Risse, Stephen C. Ropp, and Kathryn Sikkink's *The Power of Human Rights: International Norms and Domestic Change.* True to the optimism of its times (and to the painful jargon of the social sciences), our authors elaborated a "five phase" "spiral model" working on "four levels" passing through "world time" in order to demonstrate how human rights non-governmental organizations, international organizations, and Western powers could act on the state and society of non-democratic peoples so as to motivate them toward progressive change.[19]

As Larry Diamond had put it in the abstract to his 2003 article already cited on the eve of the Iraq War maintaining that "the whole world" could in fact become democratic, such a development would presumably require "robust international engagement and support." The meaning Diamond attributed to "robust" may not have involved military action or "coercive democratization" to succeed, to be sure, but then who is to know? Diamond himself later donned of a bulletproof vest in Baghdad as he labored to bring forth democracy there in early 2004. Perhaps a "demonstration" effect of the success enjoyed by the democratic world might have a "snowball" effect on others, particularly if accompanied by a lot of good advice and just a bit of arm twisting of the kind that Human Rights Watch was always prescribing. Yet if armed intervention was not called for, neither were there any proscriptions in most of this literature against its use.

One of the more innovative ways of making democracy a seemingly "universal value" was to locate in cultures that had never had such governments beliefs that could be made to endorse it. In fact, such a presumption—that Enlightenment ways are universal—goes back at least three centuries in Western liberal thinking. The tradition continues today. So in the 1990s, Hindu and Confucian traditions were closely examined for teachings on the importance of governmental responsiveness to the governed, values like freedom and equality, as well as on the state's need for honesty, transparency, and accountability. Africa was found to have traditions of village self-government. Once these values and practices were discovered, a people's openness to democratic government could be inferred. Was it not then apparent that democracy was a universal value with universal appeal?

The assertion that ideas matter was heard on every side. Based on reasoning privileging the role of ideas in their own right to make history, for example, Noah Feldman, who was active with the American occupation of Iraq as a law professor to help write a democratic constitution for the country, was able to argue with authority that the country could be democratized by virtue of what he called "mobile ideas."

> Democracy and Islam are both what might be called mobile ideas—the kind that spread across the world, appealing to many people living in far-flung, strikingly different countries and societies. Because mobile ideas claim to work always and everywhere, they can clash. But mobile ideas also tend to be very flexible, and therefore capable of coming together in intriguing ways to produce unanticipated new configurations. Islamic democracy is not a contradiction.... Islam and democracy are starting to find means of mutual accommodation.[20]

As a poster boy for mobile ideas, Feldman published a large number of promotional editorials: "Democracy, Closer Every Day," "A New Democracy, Enshrined in Faith," "Political Islam: Global Warming," "Muslim Democrats? Why Not!" and "Operation Iraqi Democracy."[21]

A Democratic International

"No bourgeoisie, no democracy," the historical sociologist Barrington Moore once famously observed. With the rise of international non-governmental organizations (INGOs), the remedy for deficiencies in middle classes in a wide variety of countries might be the support of middle-class democracy activists coming from the United States and Europe.

Political science professor Michael Barnett has confirmed what the well-known journalist David Rieff had earlier pointed out: during the 1990s, international democracy advocacy individuals and groups multiplied many times over in number and in political reach.[22] In sociological as well as political terms, INGOs had come to represent well before 9/11 an international force seriously to be reckoned with. Barnett points out that for an increasing number of these agencies, the 1990s had witnessed an enormous increase in financing that in many cases corresponded to their steady accommodation to state power. If in some instances the development may have aided the INGOs' independent objectives, in others their autonomy was compromised by serving the objectives of American power. In this spirit, Secretary of State Colin Powell in late 2001 called the INGOs "a force multiplier for our combat teams." Barnett concludes:

> States and international institutions can compel humanitarian agencies to act in ways counter to their interests and principles…the 1990s were unprecedented to the extent that states attempted to impose their agendas on agencies. Toward that end, states began introducing mechanisms that were intended to control their 'implementing partners.'… The most important control mechanism came from the power of the purse. Sometimes donors made transparent threats.[23]

Consider as an example the complaints reported by the American Council for Voluntary International Action at a meeting with Agency for International Development (AID) Administrator Andrew Natsios at a 2003 InterAction Forum of NGOs. Taking the podium, Natsios complained that the NGOs needed to recognize more clearly that when they receive taxpayer money they become "an arm of the U.S. government." "NGOs must show results; promote ties to U.S. or we will find new partners," Natsios warned.[24]

A "force multiplier"? "An arm of the U.S. government"? Small wonder, that human rights and democracy promotion agencies increasingly became seen as collaborators in consolidating American power abroad. In fact, many of them were. In an earlier era, the CIA had covertly bought support for American ambitions abroad and among intellectuals at home. Since the founding of the National Endowment for Democracy (NED) in 1983, the same activities have been carried forth, but now are on the record.

To the extent that their services are provided with funding from the NED and the AID, suspicions of their motives may be well founded. The NED describes itself as being "guided by the belief that freedom is a universal human aspiration that can be realized through the development of democratic institutions, procedures, and values," and that it is a "private, nonprofit, organization…governed by an independent, nonpartisan board of directors" with an operating budget in 2005 of some $48.5 million.[25]

In fact, government money is spent in accordance with State Department priorities. The idea that the NED is private, independent, or nonpartisan is not persuasive. For its part, AID is housed within the State Department, with an annual budget of over $4 billion, at least $500 million of which is dedicated to human rights and democracy promotion.

One mission of the NED and AID is to work directly with human rights and democracy activists in a wide range of countries around the world in an effort to further both the well-being of foreign peoples and what we have seen neoconservatives call America's "benevolent hegemony," or as the neo-Wilsonians would call it "the zone of democratic peace," or the "pacific union." In addition to aiding the general democratization process, we might expect that both organizations pay special attention to the goals of American foreign policy, restraining their efforts in authoritarian countries (as in Central Asia for example) friendly to the United States, augmenting their efforts where, by contrast, (as in Venezuela or Iran) governments hostile to Washington, even if democratically constituted, hold sway.

The president of the NED for more than twenty years now has been the neoconservative Carl Gershman. Perhaps in his younger days as a member of a Trotskyite organization Gershman had learned united front tactics and how to structure an international movement, skills that he apparently has put into use since in the NED. For example, in 1999, the NED launched a World Movement for Democracy, a "network of networks" to act as an umbrella organization to gather together the wide range of movements working for democracy internationally. As stated in 1999, its "goal of building a worldwide movement for democracy presupposes the universality of the democratic idea. We believe that human beings aspire to freedom by their very nature, and that no single culture has a monopoly on democracy values."[26] That such thinking was consonant with professional social science findings as neoliberals developed their theories on such matters should be apparent.

AID was busy organizing internationally as well. The International Federation of Election Systems (IFES) receives funding from AID and works, according to its homepage, in over twenty new and developing democracies in 2005. Its publication *Democracy At Large* is among the ways it acts to keep its disparate membership unified.[27]

At an elite level, sponsoring the interaction of states was the Community of Democracies. This initiative began in 1999 under the auspices of Secretary of State Madeleine Albright, holding its first international meeting in 2000 in Warsaw. On its Board of Directors of the Council for a Community of Democracies in 2005 were neoconservatives like Mark Palmer and Penn Kemble (d. 2005) as well as neoliberals like Larry Diamond and G. John Ikenberry. Among the initiatives it pursued in 2005 were gaining for itself a permanent "Secretariat," organizing a "Democracy Caucus" in the United Nations, bringing regional and international parliamentarians together, and fostering a revitalization of trans-Atlantic joint efforts to promote democracy.[28]

All this activity is more than a bit reminiscent of CIA efforts in the 1950s to create a counter to the communist international through covert funding for the Congress of Cultural Freedom and many other individuals and organizations. The difference this time is that it is overt: the individuals involved have their names on mastheads and the funding is reported. Front organizations, as they used to be called, now honestly advertise themselves, and propaganda to serve American security interests no longer disguises itself. The war of ideas, which requires a war of arms as well to get its message across, is run quite in the open.

The association of human rights and democracy promotion with other American interests has given rise to the understandable complaint that the former is little more than an ideological weapon to be used to forward a much more general U.S. agenda promoting its own power worldwide. So Thomas Carothers (who is at the Brookings Institution and himself appears on the editorial board of an IFES publication) talks of a "backlash against democracy promotion" on the part of states as different as Russia, China, and Zimbabwe. Carothers estimates U.S. official spending on such projects at over $1 billion annually (others put it at more than twice this amount), and points out that the president's "freedom agenda" to many seems "menacing and hostile. This is especially so since when Bush and his top advisers single out 'outposts of tyranny,' the governments they invariably list are those that also happen to be unfriendly to the United States. Meanwhile friendly but equally repressive regimes...escape mention."[29]

Let me be clear that many organizations promoting human rights and democratic government globally operate independently of U.S. government goals. Whether it be the Open Society Institute, Amnesty International, or Human Rights Watch, Doctors Without Borders, the International Commission of the Red Cross, Terror Free Tomorrow, or Oxfam, to name but a few, independent non-governmental organizations exist acting effectively to pursue a straightforward agenda of serving people in need and addressing a range of reforms that need to be introduced to make states more effectively serve the needs of their citizens. They are not committed to U.S. supremacy in world affairs as a means, much less as an end, to the accomplishment of their missions.

Still, the Democratic International is everywhere creating united front organizations that allow it to conduct the war of ideas with special efficiency. Its mission is not simply ideas but also the use of American military force to oblige compliance. Consider the selection of the former CIA director and neoconservative James Woolsey as head of Freedom House in January 2003, followed by its board of trustees' affirmation of support for the invasion of Iraq two months later: "Democracy is not a Western concept, it is a universally desired goal...for [the war] to have a lasting positive impact on the stability and peace of the region, the U.S. and other democracies must make a firm commitment to the establishment of democracy in that country."[30]

Given this tale of manipulation, is there any wonder that when the words "democracy promotion" are associated with the United States it so often sounds like a nefarious plot to serve the interests of American power? It sounds that way, because in fact that is all too often exactly their character.

From Liberal Democratic Transition Theory To Imperialist Practice

What we can now see is the emergence of a liberal imperialist agenda collaborated in wittingly or not by various arms of the liberal American academy. Thanks to neo-Wilsonian international relations theorists assuring us that the spread of democracy worldwide would be a boon for world peace, and the neoliberal comparative political analysts assuring us that democracy had a "universal appeal," we have the essential intellectual building blocks of the Bush Doctrine. And while the ideas certainly could be appropriated by the neoconservatives, once again the intellectual heavy lifting had been done for the most part by Democrats, nonpartisans, or those generally to left. For these neoliberals to arrive at the conclusions specified by democratic peace theory and democratic transition theory required hard work. But once achieved, the ideas could be readily transmitted far and wide.

Consider, once again, the example of Natan Sharansky, the right-wing Israeli politician credited by President Bush with being a major inspiration on his own thinking about democratizing the Middle East. So far as I am aware, Sharansky had done no academic work whatsoever in analyzing the global prospects for freedom. Yet he eloquently synthesized the neoliberal findings. In keeping with his times, Sharansky could conclude, in line with democratic peace theory, "While the mechanics of democracy make democracies inherently peaceful, the mechanics of tyranny make non-democracies inherently belligerent. Indeed, in order to avoid collapsing from within, fear societies must maintain a perpetual state of conflict." Sharansky also subscribed to the notion of neoliberal comparative theory promoting the idea of the universal appeal of democracy. Democracy was therefore a relatively easy form of government to sponsor, and once it occurred peace would be the result. Finally, Sharansky understood that armed force of the sort the Bush Doctrine envisaged might have to be deployed by the United Sates for the golden age to dawn.

> I believe that all people are capable of building a free society. I believe that all free societies will guarantee security and peace. And I believe that by linking international policy to building free societies, the free world can once again secure a better future for hundreds of millions of people around the world.... I am convinced that all people desire to be free. I am convinced that freedom anywhere will make the world safe everywhere. And I am convinced that democratic nations led by the United States have a critical role to play in expanding freedom around the globe...the free world can transform any society on earth, including those that dominate the current landscape of the Middle East. In doing so, tyranny can become, like slavery, an evil without a future.[31]

"Those who seek to move the earth must first, as Archimedes explained, have a place to stand," Sharanksy went on to write. "Moral clarity provides us with a place to stand, a reference point from where to leverage our talents, ideas, and energies to create a better world." How could neoliberals disagree? Sharansky's ideas were theirs after all.

Others who contributed to the Bush Doctrine could also learn from their neo-Wilsonian colleagues. Let us return to the Lawrence Kaplan and William Kristol volume, which as I indicated in the opening chapters is the most reliable guide we yet have to the thinking of those who were ideologically inclined in the Bush administration in early 2003. Here too we also find democratic peace theory and democratic transition theory, as they originated with the neoliberals, ably articulated, even though Kristol and Kaplan had done nothing to elaborate these concepts. Yet they certainly understood how to apply them. So far as democratic transition theory is concerned, our authors waxed enthusiastic about Iraq becoming, in Paul Wolfowitz's words, "the first Arab democracy," and they concluded their chapter on "regime change" with a confident assertion:

> After we have already seen dictatorships toppled by democratic forces in such seemingly unlikely places as the Philippines, Indonesia, Chile, Nicaragua, Paraguay, Taiwan and South Korea, how utopian is it to imagine a change of regime in a place like Iraq? For that matter, how utopian is it to work for the

fall of the Communist Party in China after a far more powerful and stable oligarchy fell in the Soviet Union? With democratic change sweeping the world at an unprecedented rate over the past decades, is it truly 'realistic' to insist that we quit now?[32]

Do we have here an important, if only partial, explanation for what virtually everyone agrees to have been the disastrous bungling of Iraq after the fall of Baghdad in April 2003? Was it neoconservative arrogance, reinforced by naïve neoliberal academic reassurance, that in practice put too few troops on the ground, that failed to anticipate the plundering of the capital's major cultural institutions along with the sabotage of its sources of water and electricity? If we want to explain the blindness of American leadership—the rush to occupy a country about which they knew so little and whose reality was so foreign to their expectations—suppose we explain American expectations as based not so much on ignorance as on faulty intellectual conceptualizations of what to expect once Baghdad fell.

Seen in this light, Operation Iraqi Freedom was based not so much on overoptimism as on *educated misperception*. Its origins? Not just from the neoconservatives, however culpable they might be in their own way, but also from the neoliberal establishment, which had done so much to make the democratization project seem so relatively easy to envision in Iraq.

Consider the case of Paul Wolfowitz, who many today would agree with George Packer was "the intellectual architect of the War."[33] Wolfowitz had long experience with security issues in the Middle East. Beginning in the mid-1960s, he had done research on the question of nuclear proliferation in the region, work that culminated in his doctoral dissertation at the University of Chicago in 1972. In 1977, he had joined the Carter State Department working on questions concerning national security issues in the Persian Gulf, especially the challenges of Western access to petroleum in the event of Soviet or local power grabs. In 1986, Wolfowitz had served as Ambassador to Indonesia, where he apparently met moderate Muslim clerics and came to feel that Islam and democracy were compatible value systems. Although he had not urged American troops on to Baghdad in the Gulf War in 1991, Wolfowitz felt that President George H. W. Bush had betrayed the Kurds and the Shi'a by urging them to revolt against Saddam Hussein, then leaving them to their own devices. And as the neoconservative movement increased its organizational punch after Clinton's reelection in 1996, Wolfowitz became the most prominent of those calling for military force for regime change in Iraq. Small wonder, then, if immediately after 9/11, Wolfowitz wanted to bypass Afghanistan and strike immediately at Baghdad.[34]

For our purposes, the most striking feature of Wolfowitz's thinking was the ease with which he saw democracy flowering in Iraq once Saddam was deposed. In an extended interview with Bill Keller published in September 2002, Wolfowitz criticized the State Department's skepticism that Iraq could be democratized: "You hear people mock [the idea] by saying that Iraq isn't ready for Jeffersonian democracy. Well, Japan isn't [a] Jeffersonian democracy either. I think the more we are committed to influencing the outcome, the more chance there could be that it would be something quite significant for Iraq. And I think if it's significant for Iraq, it's going to cast a very large shadow, starting with Syria and Iran, but across the whole Arab world, I think."[35]

Similarly, in the run-up to war in February 2002, Wolfowitz had publicly rebuked Army Chief of Staff General Eric Shinseki, who had said that several hundred thousand troops seemed called for to hold Iraq, calling this estimate "wildly off the mark." Mark Bowden described Wolfowitz's thinking, as he prepared to leave the Pentagon for his new position as head of the World Bank in 2005:

> [Wolfowitz] likes to tell the story of a conference in Washington where a critic of America's foreign policy stood up to denounce the arrogance of imposing "our" democratic values on the Arab world, only to have an Arab stand up to explain that true arrogance was to assume such values were "ours" when they are universal. Underlying [Wolfowitz's] faith about Iraq is the belief that mankind everywhere seeks freedom and self-government.... When a Polish interviewer suggested that his policy was about "exporting democracy," Wolfowitz objected. "'Export of democracy' isn't really a good phrase," he said. "We're trying to remove the shackles on democracy."[36]

The statement was much in line with an exchange Jeffrey Goldberg reported having with Wolfowitz. "I asked him what he would think if previously autocratic Arab countries held free elections and then proceeded to vote Islamists into power. Wolfowitz answered, 'Look fifty per cent of the Arab world are women. Most of these women do not want to live in a theocratic state. The other fifty per cent are men. I know a lot them. I don't think they want to live in a theocratic state...it's absurdly unrealistic, demonstrably unrealistic, to ignore how strong the desire for freedom is.'" When Goldberg reported these words to former National Security Advisor

Brent Scowcroft, the latter dismissed Wolfowitz saying, "he's got a utopia out there. We're going to transform the Middle East and then there won't be war anymore. He can make them democratic...where he is truly an idealist is that he brushes away questions, says 'it won't happen,' whereas I would say, 'it's likely to happen and therefore you can't take the chance.' Paul's idealism sweeps away doubts."[37]

George Packer also reported Wolfowitz's conviction "about the nature of the Baathist tyranny and the stifled talents of the Iraqi people that were just waiting to be set free." James Mann recounted still another anecdote. As early as 1976, when he discussed Henry Kissinger's book *A World Restored* with Francis Fukuyama, Wolfowitz offered a telling assessment: "'It was a good book, Kissinger's best...yet Kissinger had missed the point: The hero of this history was not Metternich, the realist. It was Tsar Alexander I of Russia, who had pushed for stronger action against Napoleon because Alexander I had stood for moral and religious principles.'" Or consider the words Wolfowitz said according to *The Weekly Standard* to a wounded serviceman in an Iraqi military hospital in October 2003, "How do you feel about building a new Middle East?"[38]

Wolfowitz was far from the only high official to speak in such idealistic terms. As Secretary of State Condoleezza Rice put it at Princeton on September 30, 2005:

> Now, to support democratic aspirations, we must be serious about the universal appeal of certain basic rights. When given a truly free choice, human beings will choose liberty over oppression, the right to own property over random search and seizure. Human beings will choose the natural right to life over the constant fear of death. And human beings will choose to be ruled by the consent of the governed, not by the coercion of the state; by the rule of law, not the whim of rulers. These principles should be the course of justice in every society and the basis for peace between all states.[39]

In a similar vein, British Prime Minister Tony Blair could declare before a joint session of Congress on July 18, 2003:

> Our ultimate weapon is not our guns but our beliefs. There is a myth that though we love freedom, others don't, that our attachment to freedom is a product of our culture. That freedom, democracy, human rights, the rule of law are American values or Western values. That Afghan women were content under the lash of the Taliban. That Saddam was beloved by his people. That Milosevic was Serbia's savior.

Ours are not Western values. They are universal values of the human spirit and anywhere, any time, ordinary people are given the chance to choose, the choice is the same. Freedom not tyranny. Democracy not dictatorship. The rule of law not the rule of the secret police.[40]

The prime minister could not outdo the president. At his West Point Commencement Address earlier, on June 2, 2002, Bush had been equally confident:

When it comes to the common rights and needs of men and women, there is no clash of civilizations. The requirements of freedom apply fully to Africa and Latin America and the entire Islamic world. The peoples of the Islamic nations want and deserve the same freedoms and opportunities as people in every nation. And their government should listen to their hopes…. Mothers and fathers and children across the Islamic world, and all the world, share the same fears and aspirations. In poverty they struggle, in tyranny, they suffer…in liberation they celebrate.

Mixing democratic peace theory, which proclaimed the desirability of democracy's worldwide spread, with democratic transition theory, which asserted that such a task should not be too difficult, was to produce the substance itself of the Bush Doctrine. On February 26, 2003, the president's vision at the American Enterprise Institute was a clear explication of the union of these two neoliberal beliefs.

The world has a clear interest in the spread of democratic values, because stable and free nations do not breed the ideologies of murder. They encourage the peaceful pursuit of a better life…. A new regime in Iraq would serve as a dramatic and inspiring example of freedom for other nations in the region. It is presumptuous and insulting to suggest that a whole region of the world—or the one-fifth of humanity that is Muslim—is somehow untouched by the most basic aspirations of life. Human cultures can be vastly different. Yet the human heart desires the same good things, everywhere on Earth. In our desire to be safe from brutal and bullying oppression, human beings are the same…. For these fundamental reasons, freedom and democracy will always and everywhere have greater appeal than the slogans of hatred and the tactics of terror. Success in Iraq could also begin a new stage for Middle Eastern peace.

In his Second Inaugural Address of January 2005, Bush was eloquent on the ease with which the appeal of the American way could be adopted across the planet.

America's vital interests and our deepest beliefs are now one. From the day of our Founding, we have proclaimed that every man and woman on this earth has rights, and dignity, and matchless value, because they bear the image of the Maker of heaven and earth. Across the generations we have proclaimed the imperative of self-government because no one is fit to be a master and no one deserves to be a slave. Advancing these ideals is the mission that created our nation. It is the honorable achievement of our fathers. Now it is the urgent requirement of our nation's security and the calling of our time.

Bush was noticeably less eloquent, but still on message, in a question-and-answer session at Johns Hopkins University on April 12, 2006, where he attested once again his faith in the relative ease of transitions to democracy from authoritarian rule. "I want you to understand this principle, and it's an important debate and it's worth debating here in this school, as to whether or not freedom is universal, whether or not it is a universal right of all men and women.... And I think it is universal. And if you believe it's universal, I believe this country has—should act on that concept of universality. And the reason I do is because I do believe freedom yields the peace...and if you don't believe it's universal, I can understand why you say, 'what's he doing, why is he doing that?' If there's no such thing as the universality of freedom, then we might as well just isolate ourselves and hope for the best."

The Achilles' Heel of Neo-Wilsonian Democratic Transition Theory

If the Achilles' heel of democratic peace theory reviewed in the preceding chapter is that it was too clever by half, the fatal flaw of democratic transition theory was that it was too simplistic by ten. To be sure, the new thinking that comparative political analysis put forth in the 1990s had its positive points. By breaking down the barriers between national, regional, and global forces, comparative politics was redefining itself in healthy ways. By highlighting the role that ideas and individuals can play at certain historical moments, comparativists were being sensitive to the realities of their times.

But the shortcomings of the new thinking far outweighed the gains. For the turn to voluntarism—the idea that where there's a will there's a way—was naïve on two principal scores, each of which made a critical contribution to the success of the Bush Doctrine in its appeal for popular support.

First, such thinking simplified the political logic of countries where the difficulties standing in the way of a democratic transition might be much greater than the new paradigm of comparative politics allowed. The result could be to underestimate by a long measure the kind of resistance that would be mounted to an invasion such as the United States launched in Iraq in March 2003 and the success of a democratization campaign thereafter.

Second, such thinking demobilized critical reactions to the Bush Doctrine, which embraced with a bear hug the notion that the United States was leading forces of liberation across the barricades of despotism the world around. Instead of deflating such extravagant ambitions, a good deal of educated opinion actually believed it.

Consider, for instance, a much ballyhooed Rand study headed by James Dobbins on the history of American democracy promotion through armed occupation from World War II until Iraq. The team of authors opened with Japan and Germany, then proceeded through a wide range of American occupations designed to promote democracy locally before 2003 (Somalia, Haiti, Bosnia, Kosovo, Afghanistan) in order to see what made for success. One might suppose such a broad ranging study conducted by a well-financed team would have something insightful to say. Yet the most striking thing about the study is that it gives virtually no role whatsoever to the character of the peoples occupied by the United States military in the making of their postwar national institutions. The lengthy study analyzes American behavior, but it disregards rather totally the character of the peoples whose countries are occupied.[41]

The inattention to local populations was no oversight; it was a deliberate methodological choice. So the Rand group explicitly dismissed "Western culture, economic development, national homogeneity" and other factors that would describe the population under American control as factors in determining the likely success of an American invasion. In other words, these "experts" dismissed internal, domestic features of the occupied countries altogether. Instead, they favored analyzing "the level of effort the United States and the international community put into their democratic transformations." When the team ran their sets of quantitative data, it looked for what to me appears to be a random set of variables centering on changes in local per capita income and levels of military and police control, both of which were assumed to depend more on decisions by the occupiers than initiatives of the local population. When the team came to its list of eight conclusions, *seven* had to do with the actions of the occupier. The single variable concerning the character of the populations subject to American military control that they considered was something I would feel to be quite minor, the "accountability for past injustices" of incumbents of the deposed regime.[42]

Is it not apparent that the intellectual assumptions of the Rand study were fatally flawed, a dangerous recipe indeed for policy makers? Were Dobbins and his team infected by the neoliberal virus in comparative studies that concluded that leaders, ideas, and outside support were all that matters for ancient civilizations to democratize? Or were they just ambitious, telling power what it wanted to hear? Where in an earlier era one might have compared various aspects of the populations under American tutelage to explain why some occupations succeeded and others failed, all this was cavalierly put aside.

Hence, there was no analysis of what an earlier generation would have been quite correct to look for: a local middle class, local experience with limited government; local sentiments of national unity and tolerance for social diversity; local democratic leaders. For the Rand team, what counted was the degree to which American willpower and resources were put to the task at hand. Accordingly, in summarizing what his team had learned from history that might apply to Iraq, Dobbins gave scant attention to internal forces, concluding instead that the primary variables for success were an abundant supply of foreign troops and other material resources, combined with the political will in Washington to commit them for the long term, not saddled with "artificial deadlines" and "premature dates" for withdrawal.

From the point of view of an earlier generation of comparativists, a study such as that produced by Rand would have been considered an intellectual scandal. Yet consider the position of the widely read Harvard professor Niall Ferguson, a historian refreshingly ready to use the words "empire" and "imperialism" to describe the American mission in Iraq. As by now we should not be surprised to learn, not the objective reality of the political dynamics of the Middle East, but rather American willpower, was his concern. Hence, the obstacle in the way to American success was not local politics—about which Ferguson had virtually nothing to say—but the lack of an American will to stay the course. So he opened one of his articles in April 2003 saying breezily: "Iraq has fallen. Saddam's statues are face down in the dust. His evil tyranny is at an end. So—can we, like go home now?" And he concludes his folksy ruminations:

> So long as the American empire dare not speak its own name—so long as it continues this tradition of organized hypocrisy—today's ambitious young men and women will take one look at the prospects for postwar Iraq and say with one voice, 'Don't even go there.' Americans need to go there. If the best and brightest insist on staying home, today's unspoken imperial project may end—unspeakably—tomorrow.[43]

Publishing a book on U.S. foreign policy in 2004, Ferguson announced that American objectives in the war, "to overthrow a vicious tyrant and to transform fundamentally the politics of the Middle East, were both laudable and attainable." The problem with Americans' efforts to attain "primacy by achieving and maintaining full-spectrum dominance" was not to be found in the character of Iraqi or Arab politics, however, but as he had insisted before lay instead "within," with "the absence of a will to power" in the American people.[44] In late 2006, Ferguson reiterated his argument, asserting that "the principal cause of [America's] ephemeral empire is not the alien-ation of the conquered peoples…but domestic constraints."[45] Unfortunately, such examples could be multiplied many times over, to the same effect: if democratization failed or succeeded it was enough to consider the willpower of the imperialist power, the United States of America. The local people were apparently to be understood as simply waiting in hopeful anticipation of their liberation.

No one has better pointed out the characteristic shortcomings of liberal hawks—their assumptions of American omnipotence and disinterested-ness, and their assurance that an unhappy world waited for its deliver-ance—than David Rieff. Rieff took as his primary target Samantha Power, whose Pulitzer prize and National Book Award for *A Problem From Hell*, a book on genocide, had gained her a high-profile reputation as a humani-tarian interventionist. Rieff warned his readers that despite her last-min-ute opposition to the Iraq invasion, the fact remained that her thinking pointed very clearly in the direction of an assault on Saddam's Iraq. Just before the invasion began, Power wrote that the 1990s was "a lost decade" for its failure to push a human rights agenda far more aggressively. Rieff was exactly on target when he described her position as "a breviary for this new military humanism," for it "offers an insight into the millenarian tenor of interventionist human rights activism…[her arguments necessar-ily] lead to endless wars of altruism—one, two, many Kosovos, to para-phrase Che Guevara." Given the number who have vied for the title, one might only disagree with Rieff when he asserted that Power "has made the case for legal imperialism more elegantly and fastidiously than any other advocate on the American scene today," yet surely he is right that she should be on the short list under consideration.[46]

As Rieff implies, the intellectual problem in Power's position is one typical of the liberal imperialist ideology more generally. She lacks a reasoned way to be selective in her call for humanitarian intervention and thus to recognize either that American power has its limits, or to comprehend that American power may have quite a different agenda than democracy promotion so one should be hesitant to support it in every instance. Instead, so far as liberal hawks are concerned, wherever dictatorship looms, there the battle lines are to be formed, behind whichever democratic state asserts that the cause of human rights is the battle standard it will raise.

The Carr Center for Human Rights Policy at the John F. Kennedy School of Government at Harvard University is a flourishing gathering point for those who see no obstacle to humanitarian intervention other than lack of vision and resolve. Samantha Power was the founding executive director of the center before becoming a professor at the Kennedy School. A prominent liberal hawk was her colleague, Michael Ignatieff, who, until early 2006, was director of the center. For Ignatieff, too, neither the limits on American power, nor the ambitions of American leaders, nor the aptitude of the people waiting for human rights activists to come to their rescue so as to enjoy the benefits of liberal democracy were for a moment reasons to decline what he called "the burden of empire" when he came out in support of the war early in 2003. As he had put it earlier, "The human rights movement's strength— and also what makes it so irritating to state leaders—has been its moral perfectionism, its refusal to allow trade-offs between principle and power, rights and expediency.... As a language of moral claims, human rights are an anti-politics, a moral code that refuses, a priori, any political justification for the denial of basic rights."[47]

But Ignatieff's purity of intention, which true to neoliberal form disregards both the intentions of the conqueror and the political reality of those to be conquered, may lead once again to a hell of consequences. By failing to recognize either that intervention could make a bad situation worse, or that it might serve ends quite opposed to those liberal internationalism traditionally seeks, liberal imperialists, of whom Ignatieff is an outstanding example, run the risk of betraying the cause they profess to serve. Ignatieff is quite right: the "anti-politics" of this "moral code," its "moral perfectionism" is indeed, to put it mildly, "irritating." A series of his own publications in the New York Times from early 2003 through June 2005, lays out the logic of his arguments in favor of a utopian human rights solution to world problems and his steadfast support for the Iraq War. All are based on impeccable neoliberal thinking, a reflection of how popular pieces may be purveyed by someone familiar with the academic literature.[48]

The Lessons of Japan and Germany

Americans, especially those possessed of the message of the Bush Doctrine, or "educated" by modern-day comparative political theory, too often imagine that everyone is waiting for something called *freedom* that in due course will lead those who cherish it to institute among themselves a democratic order. The president himself has repeatedly expressed himself in words to this effect as have any number of his supporters. The danger of embracing such a chimera is today quite apparent.

As one would think conservatives themselves would be the first to perceive, freedom can mean chaos. Freedom must be based on political order, an accomplishment difficult to achieve in a country lacking experience with limited government and without a social contract binding the various elements of society together in some kind of political consensus. The idea that elections alone can provide such a framework for democratic order is only the first of the illusions nearly four years of occupying Iraq has shattered.

That said, a transition to freedom is possible, including a type based on foreign occupation. The best example is that of Germany and Japan under American occupation after World War II. So President Bush could declare in February 2003:

> There was a time when many said that the cultures of Japan and Germany were incapable of sustaining democratic values. Well, they were wrong. Some say the same of Iraq today. They are mistaken. The nation of Iraq—with its proud heritage, abundant resources and skilled and educated people—is fully capable of moving toward democracy and living in freedom.

Six months later, then-National Security Advisor Condoleezza Rice could write in the *Washington Post*, "Much as a democratic Germany became a linchpin of a new Europe that is today whole, free and at peace, so a transformed Iraq can become a key element of a very different Middle East in which the ideologies of hate will not flourish."[49]

At the president and the secretary's invitation, let us consider a central proposition that fits Iraq into a narrative about an enormously successful American undertaking. But does Iraq bear comparison to this record of accomplishment?

The analogy does not hold. For all the invocations of Japan and Germany as precedents for the American occupation of Iraq and its hopes for reform in the "Broader Middle East" (which presumably includes Iran, and perhaps Turkey, as well as the Arab world), the unquestioned success the United States had in occupation policy after 1945 is quite unlikely to be repeated today. We may agree that the greatest achievement in the entire history of American liberal internationalism was the impact occupation policy had on Japan and Germany. By converting these two militaristic powers with autarkic economies into democracies integrated into the international economic and security system, Washington contributed wisely and well to its eventual triumph in the Cold War. But invoking this past in order to sanction the present conquest of Iraq is a specious undertaking indeed, whose spokespersons are playing fast and loose with their comparisons.

To be sure, Iraq under Saddam Hussein may legitimately be called a "fascist" country. It had a single party, totalitarian state with a populist, nationalist, militarist leader, a brutal despot supported by a cult of the personality. Not only is the resemblance to fascism striking, but apparently Saddam was informed as to how communist and fascist political systems functioned. Nevertheless, to acknowledge the similarity between Saddam's Iraq and fascism of the 1930s should not be to countenance the idea that what the United States accomplished after 1945 in Germany and Japan thanks to their democratization might be duplicated in the Middle East some sixty years later.[50]

First, unlike Iraq, Germany and Japan each had an integrated industrial economy that needed predictable, accountable governmental supervision to perform well and that counted on an educated middle class for its development to proceed. With its "rule of law," democracy was thus a form of government that corresponded to the economic stage of development and class relations that Japan and Germany had reached in 1945. The same cannot be said of Iraq, where the national wealth has long been based on oil, a notoriously anti-democratic resource as its revenues are easily captured by the state, which then uses its wealth to control the populations over which it rules. Such middle class as there is largely located in the state bureaucracy and depends rather completely on government revenues. Neither the structure of economic development nor of class relations predisposes Iraq to be a democracy in the way that Japan and Germany were predisposed.

Second, again unlike Iraq, domestic conflicts in Japan and Germany after World War II were more along class than ethnic or religious lines and never threatened to undermine a sense of national unity. Long before 1945, nationalism had become firmly entrenched in both countries and ways of resolving class conflict had emerged. Social divisions most certainly existed in both countries (and still do today), but they are greatly exceeded by the kind of splits we see in Iraq today between Sunnis, Kurds, and Shi'a—splits that are in different measure religious, linguistic, and territorial but that are most fatally lodged in fearful historical memories that the Kurds and the Shi'a have of Sunni domination. Whatever the internal divisions of postwar Germany and Japan, they pale into insignificance alongside the magnitude of the tensions within Iraq society.

Third, still again unlike Iraq, nationalists in Japan and Germany could see clearly enough that, in terms of international forces surrounding them, their choice was between accepting the terms of American occupying forces or facing alone the rising tide of world communism. The Soviets were encamped in East Germany and Mao Zedong came to power in Beijing in 1949. Understanding that the Americans were trying to enlist their aid in a global struggle, aware that their own economic strength could be increased by their participation in an American-sponsored international economic order while their essential national political institutions would be in their own hands, Japanese and Germans of different political backgrounds could agree to work with occupation forces for the sake of democratic order. Such a mood is most assuredly not present in Iraq today, where anxious or ambitious foreign forces jockey for position in a fluid political environment.

Fourth, in contradistinction once more to Iraq, in Germany especially, there was a tradition of parliamentary government that could make the democratization of the country seem a legitimate development. Parliamentary government had enjoyed a brief period of success in interwar Japan as well, but for the notion of power sharing perhaps it is better to refer back to the collaborative leadership style of the Meiji Restoration to see domestic origins there of modern democratic government. No such historical legacy is available in the Iraqi case. Worse, the legacy of totalitarianism is a fearful and angry civil order unlikely easily to be able to come up with a social contract that could endure.

Fifth, again quite unlike Iraq, in Germany especially there were leaders and popular movements that had opposed the rise of Hitler and waited out the war in hopes of an occupation that would bring the country democracy. Japan was less favored in this respect, but under the emperor the political elite cooperated with General Douglas MacArthur's plans for the country's democratization. There simply is no equivalent to the willingness to cooperate witnessed in Japan in 1945, much less to Konrad Adenauer and his Christian Democrats or to Kurt Schumacher and his Social Democrats in Germany in all the Middle East. The pretense of the Pentagon as the Iraq War began that Ahmad Chalabi was just such a figure—the leader of a "democratic opposition in exile," as the neoconservatives liked to put it—beggars the imagination.

The point of this briefly developed argument is that efforts to compare the democratization of Japan and Germany to what might be expected from a similar undertaking in the Middle East fly in the face of historical reality. Yet no comparison is more likely to be made by those who look forward to the eventual democratization of Iraq, and to the gains for American security as a result, than what was achieved after 1945 in Germany and Japan.

Partisans of the analogy are likely to denounce those who are skeptical of the validity of the comparison as being contemptuous of Arab culture or the Muslim religion, blind to the ways change may occur—racist and reactionary in a word. What is more contemptuous of Middle East reality, however, are those proponents of the war who fail to respect the character either of the "nationalist" (if we may call it that given that the Iraqi nation-state is not necessarily the first object of loyalty) resistance to an American invasion, or who fail to appreciate how the murderous subnational cleavages that exist in Iraq render stable democratic government based on popular mobilization difficult to envision.

What was also contemptuous of Middle East reality was the failure to recognize that absolute chaos could occur there in the wake of an American invasion for the obvious reason that the character of first authoritarian, then totalitarian, rule there had destroyed the social base for the kind of civic consensus that could provide anything approaching stable democratic government. An outside invasion therefore was quite likely to produce both a savage backlash and a civil implosion. The result, in short, was a human tragedy on a grand scale, not the dreamed-of birth of a modern democratic country, a force for progressive change throughout the region and friendly to American purposes on the broader world scene.

The false analogy between Iraq and the occupations of Japan and Germany should be replaced by some closer analogies having to do with the *failures* of American democratization efforts in the course of the twentieth century. Thus, not long after taking office in 1913, President Wilson authorized the occupations of the Dominican Republic and Nicaragua to save them from civil war and preserve an area important to American security by democratizing them. What the operations ultimately produced by the 1930s were stable and pro-American governments—the tyrannies of the Trujillo and Somoza families in each of these countries respectively—but certainly not democracy.

Again, in the 1960s President Kennedy hoped for a "White Revolution" to liberalize Iran and inaugurated the Alliance for Progress to bring democratic government to Latin America. In each case the idea was to promote American security by replacing authoritarian governments with democracies. And in each case, the effort failed quite completely.

Still later, in 1994, President Clinton occupied Haiti to restore the democratically elected Jean-Baptiste Aristide, "Haiti's Nelson Mandela," yet democratic stability was not to become the hallmark of that country either. Even the Philippines, which the United States occupied for nearly half a century with the support of its social elite, might today be considered only a semi-democracy.

Why do those who invoke the memory of Germany and Japan have amnesia when it comes to these other cases? In fact, the comparison with Iraq advocates of the Bush Doctrine most avoid as if taboo is Vietnam. Here, too, the United States attempted to "win the hearts and minds" (WHAM, as the bureaucrats labeled it) of the people through persuading them to embrace the liberal dream. By the time America took over the struggle in Southeast Asia from the French, however, local nationalism was firmly embedded in communist resistance to Western imperialism. The American effort to encourage democratic government in the region proved utterly quixotic. Yet who among the partisans of the Iraq War invoking American success in Germany and Japan thinks to reflect on the lessons to be learned from Vietnam? Their mood instead is to end the "defeatism" of the "Vietnam syndrome" by focusing instead on the immediate aftermath of World War II where indeed the success was spectacular.

The paradigm shift in comparative political analysis of the 1990s effectively obscured much more of historical reality than it revealed. It encouraged a voluntarism, an optimism, a Leninist-style conviction that great ideas and great men could move history. It underwrote a tendency to discount deep knowledge of specific countries and regions in favor of gross comparative generalizations. As a result, this branch of the neo-Wilsonian movement lost sight of the embedded nature of many of the obstacles to democratization and of the dangers that could arise in some circumstances should imprudent risks be run. Surely that is one of the lessons of the Rwandan tragedy of 1994, provoked in part by meddling outsiders who wished that country well but whose efforts contributed to its undoing. More importantly still for our purposes, when such optimism was taken up by the Bush Doctrine, the experts to act as a reality check were few and far between. The young guard of the academy, especially if it was to the left, was likely to share the enthusiasm for an imperialist crusade designed to help the wretched of the earth.

The result of such facile thinking was to spread human misery even further and to endanger American national security at the same time. The political vacuum in Iraq has acted as a recruiting station for terrorists from throughout the Muslim world and an as incitement to anti-Americanism as well. In the short to medium term, the winner in this deadly struggle looks to be Iran and what professor Vali Nasr calls "the Shi'a revival."[51] The combination of Tehran's growing power with its increasingly well-organized collaborators among the Hezbollah in Lebanon and the Shi'a dominated government in Baghdad suggests that in Iraq, at least, the United States and Israel are feeding the very forces that may eventually conspire against them. In the longer term, to be sure, a Sunni reaction to these developments, combined with state actors from Turkey and Pakistan to Saudi Arabia determined to counter this trend, may reverse the gains for Iran. But the greater outcome may be that political Islam sweeps all before it, making relatively irrelevant the distinction between sects. Whatever the outcome, the idea that democracy holds any promise for the future of the region or world order—much less that it has a "universal appeal"—is a chimera impossible to maintain. That the American government would have engaged in such wishful thinking is grounds for serious concern. That this thinking found its support in the academy with its overblown theories, concepts, and pretensions is a matter that so far as this book is concerned deserves of particular censure.

The Mansfield-Snyder Argument

Suppose, however, that the neoconservatives and neoliberals have their prayers answered and some form of democracy does come to the Middle East. What is its character likely to be? In all likelihood, not what they would want to see—something like a new Chile, a free Slovenia, a democratic South Korea, a proud Czech Republic freed finally from the grip of authoritarian rule, all friendly toward the United States.

In an important study published in 2005, professors Edward D. Mansfield and Jack Snyder offered powerful evidence that "emerging democracies" have a tendency to go to war with a frequency and intensity that makes them a cause for worry, not hope. If Mansfield and Snyder are correct, their findings deliver a body blow to the facile assumption of the Bush Doctrine that terrorism is more likely to come under control in the Middle East as a result of the conquest of Iraq followed by its democratization. Indeed, exactly the opposite appears likely as, in the name of an unfamiliar doctrine dictated by foreigners who in past experience have only shown themselves to be self-interested in the region, civil society is unleashed against unpopular and ineffective state institutions.[52]

Mansfield and Snyder explain the warlike propensities of immature, as opposed to consolidated, democratic orders by pointing out features of these political systems that an earlier generation of comparative theorists (but not those of the brave generation of the 1990s) would have recognized immediately as a toxic brew. In countries where authoritarian or demagogic privileged elites can mount a counterattack on the democratization process, or use it to bellicose ends (usually by mobilizing populist emotions often against foreign enemies), or where civil society is split into mutually hostile factions with little sense of overarching identity or interest, then civil or interstate war is a quite possible outcome of the mass mobilization that democratization engenders. Indeed, what the empirical evidence in their study allows our authors to conclude is that young democracies are an especially bellicose group of peoples and states.

To be sure, neither regional nor internal war need be the result of a democratic opening as the examples of Poland, the Czech Republic, Hungary, or Slovenia after 1989 all illustrate. Where there is a clear sense of national identity, established national borders, civic unity, a degree of economic development, and an elite dedicated to liberalization—that is the "preconditions" that an earlier generation of comparativists had established as important facilitators of democracy—the process of democratization may proceed rapidly and effectively. When it does so, it may well serve American interests.

But woe unto the people introduced to democracy before state institutions or a civil consensus is in place. Instead of joining the world of Kantian peace, they are much more likely slated to fall into an especially nasty Hobbesian world.

The Mansfield-Snyder study is both wide in its samples and deep historically. At one point, however, the authors draw their general conclusions together to warn against undue optimism in efforts to democratize the Muslim world. While it is conceivable that some transitions will succeed (Turkey, Lebanon, Morocco, or Jordan, for example), the likelihood is that in many countries violence will increase both domestically and internationally where such ambitions are realized.

> Although democratization in the Islamic world might contribute to peace in the very long run, Islamic public opinion in the short run is, in most places, hostile to the United States, reluctant to condemn terrorism, and supportive of forceful measures to achieve favorable results in Palestine, Kashmir, and other disputed areas...unleashing Islamic mass opinion through a sudden democratization could only raise the likelihood of war. All of the risk

factors are there: the media and civil society groups are inflammatory, as old elites and rising oppositions try to claim the mantle of Islamic or nationalist militancy. The rule of law is weak and existing corrupt bureaucracies cannot serve a democratic administration properly. The boundaries of states are mismatched with those of nations, making any push for national self determination fraught with peril.[53]

Mansfield and Snyder were not alone in expressing their concerns. Thomas Carothers and Marina Ottaway had already indicated similar worries as had F. Gregory Gause. As if in confirmation of these doubts, with the election of a Hamas government in Palestine in January 2006, recriminations were heard far and wide against the naiveté of thinking that the democratic process in and of itself would bring forth peace.[54]

Conclusion

Convinced of democracy's "universal appeal" given the "historic winds" at its back, policy makers in the Bush administration, backed by neoliberal academic theory, systematically reduced what they saw as the obstacles to the democratization of virtually all countries in the world to a simplistic formula. In their conceptualization, historic winds, plus enlightened leadership that held high the values and institutions of democratic life, plus popular hopes for honest and effective government, plus "robust" outside support—all equals democracy just about anywhere.

Combine this formula with that provided by democratic peace theory, which maintained that should the world's dominant powers become liberal democracies, peace would reign, and you have the essential combustible ingredients needed for liberal imperialism.

Whence the formula? Most certainly not from the neoconservatives, who were not doing the difficult scholarly studies such conclusions implied, but from the neoliberals who expected to come to the aid of the wretched of the earth thanks to their theoretical certainty that their mission would be welcomed locally and blessed by history. To be sure, neocons like Kristol, Kaplan, Kagan, and Sharansky appropriated these ideas and folded them in to what posterity will study as the Bush Doctrine. But the origins of these concepts lie outside the ambit of conservative or Republican thinking to such an extent that still late in 2006 leading intellectual lights in the Democratic Party continue to speak in these terms (as we shall see in the next chapter).

True to the unbridled superficiality of such thinking, the Bush Doctrine knew no limits. After Iraq, why not the rest of the Middle East? As the president put it before the UN General Assembly on September 23, 2003:

> Success of a free Iraq will be watched and noted throughout the region. Millions will see that freedom, equality and material progress are possible at the heart of the Middle East. Leaders in the region will face the clearest evidence that free institutions and open societies are the only path to long-term national success and dignity. And a transformed Middle East would benefit the entire world by undermining the ideologies that export violence to other lands. Iraq, as a dictatorship, had great power to destabilize the Middle East. Iraq, as a democracy, will have great power to inspire the Middle East.

And after the Middle East, why not the world? As the president reaffirmed in his State of the Union Message of January 31, 2006:

> Fellow citizens, we've been called to leadership in a period of consequence. We've entered a great ideological conflict...the destination of history is determined by human action, and every great movement of history comes to a point of choosing. Lincoln could have accepted peace at the cost of disunity and continued slavery.... Abroad, our nation is committed to an historic, long-term goal—we seek the end of tyranny in our world. Democracies replace resentment with hope, respect the rights of their citizens and their neighbors, and join the fight against terror. Every step toward freedom in the world makes our country safer—so we will act boldly in freedom's cause.

CHAPTER 6

Liberal Imperialism III
Militarizing Humanitarianism

If we have to use force, it is because we are America. We are the indispensable nation. We stand tall, and we see further into the future.

Madeleine Albright, February 18, 1998

Never, never, never believe any war will be smooth or easy, or that anyone who embarks on the strange voyage can measure the tide and hurricanes he will encounter. The statesman who yields to war fever must realize that once the signal is given, he is no longer the master of policy but the slave of unforeseeable and uncontrollable events.

Winston Churchill, *My Early Years*

The two preceding chapters maintained that paternity for the dimension of the Bush Doctrine that promoted free market democracy to all the world for the sake of freedom and peace should be attributed to the neoliberals, much more than to the neoconservatives. To be sure, the neocons had always stood foursquare for the superiority of liberal democratic ways, and during the Reagan years many of them had come to appreciate the advantages to the national security of the global expansion of market democracies. The thinking behind their call for democratizing regime change under the terms of a "benevolent hegemony" on the part of the United States was in good measure independent of the neoliberal idea of a "zone of democratic peace." Yet it was the neolibs, with their sophisticated theoretical arguments on both the desirability and the feasibility of expanding the "Community of Democracies" to areas where neither the market nor democracy were familiar arrangements, who gave this signature feature of the Bush Doctrine the *gravitas* it came to possess.

As the neocon emphasis on the word *hegemony* implied, their paternity was more apparent in that dimension of the Bush Doctrine that insisted on the importance of safeguarding and using American military primacy in world affairs. Their argument was based on their long-standing conviction, going back to the late 1960s, if not earlier to the inception of the Cold War, that the best hope for liberal democracy, in a world where totalitarianism was an ever-present challenge, was a powerful and vigilant United States.

In sum, Washington's bid for world supremacy reflected essentially a neo-con position on questions of this country's relative power position, while the American promise for what it would actually do with the power at its disposal grew more out of neolib thinking. If the Bush Doctrine had a pillar of power and a pillar of purpose, as Chapter 1 indicated, each ideological partner to American policy had a distinctive gift to offer.

We should not conclude from this observation, however, that the two major dimensions of the Bush Doctrine represented a neat division of labor between neoconservatives and neoliberals. Just as we should not suppose that the neocons were tone deaf to the appeals of the neoliberals so far as democracy promotion was concerned, so we should not assume that the neolibs were unaware of the need for military action in world affairs in order to spread the blessings of the Kantian peace. Each of these two schools of thought had within it ideological predispositions for the arguments made by the other, predispositions that underlay a growing convergence of viewpoints that was evident well before the 9/11 terrorist attacks.

What I am suggesting, in short, is a complicated, but important, cross-fertilization of intellectual first cousins that together produced the Bush Doctrine. What most bedeviled the coming together, nevertheless, was the question of the militarization of democracy promotion, a step many of the neoliberals were hesitant to take if this meant America would act alone. The left in general was highly allergic to the unilateral exercise of American military power, remembering as they did not only the shame of covert CIA activities in Iran and Guatemala during the Cold War, but more especially the disaster of war in Southeast Asia. In more recent times, their awareness of American involvement in human rights outrages in Guatemala and El Salvador in the 1980s was particularly acute. Nor did the administration of George W. Bush inspire much confidence that it would use responsibly the power at America's disposal. The center-left had been sparring with the neoconservatives for a full three decades before George W. Bush was inaugurated as president. Whatever respect they might have for the convictions of the neocons, they knew that they were not cut of the same cloth.[1]

Misuse of force by Washington was not their only concern. Liberals and leftists alike were suspicious of overly grand talk about the benefits of economic globalization, and they worried about the environmental effects of unregulated consumption of energy in the world at large and especially in the United States. Moreover, because they were almost genetically programmed to be multilateralists and anti-imperialists, talk of the preemptive, unilateral exercise of American military power to conquer a foreign people (even if for their own good) invariably made them worry.

Temperamentally, the two schools of thought were different as well. Neoconservatives might be called super-patriots. Since the early 1970s, if not since the late 1940s, they had championed the United States as the leader (not the first among equals) of a confederation of liberal democratic peoples. A clear view of how history had entrusted this country with a role to play in the titanic struggle between freedom and despotism was their second nature. They championed an American-led victory in the Cold War long before it was apparent such an outcome was likely, and called for Washington to deal decisively with both Slobodan Milosevic and Saddam Hussein in the 1990s, seeing these two men as modern embodiments of populist, militaristic fascism. In a word, their sense of American responsibility and purpose based ultimately on its military might was never for a moment in doubt.

The neoliberals, by contrast, tended to be multiculturalists at home and cosmopolitans in world affairs. Samuel Huntington has with reason called some members of this group "dead souls," and he endorsed the finding of Stanley Rothman that "social science faculties at elite universities are overwhelmingly liberal and cosmopolitan or on the Left. Almost any form of civic loyalty or patriotism is considered reactionary." Huntington selected out for special attention the ideas of a group of left liberals in a book compiled by Martha C. Nussbaum and others published in 1996 called *For Love of Country: Debating the Limits of Patriotism*. Therein, Princeton professor Amy Gutmann found it "repugnant" if Americans were told that they were "above all, citizens of the United States," when their "primary allegiance...should not be to the United States or to some other politically sovereign community [but to] democratic humanism." For her part, Nussbaum criticized "patriotic pride" as "morally dangerous." "I am a citizen of the world," she declared, "a person whose primary allegiance is to the community of human beings of the entire world...to no mere form of government, no temporal power, but to the moral community made up by the humanity of all human beings."[2]

As these observations imply, liberals and neoliberals alike, located as independents, in the Democratic Party or further to the left, tended to be suspicious about the kind of neoconservative talk that described America's "unipolar moment" as promising a "benevolent hegemony" that might be extended to a "unipolar epoch." World supremacy for the United States was not a liberal position.

Still, no impenetrable Chinese Wall separated these two schools of thought. Just as the neoconservatives did not have to be instructed by the neo-Wilsonians as to the value of liberal democracy for world order, so in the 1990s the neoliberals were capable, quite on their own, of seeing the need to militarize their humanistic purposes. For that matter, so was the Democratic Party more widely considered. Under the tutelage of Secretary of State Madeleine Albright especially, mainstream Democratic thinking came more and more to the conclusion that whatever the problem it needed a solution made in America, a solution that well might mean the use of force.

The problem for the liberals was that they were hobbled by their dedication to international law and organization to work multilaterally in exercising armed force. As we saw in Chapter 4, the most sophisticated of the neo-Wilsonians were committed by virtue of their theory of world affairs to a collaborative form of multilateralism that eschewed American unilateralism. Instead, these liberals preferred to rely on the concept of "muscular multilateralism" advanced by Secretary Albright, the use of force presumably to be exercised under the command of another of her intellectual constructions, the "Community of Democracies."

The question for Wilsonians in the 1990s, then, was how to make international law and multilateral cooperation, particularly in the form of United Nations sanctioned peacekeeping forces, better able to address with military force issues like genocide in Rwanda and the Sudan, military despotisms such as Haiti, populist militarists like Saddam, terrible civil wars as in Cambodia, Indonesia, and Sri Lanka, and regional wars such as those consuming the Balkans and Central Africa. To the chagrin of leftist activists, the political elites in the democratic world were focusing not on human rights but on nuclear proliferation, economic exchanges, and military buildups. To read through the annual *World Wide Reports* of the influential Human Rights Watch in the 1990s is to see an example of the frustration of the human rights community in general with Washington's reluctance to take up the charge to use the window of opportunity history had afforded with the end of the Cold War to improve the human condition. In seeing that something urgently needed doing, but nothing was happening, neoconservatives and liberals could be on the same page. Although they pursued different lines of reasoning, their thinking converged on the belief that the failure of the United States to take a firm stand on military grounds in the Balkans had been a serious mistake. Here more than anywhere else, in the drama surrounding the despotism of Milosevic, was fertile ground for these two schools to make a joint reaffirmation of the pledge: "Never Again."

The task for liberals, then, was to spell out how military intervention for the sake of human rights and democracy promotion might be handled multilaterally. In the process of coming up with a legalistic framework for action, another current of neoliberalism arose. Now, neoliberalism had three arrows in its quiver. In addition to democratic peace theory, and democratic transition arguments—the first of which declared the desirability of the expansion of democratic government, the second its relative ease—a redefinition of the meaning of sovereignty was the final blessing for battle. Enter neoliberal international jurisprudence.

Muscular Multilateralism

UN Secretary-General Kofi Annan put the concern of liberal internationalist jurists well in an address to the General Assembly on September 20, 1999: "If states bent on criminal behavior know that frontiers are not the absolute defense, if they know that the Security Council will take action to halt crimes against humanity, then they will not embark on such a course of action in expectation of sovereign immunity." And again on December 11, 2001 in accepting the Nobel Peace Prize: "The sovereignty of States must no longer be used as a shield for gross violations of human rights.... Only in a democratic environment based on respect for diversity and dialogue, can individual self-expression and self-government be secured, and freedom of association be upheld."[3]

In effect, the secretary-general was calling on the world's leaders for a reformulation of just war theory that would render illegitimate governments that were human rights violators and open them to outside attack in the name of human rights and democracy. His timing was excellent. More than a decade before Annan spoke, liberal internationalist lawyers had begun to focus

renewed attention on the normative basis of sovereignty, that is on the terms
by which states in the world system recognized each other as legitimate.

The job for these neoliberal jurists proved to be a difficult one. First, their
aim had to be to overturn long-established precedent that a government could
not be attacked for the way in which it treated its own citizenry, provided
it exercised effective control over its population and territory. Any effort to
revise this understanding was sure to arouse the consternation of governments
that might feel such a determination was only a pretext to permit them to be
attacked (which, in fairness, it well could be). Second, the neoliberals had to
articulate what organization or group had the legitimacy to decide on whether
sovereignty could be extended, suspended, or withdrawn to a state based on its
organization and conduct. Implicit in these deliberations was the most important question of all: under whose authority could force be used? In Annan's
thinking, that organization had to be the United Nations or, more likely, the
Security Council. But the obvious objection was that the conduct of this body in
the 1990s—whether with respect to Rwanda, Iraq, or Serbia—had shown itself
to be terribly wanting for reasons that did not seem open to basic reform.

The first task, which was largely definitional, was the easier of the two. It
was a rather strictly theoretical matter, after all, to come up with the reasoning
for a new form of just war, one waged in defense of human rights and democracy promotion against oppressive regimes. Lawyers are by profession excellent at writing and rewriting rules. By the late 1980s they were lending their
talents to redefining the juridical basis of a state's claim to sovereignty.

By contrast, the second task was inherently more difficult. It meant finding, or founding, an international institution capable of exercising jurisdiction
over the world community with respect to the promotion of human rights
and democratic government, including the ability to use force where the need
arose. Could the United Nations exercise this role through the Security Council? Or could a Community of Democracies be set up, an expanded NATO
perhaps, that could be judge, jury, *and executioner* with respect to the behavior
of the non-democratic world so far as the safeguard of basic human rights was
concerned? Both Annan and Albright were suggesting that this was the practical political task of the late 1990s, but could it be accomplished?

To make the case that non-democratic governments were illegitimate, the
main line of attack for neoliberal jurists was to show that during the course
of the twentieth century, and especially since 1947, most states in the international community had pledged themselves through a variety of resolutions,
covenants, and treaties to what might be called a common law for the world's

states. The outcome was an implicit moral contract that bound them to a set of obligations to respect human rights for their citizens and in due course to be democratic themselves if they were not so already. Those states that failed to live up to international norms—gross and systematic human rights abusers—might by virtue of their own agreements find their legitimacy withdrawn by the world community, leaving them in effect pariahs of the global system.

It was but a short step from withdrawing their legitimacy to sanctioning an attack on them in the name of their failure to respect human rights. As early as 1987, Bernard Kouchner, a founder of Doctors Without Borders, was working with the French jurist Mario Bettati on an idea the latter called "the right to intervene." Immediately thereafter, the "right" became a "duty," one that Bettati argued was vigorously promoted by countries like France under the auspices of the United Nations. In short, at the very time the Cold War was ending, the legal grounds were being formulated for the expansion of the zone of democratic peace under the auspices of the Security Council, the organization that had the authority, and now the obligation, to call for the use of force in instances where it was warranted by the circumstances.[4] The problem, of course, was that as the genocide in Rwanda vividly illustrated, the Security Council lacked the will to act. How then were neoliberals to respond?

The Case of Thomas M. Franck

To see how persuasive the neo-Wilsonian argument in favor of the forceful imposition of democratic government could be, let us consider its terms in the reasoning of one of its most articulate American spokespersons, New York University law professor Thomas M. Franck. Writing in a widely cited essay in the flagship scholarly journal of the American international legal profession *The American Journal of International Law* (AJIL) early in 1992, Franck declared that what was once a "radical notion" was fast becoming standard fare: that to be seen as legitimate in the eyes of the international community, sovereignty must rest on the consent of the governed. "Democracy, thus, is on the way to becoming a global entitlement, one that will be increasingly promoted and protected by collective international processes." Should one doubt how intensely Franck felt, he left no doubts: "The question is not whether democracy has swept the boards, but whether global society is ready for an era in which only democracy and the rule of law will be capable of validating governance."[5]

Such a watershed development was not restricted to "a small enclave of Western industrial states" in Franck's opinion, but was global in scope: "this almost complete triumph of the democratic notions of Hume, Locke, Jefferson and Madison—in Latin America, Africa, Eastern Europe and, to a lesser extent Asia—may well prove to be the most profound event of the twentieth century and, in all likelihood, the fulcrum on which the future development of global society will turn." Hence he proclaimed, "a sea change in international law, as a result of which the legitimacy of each government someday will be measured definitively by international rules and processes...we can see the outlines of this new world in which the citizens of each state will look to international law and organization to guarantee their democratic entitlement."

To make his case, Franck reasoned as many other neoliberal jurists would by reaching back to the peace settlement that followed World War I and that established a right of national self-determination. Self-determination, in turn, required those entrusted with state power to act on behalf of their citizenries. Franck's emphasis fell on the years since World War II with the creation of the United Nations, whose various instruments had been agreed to by the states who composed its membership. Among the landmarks he cited:

> The Universal Declaration of Human Rights; the International Covenant on Civil and Political Rights; the International Convention on the Elimination of All Forms of Racial Discrimination; the International Convention on the Suppression and Punishment of the Crime of Apartheid; the Declaration on the Elimination of All Forms of Intolerance and of Discrimination Based on Religion or Belief; and the Convention on the Elimination of all Forms of Discrimination against Women. These universally based rights are supplemented by regional instruments such as the European Convention for the Protection of Human Rights and Fundamental Freedoms; the American Convention on Human Rights; the African Charter on Human and Peoples' Rights; the Copenhagen Document and the Paris Charter.

Franck concluded his article with an appeal to his fellow internationalists to push legal arguments forward: "Both textually and in practice, the international system is moving toward a clearly designated democratic entitlement with national governance validated by international standards and systematic monitoring compliance. The task is to perfect what has been so wondrously begun."

Despite these brave words, Franck was careful to recognize that some might feel such arguments amounted to an effort "to re-impose a form of neocolonialism under the banner of establishing democracy." Here Franck hesitated:

"History has warned, repeatedly, that the natural right of all people to liberty and democracy is too precious and too vulnerable to be entrusted entirely to those who govern." He nonetheless concluded that his position did "not necessarily implicate military enforcement action." His concern was to distinguish the emerging right to democratic governance "in the clearest fashion from the long history of unilateral enforcement of a tainted colonialist 'civilizing' mission.... This requires that all states unambiguously renounce the use of unilateral, or even regional, military force to compel compliance with the democratic entitlement in the absence of prior Security Council authorization under Chapter VII of the Charter."

In 1997, again in the AJIL, Franck returned to the question of the universal relevance of his argument, in "Is Personal Freedom a Western Value?" While showing his respect for those who insisted that certain cultures (including some subcultures in the West) might properly place communal over individual rights, Franck argued that what was initially a Western value was becoming increasingly global. He specifically included the Islamic world as opening up to his view of the meaning of freedom. His conclusion was that a convergence of values was occurring, which suggested that the "global entitlement" enshrined in international agreements coincided with an increased recognition among cultures that certain rights were universal.[6]

Faced with the Taliban in power in Afghanistan, however, Franck became emphatically belligerent. Writing early in 2001, he assailed the Afghan government, asking, "Are Human Rights Universal?" and answering unequivocally in the affirmative. Not Western culture (whose history showed much opposition to a modern notion of human rights, he asserted) but worldwide changes such as "universal education, industrialization, urbanization, the rise of a middle class...generated the move to global human rights." Taking the Taliban as his example of the retrograde forces that must be combated, Franck called for "joining the battle."

> [I]f the fight...is to be effective, it needs military and fiscal resources. It needs a common strategy involving governments, intergovernmental organizations, NGOs, business and labor. But let there be no mistake: the fight is essentially one between powerful ideas, the kind that shake the pillars of history.... This, then, is a wake-up call. Waging this war of ideas successfully—and it cannot be evaded or postponed for long—will require intellectual rearmament for thinkers lulled by the warm, fuzzy triumph of liberalism and the supposed end of ideology.[7]

In a period of nine years, Franck's message had evolved in a way that paralleled the thinking of an important part of the liberal international legal community. In early 1992, he expressed himself as hesitant that the right to democratic government could be enforced militarily by the international community because international law was not yet able to validate an institution with authority to come to such a determination. Subsequently, he indicated progress toward a convergence of values. Then, by early 2001, he was issuing an unambiguous call for military action, even if the exact political body or bodies properly invested with a right to attack a sovereign state because of its domestic policies remained to be determined.

We should not conclude from the preceding discussion that Franck supported the American invasion of Iraq in March 2003. As a fastidious lawyer committed to multilateralism and to respect for the emergence of a body of law that would legitimize war if it cannot be avoided, Franck had grounds to oppose the Bush administration's determination unilaterally to be rid of Saddam Hussein. Nevertheless, the argument was there thanks to him for others to borrow to their own purposes, whether it be preemptive war as "anticipatory self-defense" or as military humanitarian intervention. Franck had clearly laid the groundwork for a juridical blessing of progressive liberal imperialism.[8]

Muscular Multilateralism at the End of the Decade

Appeals like Franck's were far from isolated voices. On September 20, 1999, Kofi Annan had asked the UN General Assembly, "if humanitarian intervention is, indeed, an unacceptable assault on sovereignty, how should we respond to a Rwanda, to a Srebrenica—to gross and systematic violations of human rights that affect every precept of our common humanity?" The answer came from the Canadian government, which in 2000 offered to host an international body to make recommendations to the world community on a framework for action. In short order, the International Commission on Intervention and State Sovereignty convened, headed by Gareth Evans, a former Australian foreign minister, and Mohamed Sahnoun, a senior Algerian diplomat, supported by ten members of the world community respected for their commitment to human rights, including Michael Ignatieff, a neoliberal who appeared earlier in these pages.

At the end of 2001 (but its work completed before 9/11) the commission published a document entitled "The Responsibility to Protect." The high-profile statement constituted a sensitive and detailed analysis of the dilemma of respecting sovereignty, yet defending peoples when governments were unwilling or unable to protect them or was itself the cause of their suffering. Ultimately, it fulfilled its mandate by providing the rationale and methods that permitted what should be called "militarized humanitarianism."

While the commission recognized that under Article 2 of the UN Charter, states were presumed to be free of outside intervention based on their management of their internal affairs, the panel could nonetheless point to other features of the UN Charter that qualified the recognition of a state's sovereignty if its conduct toward its subject peoples was abhorrent to international norms. The commission also referred to the variety of later declarations and covenants, invoked as we have seen by Franck, that made a state's legitimacy more conditional yet, a kind of contract law that obligated states that had joined the United Nations to respect the accumulation of agreements that had been made by the club of which they were now members.

The commission's finding: "What has been gradually emerging is a parallel transition from a culture of sovereign impunity to a culture of national and international accountability." As a consequence, the commission asserted not simply the right in extreme circumstances, to intervene but *the responsibility* of the international community—ultimately defined as the UN Security Council—in effect to put a state into receivership, and to puts its people in what another time would have been called a trusteeship, until such time as a more responsible government, defined as being a democracy, could be created.[9]

An essential dilemma for the commission was to protect itself from the charge of fostering imperialism: "What is at stake here is not making the world safe for big powers, or trampling over the sovereign rights of small ones, but delivering practical protection for ordinary people, at risk of their lives, because their states are unwilling or unable to protect them."[10] Accordingly, in several of its provisions, the report strived to construe its mission as narrowly as possible to protect the suffering, not to promote the ability of outside powers to use an intervention to serve their own purposes.

Still, the fact that the report justified liberal imperialism is quite impossible to deny. That was its mandate after all. As a first step, the commission licensed the international community to pass on a state's legitimacy: "International organizations, civil society activists and NGOs use the international human rights norms and instruments as the concrete point of reference against which to judge state conduct." Ultimately the commission anointed the United Nations as "the main arena for the jealous protection, not the casual abrogation, of state sovereignty." Applying for and receiving membership in the UN implicitly meant accepting the standards of this organization as the guardian of the set of international conventions that have evolved over time. "The state itself, in signing the [UN] Charter, accepts the responsibilities of membership flowing from that signature. There is no transfer or dilution of state sovereignty. But there is a necessary re-characterization involved: from *sovereignty as control to sovereignty as responsibility,* in both internal functions and external duties."[11]

Suppose exhortations from the international community were of no avail? As a second step, when other remedies have been exhausted, the commission concluded that military force might be used to fulfill "the responsibility to protect" against a state that was unable to defend its population from gross human rights abuses or was itself guilty of these outrages. "The emerging principle in question is that intervention for human protection purposes, including military intervention in extreme cases, is supportable when major harm to civilians is occurring or imminently apprehended, and the state in question is unable or unwilling to end the harm, or is itself the perpetrator." After citing examples of such interventions including NATO in Kosovo, the Economic Community of West African States in Liberia and Sierra Leone, and the UN in Somalia, the commission reiterated its finding that, "the Charter's strong bias against military intervention is not to be regarded as absolute when decisive action is required on human protection grounds."

The commission further asserted that the "responsibility to protect" carried with it a "responsibility to rebuild." For the commission, "this might involve democratic institution and capacity building; constitutional power sharing; power alternating and redistribution arrangements; confidence building measures between different communities or groups; support for press freedom and the rule of law; the promotion of civil society; and other types of similar initiatives that broadly fit within the human security framework."[12] Part 6 of the report was entitled "The Question of Authority." While there was no question but the ideal institution to call for military intervention was the United Nations, regional organizations may exercise this authority if need be.

In the fall of 2005, the UN General Assembly was presented with a High-Level Plenary statement that it adopted in a text entitled "In Larger Freedom." "Member States said they would spare no effort to promote democracy and strengthen the rule of law," the document declared, but "without action, promises are meaningless.... The world must move from an era of legislation to implementation." Explicitly endorsing "the responsibility to protect," the document turned to a variety of ways the UN could be strengthened, but the document expressly delegated to regional organization "conflict prevention or peacekeeping" operations without insisting on the UN's sanction for decisions taken.[13] One might doubt that such a conclusion meant the international community would act effectively should the need arise, but the legislative basis to defend human rights internationally at least seemed securely in place.

From Theory To Practice

In the long decade that stretched between the fall of the Berlin Wall to the attack of 9/11, neoliberal international jurists had redefined the concept of sovereignty so as to make it conditional on a government's respect for what might be called the body of international common law that defined a people's basic human rights. Despite the inability of the neo-Wilsonian community to answer the vexing question of what group would have the authority to deem a state illegitimate, and how it would then act to remove it from power, the ground covered by these liberal international jurists was impressive. With the end of the Cold War, a new standard of sovereignty had been formulated, one to be enforced where necessary by military means, under the leadership of the UN Security Council where possible, under the authority of other multilateral organizations where necessary.

To be sure, unilateralism of the kind implicit in the Bush Doctrine remained unacceptable. But a great divide had been crossed, one that previously had separated the neocons from the neolibs, but that now seemed increasingly insignificant. Given the outrages committed by Saddam Hussein—crimes against humanity widely recognized as such by the international community and behavior repeatedly in violation of UN Resolutions—there was only a small step to take to from supporting multilateral military intervention to that which was American and unilateral.

As Michael Ignatieff put it when he took just that step himself in January 2003, in practical terms to join hands with the neoconservatives, "human rights groups [objecting to American unilateralism] seem more outraged by the prospect of action than they are by the abuses they once denounced.... Multilateral solutions to the world's problems are all very well, but they have no teeth unless America bares its fangs." Recognizing that America was creating an empire—"if America takes on Iraq, it takes on the reordering of the whole region"—Ignatieff endorsed Herman Melville's words that Americans "bear the ark of the liberties of the world."[14]

Nor was Ignatieff to change his position once the war was well underway. "Just remember how much America itself needed the assistance of France to free itself of the British," he declared in a surprising historical analogy in mid-2005. "Who else is available to sponsor liberty in the Middle East but America? Certainly not the Europeans who themselves have not done a very distinguished job defending freedom close to home...when the chips were down, in the dying years of Soviet tyranny, American presidents were there and European politicians looked the other way."[15]

In short, over the course of the 1990s, neoliberal and neoconservative arguments tended to converge with respect to human rights and democracy promotion. Both would use military force, even if the former, favoring adherence to international law and working through multilateral organizations, was much more circumspect than the latter, a trigger-happy group that repeatedly looked back to the character building days of Theodore Roosevelt with his rough-riding invocations of duty and heroism, and his warnings that the greatest danger America faced was its own lack of vision and courage. As Harvard law professor David Kennedy wrote, a "new law of force" had come into being, one with a "common vocabulary," "an audacious and astonishingly successful—conception" that led to a "vocabulary for statecraft" and a "merger of military and humanitarian roles."[16] At the end of the day, then, as the itinerary of Michael Ignatieff suggests, many neoliberals had come to resemble their neoconservative first cousins. Together they would march to conquer Baghdad.

Neo-Wilsonians and Weapons of Mass Destruction

An additional concern that pulled the neo-Wilsonians increasingly to the side of the neoconservatives became more concrete with 9/11: the danger posed to the liberal democratic world by terrorist groups in possession of weapons of mass destruction (WMD) furnished them by hostile non-democratic states. As Michael Ignatieff phrased it in 2003, "Iraq represents the first in a series of struggles to contain the proliferation of weapons of mass destruction, the first attempt to shut off the potential supply of lethal technologies to a global terrorist network."[17]

Because the states that would harbor such weapons with malicious intent or transfer them to terrorists were all non-democratic, nothing could be easier for liberal internationalists than to transpose the argument that states that failed to respect a human rights regime for their citizenry, and so were provisionally illegitimate, were also illegitimate and open to attack if they possessed, or were trying to amass, WMD. As President Bush had put it in his State of the Union Address of January 29, 2002, what made the regimes composing the "axis of evil" so dangerous was their development of weapons of mass destruction and their potential willingness to provide them to terrorists or otherwise to "threaten the peace of the world." Over the next several years, the president reaffirmed the conclusion that such a process could be a cause for war.

If rogue or backlash states could be attacked not only on the basis of their human rights record but also because of their efforts to acquire nuclear weaponry, then a clear-cut, major security concern would be addressed at the same time that the cause of protecting human rights would be served. Washington was concerned by more than Iraq. In President Bush's words on November 6, 2003, for example:

> In Iran the demand for democracy is strong and broad.... The regime in Teheran must heed the democratic demands of the Iranian people, or lose its last claim to legitimacy.... The United States has adopted a new policy, a forward strategy of freedom in the Middle East. This strategy requires the same persistence and energy and idealism we have shown before. And it will yield the same results. As in Europe, as in Asia, as in every region of the world, the advance of freedom leads to peace.

By the time of his State of the Union Address on January 31, 2006, Bush had linked Iranian development of WMD to their authoritarian state structure and threatened an armed reprisal:

> Yet liberty is the future of every nation in the Middle East, because liberty is the right and hope of all humanity. The same is true of Iran, now held hostage by a small clerical elite that is isolating and repressing its people. The regime in that country sponsors terrorists in the Palestinian territories and in Lebanon—and that must end. The Iranian government is defying the world with its nuclear ambitions, and the nations of the world must not permit the Iranian regime to gain nuclear weapons.
>
> Tonight let me speak directly to the citizens of Iran. America respects you, and we respect your country. We respect the right to choose your own future and win your own freedom. And our nation hopes one day to be the closest of friends with a free and democratic Iran.

For neo-Wilsonians there was little problem enlisting in the cause laid out by President Bush. Consider the reasoning of the well-known American neoliberal legal scholar Anne-Marie Slaughter. After providing a justification for the United States to attack Iraq without the appropriate UN approval (she

found the example of NATO's attack on Serbia in 1999 might be used as a precedent), Slaughter discovered a way to argue that a country trying to develop
a nuclear weapons capacity that was not democratic might legitimately be
treated as an outlaw state against which military intervention would be a
legitimate option.

Writing with Lee Feinstein in *Foreign Affairs* in 2004, Slaughter came to
what many might find the astonishing conclusion that, "the biggest problem
with the Bush preemption strategy may be that it does not go far enough."
Explicitly working from the Canadian-sponsored International Commission's
work analyzed above, Slaughter and Feinstein invoked a "collective 'duty to
prevent' nations run by rulers without internal checks on their power from
acquiring or using WMD." They then called to "shift the burden of proof from
suspicious nations to suspected nations" so that inspection regimes might be
expected to become far more intrusive. "Ours is not a radical proposal," the
authors declared in their conclusion: "It simply extrapolates from recent developments in the law of intervention for humanitarian purposes—an area in
which over the course of the 1990s old rules proved counterproductive at best,
murderous at worst."[18]

Theirs was "not a radical proposal"? Most certainly it was. Slaughter and
Feinstein were asserting that democratic governments could legally (that is,
morally) suspend the sovereignty of non-democratic states whenever the concern arose that a non-democracy might harbor weapons of mass destruction.
As neo-Wilsonians, Slaughter and Feinstein surely preferred that an inspec-
tions regime be authorized by a multilateral group such as the United Nations,
or perhaps the Community of Democracies, which the Clinton administration had proposed. Should such an association not issue the proper finding
to investigate, however, then they raised no objection to a democracy acting
unilaterally and preemptively to defend its security. Recall their injunction
that the Bush Doctrine "does not go far enough."

Echoing this line of reasoning, Ivo Daalder and James Steinberg late in 2005
coined the phrase "conditional sovereignty" to designate governments guilty of
human rights violations against their own citizens and active participants in the
proliferation of weapons of mass destruction. Like those who had gone before
them in this realm, Daalder and Steinberg found the Security Council "the preferred vehicle" for authorizing military action, failing which regional organizations might legitimize a preemptive strike. Should that too fail, they concluded
by explicitly affirming, with the Bush Doctrine, that the "underlying logic of the
limited use of preventive force in appropriate contexts is compelling."[19]

Amitai Etzioni was of the same mind. A well-known liberal internationalist Israeli writer who was a founder of the "communitarian" movement, Etzioni in 2004 heralded the expansion of American power after 9/11 if it led to a U.S. headed "Global Safety (or Security) Authority." The development Etzioni forecast was one that might in due course lead from "empire to community." Making the leitmotif of his book the Biblical injunction that "from might came sweet" (*Judges* 14), Etzioni speculated on how the East (with its values centered on the collective good), and the West (centered on individual freedom), might blend toward "a form of world government" thanks to the establishment of "a new safety architecture" based on an "emerging global normative synthesis." Invoking democratic peace theory, asserting without hesitation that "the value of humanitarian intervention trumps that of national sovereignty," Etzioni found that promoting "nuclear de-proliferation" was a more critical task than democracy promotion because it could be accomplished more cleanly, clearly, and quickly. As one might expect, Etzioni found no problem on moral grounds with Israel's nuclear weaponry (its democratic credentials were quite in order, after all) but determined that because of its system of government, Iran had no right to make an equivalent effort itself.[20]

Examples of this line of reasoning could be multiplied, but the point should be clear. Quite on their own, without the aid of the neoconservatives, neoliberals were able to embrace the notion of using military force to expand the zone of democratic peace by promoting the transition to democratic government of peoples living under regimes that were gross and systematic abusers of human rights or that were non-democratic and harbored weapons of mass destruction. Neither the unilateralism nor the claims to primacy championed by the neoconservatives corresponded to neoliberal liking, to be sure, but when it came to the practical politics of war making, these two camps could unite in a common cause.

The Neoliberal Call To Arms: The Progressive Policy Institute of the Democratic Leadership Council

By the nature of their intellectual origins to the left, most usually in association with the Democratic Party, the neo-Wilsonians we have been considering had relatively little to do directly with the actual formulation of the Bush Doctrine so far as we know today. Yet many of them not only found themselves supporting the Republican grand design (if for their own reasons), but they actually offered it far more intellectual substance than it was able to muster from the thinking provided by neoconservative ranks alone. In doing so, these neoliberals put a severe damper on whatever anti-war movement might have been expected to have arisen in the United States against this conflict, for they carried the message of progressive liberal imperialism deep into the heart of the Democratic Party.

A leading vehicle for the dissemination of attitudes favorable to the war among the Democrats was the Progressive Policy Institute (PPI), which described itself as "the think tank for the Democratic Leadership Council" and was called "Bill Clinton's idea mill" by others. Founded in 1989 by Will Marshall, its president still in 2006, the role of the PPI was to formulate a broad range of ideas for the Democratic Party so as to provide unity and direction for national political campaigns. Among those liberal hawks who became public signatories of PPI position papers on American foreign policy were Ronald Asmus, Larry Diamond, Philip Gordon, Bob Kerrey, Will Marshall, Michael McFaul, Kenneth Pollack, Jeremy Rosner, and James Rubin. Among the Democratic political leadership, the PPI could count on signatures for various of its publications from Senator Evan Bayh (IN), and Representatives Jim Cooper (TN), and Artur Davis (AL), Adam Schiff (CA), Stephen Solarz (NY), and Ellen Tauscher (CA). Others whom the PPI commented on favorably included Senators Joseph Biden (DE), Hillary Clinton (NY), John Kerry (MA), and Joseph Lieberman (CT).

From its first pronouncements on Iraq, the PPI was militantly in favor of armed invasion, to a degree and in a fashion that made it virtually identical with the neoconservatives grouped in the Project for a New American Century (PNAC). (That *The Weekly Standard* frequently cited these Democrats favorably should come as no surprise.) In October 2003, the PPI published a document it entitled "Progressive Internationalism" in which its argument for "tough internationalism" appeared in a language that neo-Wilsonians could respond to every bit as much as war hawks in the Republican Party. Invoking the American traditions embodied in Democratic Presidents Roosevelt, Truman, Kennedy, Carter, and Clinton, the PPI called for "a new generation of Democratic leaders to step forward and provide the same caliber of leadership as their twentieth century predecessors…. Like the Cold War, the struggle we face today is likely to last not years, but decades. Once again the United States must rally the forces of freedom and democracy around the world to defeat this new menace and build a better world."[21]

In document after document over the years to follow, the members of the PPI pledged their allegiance to the logic of expanding the zone of democratic peace as well. As the institute put it in October 2003, in language that came directly from democratic peace theory as it was laid out in Chapter 4:

> Democrats believe that America should use its unparalleled power to defend our country and to shape a world in which the values of liberal democracy increasingly hold sway. History amply demonstrates that true peace and security depend not only on relations between states but also between state and society. Rulers who abuse their own people are more likely to threaten other countries, to support and spawn terrorism, to violate treaties, and otherwise flout norms of civilized conduct.

As Democrats, the members of the PPI had to find some way to criticize the Republican administration. An obvious way that was in keeping with the Wilsonian tradition was for its unilateralism: "the United States should have done much more to win international backing and better prepare for postwar reconstruction." Hence, the Democrats should stress multilaterialism, "strengthening and reforming international institutions—the United Nations, the international financial institutions, the World Trade Organization—which, for all their obvious flaws, still embody humanity's highest hopes for collective security and cooperative problem-solving."

I know of no way to calibrate the stridency of appeals in political arguments. As one who has read most of the documents available online through 2006 with respect to world affairs written by PNAC and by the PPI, I can nevertheless affirm that the latter seems to me to be the more shrill of the two organizations in its calls for action against a clear and present danger and in its assurance that the export of democratic institutions to the Middle East means success. Beginning in October 2003, the institute repeatedly declared that the Bush administration "has not been ambitious or imaginative enough" when it comes to "belief that America can best defend itself by building a world safe for individual liberty and democracy."

> We therefore support the bold exercise of American power, not to dominate but to shape alliances and international institutions that share a common commitment to liberal values. The way to keep America safe and strong is not to impose our will on others or pursue a narrow, selfish nationalism that betrays our values, but to lead the world toward political and economic freedom.

In March 2004, PPI members Ronald D. Asmus and Michael McFaul published a policy brief focusing on Iraq entitled "Let's Get Serious About Democracy in the Greater Middle East." Its core proposition duplicated exactly the neoconservative refrain: that the war on terrorism "must be won politically and with ideas. We need a grand strategy to help these countries transform themselves into the kinds of societies that focus on the needs of their peoples—ones that do not produce people who want to kill us and have the capacity to do so. Unless we help the Greater Middle East resolve its own internal pathologies, we will not stem the root causes of terrorism." To back this cause, Asmus and McFaul call for NATO's involvement, an enormous increase in budget appropriations for groups such as the National Endowment for Democracy (whose budget they proposed should be increased "tenfold or more") so that the NED and various NGOs could work with "democrats in the region," "moderate Arab states," and "democratic leaders." Among their more fanciful ideas was the creation of a Department of Democracy Promotion headed by an official with cabinet-level position to assist the president in making effective foreign policy for the country.

In February 2005, the PPI issued "Our National Security Challenge: An Open Letter to Democrats." Signed by a number of intellectuals, the letter warned: "Today's Islamist terrorists could prove more dangerous than our Cold War adversaries...the Jihadist creed, in its bigotry and intolerance, its sanctification of murder and its contempt for liberal democracy, bears a sinister resemblance to the totalitarian ideologies of twentieth century Europe." Consequently, "moral clarity in this fight is essential...Jihadist extremism will be the Democratic Party's first priority this year and every year until the danger recedes."

The very phrasing of these declarations was strikingly similar to the positions taken by the neoconservatives. True, if taking a stand for multilateralism was one way these Democrats could mark their distance from the Republicans, they might also criticize the administration's reluctance to plan for an adequate missile defense shield, or call for "a smarter fight" by publicizing ideas on counterinsurgency strategy for Iraq that were not being considered. However, neither of these positions was critical to the main question: their allegiance to the decision to invade Iraq in March 2003, their commitment not simply to stay the course until "victory" was achieved, but to expand the benefits of "freedom" elsewhere in the Middle East. Through 2006, these liberal hawks were thoroughly committed to making the secular religion of American democracy promotion the keynote of the Democratic Party's position on world affairs.[22]

Perhaps the most dramatic way these Democrats criticized Bush was by calling for *more robust* intervention to curb the proliferation of weapons of mass destruction. Thus "the White House stood by passively" in the face of both North Korean and Iranian nuclear ambitions we are told. In this spirit, for example, Philip Gordon, PPI signatory and director of the Center on the United States and Europe at the Brookings Institution, called for "Bringing Democracy to Iran" as a joint EU-U.S. initiative designed to control the development of WMD in that country. The fact that multilateralism had been effectively destroyed by the Bush administration, first in its strong-arm tactics, then in its inglorious conquest of Iraq, and that even were liberal democracy to come to Iran nuclear weapons would in all probability not be far behind, did not detain these Democrats for a minute from asserting again and again the need for a collective undertaking ever harder to imagine ever occurring.[23]

As president of the PPI, Will Marshall was the person most prolific in writing for the organization on the Iraq War. His titles alone convey his message.

- *Stay and Win in Iraq*—January 2004: "The escalating violence prompted facile and mostly misleading analogies between Iraq and Vietnam."
- *Heartland Strategy*—December 2004: Democrats should "challenge our allies to join the United States...by creating a new anti-terror NATO focused on the greater Middle East, toughening their stance on Iran's nuclear ambitions."
- *Thinking Bigger*—December 2004: "Turn NATO into a new anti-terrorism alliance...if some of our European partners balk, the United States should forge a new mutual defense pact that would include willing European allies as well as Russia, India and possibly even China."
- "Valuing Patriotism"—July 2005: The "Democrats' most important task is to articulate a tough but smart strategy for winning the ideological struggle against Jihadist extremism...more than anything else they need to show the country a party unified behind a new patriotism—a progressive patriotism determined to succeed in Iraq and win the war on terror, to close a yawning cultural gap between Democrats and the military, and to summon a new spirit of national service and shared sacrifice." This essay appeared in an edition of the PPI's *Blueprint Magazine* under the editorship of Al From and Bruce Reed given the upbeat title "How America Can Win Again."
- *Confronting Jihad*—July 2006: "Bush's 'war on terror' has focused too narrowly on terrorists' means rather than their ideas.... The United States needs a smarter strategy for undercutting the ideological appeal of the global jihad. For starters, we need to rally the world's democracies to a stouter defense of their liberal ideas.... Next, the West must make common cause with the majority of moderate Muslims who

want no part of the global jihad.... It's time for America to speak to the Muslim world less in the language of war and more in the common vocabulary of universal human aspirations for freedom and justice."

As if to illustrate the convergence between the Democrats and the neoconservatives, in the summer of 2005, the Council on Foreign Relations published an independent task force report co-chaired by Secretary of State Madeleine Albright and PNAC member Vin Weber entitled "In Support of Arab Democracy: Why and How." In a similar meeting of minds, on March 6, 2006, William Kristol published an editorial in *The Weekly Standard* positively citing Democratic Leadership Council member Marshall Wittmann: "We are in the midst of a Jihadist offensive. The bombing of Iraq's Askariya Shiite Shrine is another indication of the worldwide Jihadist offensive against the West. From the cartoon Jihad to the Hamas victory to the Iranian effort to obtain nuclear weapons to the attempt by al Qaeda to foment an Iraqi civil war—our enemy is taking the initiative. And the West is on its heels." Republicans and Democrats may have had their differences, but by 2006 more critical attacks were to be heard against the Iraq War from the realist wing of the Republican Party (connected to Henry Kissinger and to George H. W. Bush and Brent Scowcroft) than from notable Democrats, most of whom seemed to be supporting the war, thanks in good measure to the PPI.

In May 2006, the PPI published a volume Marshall edited entitled *With All Our Might: A Progressive Strategy for Defeating Jihadism and Defending Liberty.* Among its lineup of familiar neoliberal authors were Anne-Marie Slaughter, Larry Diamond, Michael McFaul, Ronald Asmus, Kenneth Pollack, and Stephen Solarz. The difference between a volume like this and something PNAC would produce is negligible, a point illustrated by a favorable review it received in *The Weekly Standard* from Tom Donnelly on May 22, 2006.[24]

The book presents itself as oriented around "five progressive imperatives for national security:"

> We must marshal all of America's manifold strengths, starting with our military power, but going well beyond it.
> We must rebuild America's alliances.
> We must champion liberal democracy in deed, not just in rhetoric, but because a freer world is a safer world.
> We must renew U.S. leadership.
> We must summon from the American people a new spirit of national unity and shared sacrifice.[25]

Through election year 2006, the Democratic Party was thus not collectively in opposition to the Iraq War. Whatever the growing desire of the electorate in the Democratic Party for a new course of action in the Middle East, to the extent there was an organized intellectual caucus, its members supported the terms of the Bush Doctrine as their own. These self-proclaimed "progressives" supported American primacy militarily over all the globe (which they understood to mean expanding the country's armed forces), and they saw democracy promotion and global markets as the key to world peace. "Make no mistake," wrote Marshall and Jeremy Rosner in their introduction to the PPI volume just quoted, "We are committed to preserving America's military preeminence. We recognize that a strong military undergirds U.S. global leadership." "Progressives must champion liberal democracy in deed, not just in rhetoric, as an integral part of a strategy for preventing conflict, promoting prosperity, and defending human dignity. ... We believe Democrats must reclaim, not abandon, their own tradition of muscular liberalism...violent jihadism, like fascism and communism, poses both a threat to our people's safety and a moral challenge to our liberal beliefs and ideals." "Progressives and Democrats must not give up the promotion of democracy and human rights abroad just because President Bush has paid it lip service. Advancing democracy—in practice, not just in rhetoric—is fundamentally the Democrats' legacy, the Democrats' cause, and the Democrats' responsibility."[26]

The individual contributions to the volume are mostly variations on these themes. A Muslim American writes of how important it is to be victorious in the war of ideas to overcome "the cosmic war" of terrorism so as to win "The Struggle for the Soul of Islam." Another chapter addresses the youth of America as "The 9/11 Generation." Several essays deal with making the military dimension of the struggle in the Middle East more effective. Stephen Solarz worries about Pakistan, Anne-Marie Slaughter would "Reinvent the UN." Larry Diamond and Michael McFaul are once again "Seeding Liberal Democracy." And Kenneth Pollack, whose 2002 book *The Threatening Storm: The Case for Invading Iraq* was as influential as any single writing in justifying the invasion of Iraq in 2003, is still at it with a chapter entitled "A Grand Strategy for the Middle East."

"For better or worse, whether you supported the war or not, it is all about Iraq now," writes Pollack. His political vision? "The end state that America's grand strategy toward the Middle East must envision is a new liberal order to replace a status quo marked by political repression, economic stagnation and cultural conflict." The problem with the Bush administration? "It has *not* made transformation its highest goal.... Instead the administration seems to have made advancing reform in the region its lowest priority. Iran and Syria's rogue regimes seem to be the only exceptions. The administration insists on democratic change there in a manner it eschews for Egypt, Saudi Arabia, and other allies.... The right grand strategy would make transformation of our friends and our foes alike our agenda's foremost issue." Several contributors to the volume, Diamond and McFaul most explicitly perhaps, might agree wholeheartedly with Pollack's suggestions.[27]

To be sure, these Democrats felt that acting multilaterally was strongly to be preferred in order to spread the zone of democratic peace (although how such a virtually inconceivable development was to occur was nothing they could specify), and they could be found criticizing the Bush administration for not pushing more forcefully a campaign against nuclear proliferation. But their main complaint was that Bush should have conducted the war more effectively. Given their chance at power, they would know how to be progressive imperialists far better than the Republicans—or such was their clear implication of the message repeated far and wide.[28]

In due course, "progressives" such as those in the PPI reached out beyond the Democratic Party. In March 2006 a group in Great Britain stepped forth with a statement of principles by "democrats and progressives" called the Euston Manifesto. Its first statement of principle was to be "for democracy" while its second was "no apology for tyranny." "Human rights for all" was its third principle, basic to what was its tenth principle, "a new internationalism" that could involve "humanitarian intervention." It was not difficult to see the affinity of this group with the PPI.[29]

By September 2006, an American counterpart to the Euston Manifesto had formed called New American Liberalism. References on this group's website in October 2006 showed its proximity as well to the Progressive Policy Institute, especially in its "books and articles" section, where works by people like Will Marshall were listed. A close reading of their text here and in other publications suggests an equally close affinity to the Project for a New American Century so far as world affairs is concerned.

These self-described progressives stated that they "regard anti-Americanism as a low and debased prejudice," "reject all forms of racism, including antisemitism, and also invoke the leaders of the American civil rights movement," denounced "retrograde attitudes about women and homosexuals emerging from the Islamic fundamentalists" for they were "advocates of the universality of human rights." While for the sake of the struggle against "radical Islam" some signatories urged a speedy American withdrawal from Iraq, all were committed to the notion that here was the struggle for our times.

The statements by these "progressives" were reminiscent of nothing more than communist "united front" tactics of the interwar and Cold War eras. That is, these liberal imperialists sought to find ground on which to cooperate with those concerned by matters other than the Middle East—be they women, homosexuals, or labor and environmental activists—in order to persuade them that there was one struggle that united them all above any other, that whatever their more parochial objectives, their primary concern should be the defeat of "Islamofascism."[30]

Consider as an example that could be multiplied many times over among those advocating coercive democratization in the ranks of the Democratic Party, the position of Peter Beinart, an editor of the *New Republic*. Calling for Democrats to rally to support the war, Beinart was widely cited for his essay "A Fighting Faith: An Argument for a New Liberalism" which appeared in his journal on December 13, 2004. After reporting on the "barbaric interpretations of Islam" that underlie "totalitarian Islam," Beinart asserted that for Democrats, "the struggle against America's new totalitarian foe [must be] at the center of [our] hopes for a better world." Today's "softs," as he repeatedly called those who failed to take with utmost seriousness the menace of "Islamofascism" were similar to those who failed to take the Soviet menace seriously in the 1940s. Beinart recalled what Arthur Schlesinger, Jr. accomplished for the Democratic Party in the late 1940s when he got it to take the communist menace seriously with his book *The Vital Center*. For our day, Beinart declared, Democrats had to come to understand that defeating "Islamist totalitarianism…must be liberalism's north star."

In 2006, Beinart published a widely read book wherein he persisted in his admonitions. The volume's title strikingly sums up its bombastic, militaristic message: *The Good Fight: Why Liberals—and Only Liberals—Can Win the War on Terror and Make America Great Again.*[31] The volume's cover describes it as "a passionate rejoinder to the conservatives who have ruled Washington since 9/11…an intellectual lifeline for a Democratic Party lying flat on its back…a call for liberals to revive the spirit that swept America and inspired the world." Its primary purpose is to challenge the "narrative" produced by the conservatives that established and justified a grand strategy for American foreign policy with a narrative suitable for liberals in today's world.

Whatever the brave ambitions of its author and its publisher, the Beinart book summed up the dilemma of the war party among Democrats late in the

election year of 2006: they could not find any serious ground on which to distinguish themselves from the Bush administration. These Democrats agreed
that "totalitarianism" was on the march, and that fighting it with an expanded
military force was the answer to the challenge. They also agreed that once the
struggle of arms had been concluded, then to consolidate victory, state and
nation building based on democratizing the conquered peoples was the proper
way to proceed. Nor did they see any limit to such ambitions; Iraq was understood to be only the beginning of the challenge. Finally, they saw the challenge
as character building and morally uplifting, a fitting international accompa-
niment to what they hoped to see flower domestically if ever they again took
control of the national government.

In short, just like the war party among the Republicans, these Democrats,
allowance made for nuances among them, to be sure, endorsed America's bid
for world supremacy, saw that promoting this agenda meant military domination of the Middle East, were prepared to act aggressively outside Iraq,
indeed outside the Middle East, if the case was warranted, expected democratic regime change to consolidate politically the victories gained militarily, and saw American patriotism as enhanced for domestic reform thanks to
the country's imperial mission. Beinart even had the nerve to invoke not only
Arthur Schlesinger, Jr., but also Hannah Arendt (for her analysis of totalitarianism) and Reinhold Niebuhr (for his urging that we "make the tragic choices
that defending freedom requires") as patron saints of his proposed framework
of action.[32]

What these Democrats criticized, then, was the handling of the war, not
the invasion of Iraq itself, nor the pretensions to world primacy of the Bush
Doctrine. For a final instance, let us return to Larry Diamond, an active
member of the PPI, who damned the handling of the war in a book entitled *Squandered Victory: The American Occupation and the Bungled Effort
to Bring Democracy to Iraq*, modestly dedicated "to my students, may they
learn from our mistakes." Yet the "mistakes," it turns out, were not to attempt
to assert American military and ideological primacy over the entire international system, or even the Broader Middle East, or even simply Iraq, but
instead to have botched the job. In a companion article to his book published
in January 2005 in the *Journal of Democracy* entitled "Lessons From Iraq,"
Diamond presented a series of considerations for future armed, democracy
promoting interventions elsewhere, including: "1. prepare for a major commitment;…. 2. commit enough troops;…. 3. mobilize international legitimacy and cooperation."[33]

Diamond did not criticize the Bush Doctrine. Like most Democrats involved with the war, he was rather working day and night instead to make the terms of the doctrine more effective. One might say no more for Richard Perle, whose testimony before the House Committee on Armed Services of April 6, 2005, entitled "Four Broad Lessons from Iraq," had nothing in it to which Diamond could conceivably object. The neocon Perle and the neolib Diamond were Tweedledum and Tweedledee. The only apparent difference was that Diamond could list seven lessons to be learned, not just four.

The election of November 2006 could be seen as spelling the end of the Bush Doctrine. The Democrats took control of both houses of Congress in a stunning victory widely interpreted to be a rejection of the Iraq War and thus implicitly to be a rebuff to American claims to world hegemony as well.

Nevertheless, as the preceding pages have indicated, powerful forces among the Democrats continued to favor a mission to secure American supremacy whatever the travails of Iraq. A marker of the fortunes of Democrats linked to continued hopes for pursuing more effectively the essential ambitions of the Bush Doctrine was Rahm Emanuel, Democratic representative in the House from Illinois. As chair of the Democratic Congressional Campaign Committee, Emanuel was given major credit for organizing his party's take-over of the House in November 2006. And as president of the Democratic Leadership Council, Emanuel could work closely with the PPI.

Shortly before the November elections, Emanuel published with Bruce Reed, editor of the PPI magazine *Blueprint*, a book entitled *The Plan: Big Ideas for America*. In it, Rahm and Reed salute Marshall's book described above as an "outstanding anthology" that "breathes new life" into traditional Democratic thinking, endorse Beinart's "fascinating book," and declare, "Winning at war is not a partisan or ideological question…but a fiercely pragmatic one."[34] Although Rahm called himself a "centrist," and criticized the Republican strategist Karl Rove as a "polarizer," under Rahm's more gentle exterior lurked much the same dedication to the war that Rove exhibited.

The position the Democratic Party will take in the 2008 election year on foreign policy is impossible to forecast. Even if the party's November 2006 victory depended in important measure on calls to end the military involvement in Iraq, we might recall that in 1968, Richard Nixon had claimed "new leadership will end the war," a phrase often referred to as Nixon's secret plan" to arrange an American withdrawal from Vietnam. In the event, his hope was not to end the conflict but for the United States to prevail. Will the Democrats follow his example forty years later, saying they intend to recast American foreign policy only to press on for victory In the Middle East? The dream of hegemony dies hard, and the range of interests that stand to suffer should Washington change course is sure to mobilize to keep the ship of state headed in the direction the Bush administration chose in 2002.

The Bush Doctrine As A Marriage Consummated

Between the late 1980s and 2001, neoliberals came up with three concepts that converted liberal internationalism from a doctrine of hegemony into a creed of empire. As this and the two preceding chapters have described, their core conclusions were: (1) that the anarchy of world affairs and the despotism of authoritarian states that bred war could be replaced with peace by the enlargement of the Kantian zone of market democratic peoples; (2) that the incorporation of the Hobbesian world of people living under despotic rulers into the Kantian "pacific union" might not be as difficult to bring about as once believed; and (3) that sovereignty could legitimately be revoked by the Community of Democracies (or some other multilateral organization possessed of the "moral clarity" to see the fundamental distinction between democratic and non-democratic governments) from states that were gross and systematic human rights abusers or amassing weapons of mass destruction. If these three core assertions were assented to, then it was relatively obvious to many neoliberals that they should endorse the Bush Doctrine as well as the invasion of Iraq that took place in March 2003. After all, by 2002 the voice of American nationalism in world affairs had become liberal internationalism. When the alarm bells rang, how could the proponents of progressive imperialism fail to muster for the cause?

The neoconservative contribution to the process was nonetheless indispensable. Their insistence on the need for resolute American leadership, acting if necessary in a preemptive and unilateral fashion, articulated an argument altogether lacking to the neo-Wilsonians with their focus on multilateralism. A tension thus remained over the means to be used to redeem the human condition. Would it be multilateral or unilateral? But this difference was trivial. That the Pax Americana would extend its reach coercively was no longer in question by the neoliberals any more than the neoconservatives, just as both groups agreed that the hallmark of American power would be that it would sponsor free market democracies to consolidate its military victories.

By virtue of neoliberal thinking that had grown up in the American Academy during the 1990s, the Bush Doctrine as it emerged in 2002 at neoconservative prompting could become very much bipartisan in spirit. These two schools shared six essential propositions in common. First, both subscribed fully to the belief in the cultural superiority of liberal democracy over every other form of government and championed open markets globally. Second, both saw authoritarian and totalitarian states as inherently untrustworthy and aggressive. Third, both believed that the promotion of democracy abroad would serve American security interests by expanding the democratic zone of Kant against the authoritarian order where Hobbesian logic prevailed. Fourth, both disregarded the difficulties in fostering democracy abroad such that democratic regime change came to be a practical option for American statecraft. Fifth, both agreed that the United States was, in Madeleine Albright's phrase, "the indispensable nation," whose leadership of the world community was necessary should all manner of trouble be addressed. Sixth, both were ready to use military force against non-democratic states should they challenge the Pax Americana.

In effect, there was no "war of ideas" between the Republican and Democratic parties so far as much of their elite intellectual thinking was concerned. The convergence of neoconservative and neoliberal thinking was so complete that all that could be debated was how well the invasion of Iraq was being executed, not whether it should have been launched in the first place nor whether America's supremacy in world affairs was a responsibility Washington could successfully exercise.

Or does this account exaggerate the convergence? Was this a marriage in fact of scoundrels and saints? By virtue of caring as much as they did about American supremacy in world affairs, one can legitimately ask whether that many neoconservatives actually subscribed sincerely to the democracy promotion aspect of the Bush Doctrine. What they wanted above all else was world domination; how it was made to appeal to the country at large might be seen as of relatively little concern. Were the neocons, then, all Elmer Gantrys? Democracy promotion might easily enough be a code word for puppet governments abroad friendly to Washington. Were most of them then "scoundrels"?

Similarly, by virtue of focusing so intently on the desirability and feasibility of democracy promotion, one can legitimately ask whether that many neo-Wilsonians actually understood just how ambitious the Iraq War was. Did they understand that its architects had no intention of stopping in Baghdad but were keeping the Broader Middle East in their sights if not the entire world order? Intoxicated by their message of universal redemption, were most of these neoliberals little more than naïve "saints"?

While we are debating these terms, which is worse, the scoundrels or the saints? The former at least are aware of their artfully camouflaged motives and so may pragmatically adjust to circumstance. But the latter may persist in the vain illusion that ultimately a brighter day will surely dawn, when the ends reached will finally be seen to justify the means that had to be used to secure them.

The chief concern of this book has been with the saints. Their betrayal of liberal internationalism and the American promise had two chief characteristics. First, the neoliberals signed on to the Bush Doctrine's charter for democracy promotion for the beneficial features they naively anticipated it would bring. In this respect, they were undone by the vanity of their theories to suppose they actually had a key to history and could make the world a better place in which to live. In fact, both democratic peace theory and democratic transition thinking were badly flawed intellectually. At closer inspection they were more partisan expressions of American nationalism in a period of unipolarity than they were findings of a disinterested social science establishment. Second, by virtue of their self-imposed distance from realist thinking, the liberals had blinded themselves to the dynamics of power relations, assuming a historical dispensation for the exercise of American power that no one possessed of ordinary common sense would believe.

The bottom line was that neoliberal social science thinking could not impose limits on Washington's bid for control of world order. Such thinking could appreciate neither the limits on American power nor the variety of self-interested ends American imperialism was sure to pursue quite apart from promoting world peace. Their ideology itself, with its sense of redemptive promise, drove these neoliberals over a Niagara Falls suicidal to their intellectual pretensions.

We observe often enough that the road to Hell is paved with good intentions, and here is an historical example in American history second to none. Blaise Pascal had already warned us in the seventeenth century, "who would be an angel becomes a beast." Liberal internationalists might well have recalled Machiavelli's warning in his *Discourses* (2:27): "Men always commit the error of not knowing where to limit their hopes, and by trusting to these rather than to a just measure of their resources, they are generally ruined."

This book's title, *A Pact with the Devil*, refers, then, to two encounters with destiny. The first was sealed with neoconservatives, who thought that America could leave its imprint on history thanks to its victory in the Cold War by using its military primacy to secure the spread of market democracy the world around. The second was sealed with neoliberals who gave the blessing of their academic findings to embarking upon such a dangerous historical mission. In short, an ideology appeared that sanctioned war in the name of peace and actually had the cheek to interpret protests against the global domination of this system of market democracies as an attack on civilization itself, challenges to be met with unrelenting force.

In liberal internationalism's maturation lay its downfall. As its argument became tighter in the 1990s, those who embraced its new formulations became victims of the watertight logic of their way of thinking. Exhilarated by the promise of world peace thanks to the expansion of democratic government, emboldened by the conviction that all the world was waiting for the liberal sunshine, convinced that pariah states could and should be eliminated, unaware of the pitfalls of an American leadership acting on the basis of a will to power and with a long list of self-interested objectives, many neoliberals were quite unable in intellectual terms to oppose the Iraq War and instead allowed their creed to become the consummate expression of war-making American nationalism.

Hoisted by their own petard. In intellectual terms, the result was scandalous.[35] A progressive ideology born of an anti-imperialist concern to spread liberal democracy so as to enhance the prospects for "perpetual peace" had joined forces with an imperialist enterprise that made perpetual war more likely. Just as fascism and communism had met their historical limits, so now too has liberal democratic internationalism. For the American defeat in Iraq can be nothing but the defeat of the global ambitions of liberal internationalism as well, exposed as it now is as the ideological justification for an imperial power grab as old as human history.

Liberal Internationalism: The Way Ahead

The need for a doctrine that promotes human rights and democratic government the world around is apparent. Failed states, oppressed or abandoned populations, terrorist threats, rogue regimes with weapons of mass destruction—none of these dangers is likely any time soon to pass from the scene and to all of these challenges liberal internationalism has its answer. Here is a creed that contributed mightily to the defeat of both fascism and communism. In the combined efforts to the market democratic states might still lie the strength to carry us through today's difficulties.

Nevertheless, the problem with any rosy scenario about the prospects for liberal internationalism is that its hubris and self-righteousness may actually harbor the potential for still greater calamities in the years ahead. For thanks to the developments in the Wilsonian creed in the 1990s, it is easier to polarize the world into the good and the evil than before, in the process inflating the dangers, and exaggerating the likelihood of success if we but stay wedded to the vision of global peace and freedom under the protection of American power deployed worldwide. Thus, rather than speculate on how liberal internationalism may be salvaged from the debacle of American involvement in the Middle East, prudence today dictates that we should rather be on our guard against its continued excesses. For there is good reason to think that liberal internationalism as an expression of American nationalist imperialism has not reached its last gasp. Enormous sums of money (more than $2 billion a year by one estimate) continue to be showered on those who say the emperor is fully clothed.[36] Moreover, the ideology itself continues to be robust. Indeed, the rise after 9/11 of a kind of liberal fundamentalist thinking that is strikingly similar to fundamentalist reasoning elsewhere might yet mean that the life cycle of this doctrine as an international force had not yet reached its end. Another terrorist attack, the question of Iranian nuclear capacity—here are but two examples of the kinds of challenges that could sustain the liberal internationalist argument in its imperialist form.

Enter the liberal Jihadists, neoconservatives and neo-Wilsonians alike, convinced that in the face of reversals in the Middle East, the United States had no choice but to redouble its efforts for victory. For these people, defeat in Iraq was not an option. "Victory" there and in the "Broader Middle East," defined still as the liberation of oppressed peoples whatever the cost, remained their mantra. To this subject—that of a fifth stage of liberal internationalism I will call liberal fundamentalism—we turn in the following chapter.

CHAPTER 7

Liberal Fundamentalist Jihadism

We are living in a time of premeditation and the perfect crime. Our criminals are no longer helpless children who plead love as their excuse. On the contrary, they are adults, and they have a perfect alibi: philosophy, which can be used for any purpose, even for transforming murderers into judges.

Albert Camus, *The Rebel*

Woe unto the world because of offenses! for it must needs be that offenses come; but woe to that man by whom the offense cometh!

Matthew 18:7

Is liberal internationalist fundamentalism a possibility? Is liberal terror conceivable, with the murder of innocents and the deliberate destruction of any possibility of world peace due to a holy war, a liberal Jihad? Still more unthinkable: Can we imagine a totalitarian state organized in the name of liberalism?

The unsettling answer is that these developments are indeed possibilities, as after 9/11 an extremist movement emerged using the concepts of liberal imperialism to conjure up phantasmagoric ideas of an inferno that awaited us all in the war on terror. Here were individuals capable of igniting hellfires burning across the globe, conflagrations lit by a redemptive crusade to expand the zone of democratic peace in the name of American security interests.

Were liberal fundamentalism to gain a serious following, it would constitute a "fifth stage" of liberal internationalist thinking. Chapter 3 of this book proposed that changes in the character of liberal internationalist thinking be considered in terms of historical periods. In a long *pre-classical* stage lasting from revolutionary times to the early twentieth century, many Americans saw themselves, thanks to their republican form of government, as "the ark of the liberties of the world" (Melville) and "the last, best hope of earth" (Lincoln). Such a point of view could not be called ideological so far as foreign policy was concerned, however, for from such thinking no grand design emerged for world affairs, nor was any way set forth for America to secure a progressive vision for the rest of humanity.

During Woodrow Wilson's presidency (1913–1921), liberal internationalism entered its second, or *classic* phase, thanks to the president's ability to formulate a general framework for American foreign policy that foresaw making the world safe for democracy by promoting democratic government, economic openness, and multilateral organizations among the great powers of the earth. While we can now speak of a liberal ideology, the failure to put into practice the ideas Wilson formulated during the interwar years meant that the doctrine remained little more than a blueprint for world order, one lacking in tried institutional design.

During and following World War II, FDR and Truman oversaw the development of a third, *hegemonic* stage of this doctrine, using its terms to form the alliances and institutions that eventually won the Cold War. Now for the first time we can speak of liberal internationalism, or Wilsonianism, more seriously as an ideology for world affairs as it gave birth to wide-scale collective action on the part of a significant group of peoples united by a common understanding of mutual interest and purpose. Liberal internationalism nonetheless played a secondary role to containment during these years, in a "two-track" approach to world affairs.

With the collapse in 1989 of the Soviet Empire, and then the Soviet Union itself in 1991, a fourth stage arose, one I have labeled *liberal imperialism*. Its sense of hope was built on the institutions the "free world" had created in its struggle with communism, organizations that were economic, military, and political. Its sense of urgency was based on perceiving America's lone superpower status as a historical window of opportunity to push to achieve for the entire globe the victory of peace through democratic freedom. In the 1990s, we can speak for the first time of liberalism as an ideology in the fullest sense of the term, a worldview that announced its superiority to any other form of political organization whether domestic or international, one that organized itself to use force to pursue its expansion wherever the opportunity or the need arose.

Certainly there is reason to see the Bush Doctrine as the continuation of an American desire to achieve world supremacy, a goal that can be seen as rather fully formed by the time planning for postwar order was begun in Washington in 1944.[1] Yet we must be careful not to diminish the singularity and the magnitude of Bush Doctrine by dwelling overly on its historical or cultural origins. The doctrine must be understood in essential terms as a post-Cold War product of the 1990s and therefore as unique in its formulation of a grand design for American power and purpose. Never had the United States been possessed of an ideological conviction such as now, a worldview that gave it a vision of human history in which Washington was given a dispensation to achieve global hegemony so as to create a stable international order based on freedom, justice, prosperity, and peace.

Given the unanticipated rigors of the Iraq War, the question obviously arises of what the future of liberal internationalism is likely to be in what we might call a fifth stage of its development. One possibility is a retreat to the thinking of the hegemonic or third period of the doctrine, when multilateralism was embraced and the expansion of market democracies was seen as a desirable, but not too likely, occurrence on a grand scale. Francis Fukuyama, a lapsed neoconservative, seemed to be suggesting such a course when he prescribed in 2006 a "realistic Wilsonianism" as the future framework for American thinking about how to act in the world arena after Iraq. So too in 2005, Richard Haass, a man identified with policy-making circles in the Republican Party, brought out a book with an upbeat title, *The Opportunity: America's Moment to Alter History's Course*. At about the same moment, Michael Mandelbaum, a supporter of the Iraq War identified with policy-making circles in the Democratic Party, appeared to be unperturbed by events in the Middle East, for he named a book published late in 2005, *The Case for Goliath: How America Acts as the World's Government in the Twenty-First Century*. In 2002, Mandelbaum had published a book named *The Ideas That Conquered the World*, wherein his first chapter was entitled "Wilson Victorious," while other chapters were devoted to "The Democratic Peace" and "The Triumph of the Market."[2]

How are we to understand such happy talk? Perhaps our hopeful future leaders are concerned that the nation's self-confidence not be endangered at this critical juncture in world events. Rather than nourish a collective trauma, they will salvage what they can from the disaster and bravely move ahead. At any rate, despite the setback in Iraq, America's power does remain supreme. So what better way to think of the future than to retreat to a safer era, to the 1990s. Those were the days that combined prudence derived from realism, and hopes for a better tomorrow derived from liberalism, a period that no longer looks like a "squandered decade," to use a term favored by the neoconservatives, but halcyon days when indeed we had a "holiday from history" (to use another term meant to be one of abuse from this school).

But retreat is unlikely to be so easy. The legacy of the Bush Doctrine weighs heavily on the future. What is likely to occur now that the United States has spurned the United Nations and acted in such a fashion that NATO's unity has been fractured? The continued weakness of the European Union, the thin ice we skate across in terms of the international economy, the rise of China, the likelihood of another serious terrorist attack, and the blow suffered by America's global leadership for getting the United States into the Iraq War—all these issues combined together means that putting Humpty Dumpty together again is probably not possible.

Instead of thinking we may turn back the clock to the happier era of the 1990s, we are more likely to plunge ahead into new territory where past lessons are increasingly irrelevant. One possible scenario worth considering is that liberal internationalism has not been either sobered, nor has it died a natural death, as a result of its miscalculations in the Middle East. Instead, it may be gathering its strength for a fifth phase in its development: the stage of *liberal fundamentalism*.

A first reaction to the suggestion that liberal internationalist ideology could emerge as a form of fundamentalism might well be to insist that liberalism and political fundamentalism of whatever sort are polar opposites: How could the former evolve into the latter? Liberalism promotes individual freedom, an ethic of toleration, a respect for personal choice and group diversity; governments based on the informed consent of the governed. It is a doctrine of reasoned analysis, personal moderation, and limited government to which terms like "extremist" or "fundamentalist" seem totally inappropriate, indeed antithetical. The problem of liberalism—as the neoconservatives would be the first to affirm—is its "live and let live" attitude. How can a liberal order rally its citizens to its defense unto death when in practice it has nourished narrow individual self-interest and loyalties to sub-national groups that may find patriotism a cold substitute for the warmth of their parochial concerns? How could it give birth to fanatics?

Fundamentalism, by contrast, connotes doctrinal orthodoxy, and social and personal conformity enforced by an authoritarian state, sometimes with inquisitional violence. It is the doctrine of the straight and narrow, the thinking of extremists of whatever stripe, dangerous on its face for its intolerance, self-assurance, and sense of evangelical mission. Many fundamentalists do not proselytize. Others, however, seem compelled by the message they carry to move the world to conversion to their ideology. They often are willing to defend their convictions by the sword, acting heroically, even at the expense of what would seem to be their own self-interest.

To a fundamentalist, a liberal may seem egotistical, decadent, and rootless. To the liberal, a fundamentalist may seem dogmatic, closed minded, an enemy to reason and the scientific spirit, the fanatical proponent of utopian violence. The fundamentalist returns the compliment by finding the liberal devoid of spirituality, fearful of death because unsure of life.

In a word, given what appear to be the antibodies built into the genetic code of liberalism to protect it from fundamentalism, how can we believe it could metamorphose into its seeming adversary and polar opposite? Moreover, given the manifest failure of American efforts in the Middle East to bring forth democracy, one might think liberal internationalists had received a healthy lesson from reality and would lower their sights, not be emboldened by events to press on all the harder.

Such a conclusion would be mistaken. There are liberal extremists afoot in the land, liberal Jihadists we might say. In the war on terrorism they are calling for liberalism to become a form of fundamentalism, "a fighting faith," as Peter Beinart calls it,[3] a faith militant, a holy war. If for the moment, the danger of American extremism seems contained, what might happen in the aftermath of a dreadful terrorist attack tomorrow? Could struggle lead a liberal ideology into becoming a form of populist nationalism dedicated to military supremacy every bit the equal in barbarism of its fundamentalist opponent be it fascist secularism or theocratic fundamentalism in the Middle East?

The answer is that it most certainly could.

Profiling the Fundamentalist Argument

There are studies of the "authoritarian personality" as well as of situations that breed fundamentalist movements. Certain personality types, we are told, become fundamentalists, or certain historical conditions give rise by virtue of stressful circumstance to utopian proselytizing and violence. All this is certainly true. However, the focus here, by contrast, will be on the structure of the fundamentalist argument itself, on a system of thinking analyzed independently of the situation that nourishes it or the person who embraces it, on the way ideas are constructed into concepts that, if embraced, lead to extremist thinking and perhaps to militant action. Not sociology or psychology is the method to be used here but logical analysis of ideological structure.

What is striking about extremist thought, whatever the ideology that organizes it, is that its argument proceeds in certain respects under a logic all its own, whose terms need to be understood as a formal paradigm of thinking. Of course, psychological and historical explanations of fundamentalist movements matter. But a unified, comprehensive, adaptable, and directive form of thought bent on orthodoxy, conformism, and utopian violence must be seen in terms of its unique logic. We might compare it to the manner a language is analyzed by linguistics, distinctive in its own terms yet related structurally to other ideologies in the fundamentalist family.[4] Especially when a war of ideas is underway, as the proponents of the Bush Doctrine tirelessly tell us is the case, then how the argument for the invasion of Iraq was *structured ideologically* has to be our central concern.

Such an approach to understanding the horrors of the twentieth century may be found in Hannah Arendt's landmark book, *The Origins of Totalitarianism*, whose first edition appeared in 1951. In her last chapter dedicated to the subject of "ideology and terror," Arendt warns us that fundamentalist systems of thought "are known for their scientific character; they combine the scientific approach with results of philosophical relevance and pretend to be scientific philosophy.... Ideologies pretend to know the mysteries of the whole historical process—the secrets of the past, the intricacies of the present, the uncertainties of the future—because of the logic inherent in their respective ideas."[5] Or again, they "pretend to have found a way to establish the rule of justice on earth.... All laws have become laws of movement."

For ideologies with their claim to "total explanation" to become terrorist, however, they must take flesh in political movements. These movements, in turn, serve the ideology through utopian violence. In Arendt's words:

> Ideologies are always oriented toward history.... The claim to total explanation promises to explain all historical happenings.... Hence ideological thinking becomes emancipated from the reality that we perceive with our five senses, and insists on a 'truer' reality concealed behind all perceptible things, dominating them from this place of concealment and requiring a sixth sense that enables us to become aware of it.... Once it has established its premise, its point of departure, experiences no longer interfere with ideological thinking, nor can it be taught by reality.[6]

Arendt was thinking primarily of the murderous doctrines that legiti-mized Stalin and Hitler when she wrote her book, but her analysis could be extended to other creeds as well. While there are no doubt Arabs and other Muslims who may rightly be called extremist fundamentalists—both terror-ists and totalitarians according to her definition—there should equally be no doubt that many Christians and Jews fall into the same category. But why limit the terms "extremist" or "fundamentalist" to adherents of a religion? Arendt's focus was on communism and fascism, both secular doctrines that attracted extremist fundamentalists to their ranks and led to the deaths of tens of mil-lions of people. And why stop with modern movements, when in centuries past there were ways of thinking capable of mobilizing vast numbers of people for the purpose of a murderous crusade?

Paul Berman offers another example of how the fundamentalist message might be depicted. In what he calls "the ur-myth" of a doctrine whose ulti-mate mission is terror and totalitarianism, he finds that there is:

> always a people of God, whose peaceful and wholesome life had been under-mined. They were the proletariat of the Russian masses (for the Bolsheviks and Stalinists); or the children of the Roman wolf (for Mussolini's Fascists); or the Spanish Catholics and the Warriors of Christ the King (for Franco's Phalange); or the Aryan race (for the Nazis). There were always the subver-sive dwellers in Babylon, who trade commodities from around the world and pollute society with their abominations. They were the bourgeoisie and the kulaks (for the Bolsheviks and Stalinists); or the Freemasons and cosmopoli-tans (for the Fascists and Phalangists) and sooner or later, they were always the Jews....
>
> The subversive dwellers in Babylon were always aided by Satanic forces from beyond and the Satanic forces were always pressing on the people of God from all sides.... [Nevertheless] the reign of God always beckoned in the future. It was going to be the Age of the Proletariat (for the Bolsheviks and Stalinists); or the resurrected Roman Empire (for the Fascists); or explicitly the Reign of Christ the King (for the Spanish Phalange); or the Third Reich, meaning the resurrected Roman Empire in a blond Aryan version (for the Nazis). The com-ing reign was always going to be pure...the purity of unexploited virtue...the purity of Catholic virtue...the biological purity of Aryan blood.[7]

Both Arendt and Berman have offered compelling, if different, depictions of the fundamentalist message. Each sees in such an ideology its conviction that it has perceived the logic of history, its imperviousness to reason, its appeal to the most basic of human emotions including not only fear and hatred but also hope for justice and freedom, its utopian violence, and ultimately its effort to organize itself in terms of totalitarian institutions so that its dogmatic orthodoxy can be enforced and expanded.

I have no quarrel with Arendt or Berman in their definitions, nor in their alarm over the character of totalitarian mind and its origin in fundamentalist doctrine. Nevertheless, I would like to suggest another way of categorizing fundamentalist thinking, one compatible with theirs in that it lends itself to sifting through ideologies to see if they correspond to an extremist template. Let me suggest that whether a fundamentalist doctrine be religious or secular, modern or ancient, it is useful to consider its message as having three basic dimensions, each one of which corresponds to an essential dynamic of the ideology essential for its success in becoming a murderous popular movement.

Political fundamentalism's first dimension rests on the depiction of an *apocalyptic struggle* that in *Manichean* fashion divides the world into good and evil, with the forces of dark on the assault against the forces of light. In portraying the relative position of the sides engaged in conflict, there are no shadows—"moral relativism" or "moral equivalence" is excluded. "Moral clarity" reveals that what is good is good, what is evil is evil. Nor does any doubt exist as to the existential nature of the combat that is enjoined on the forces of light: this is a no-holds-barred fight to the finish, where compromise is excluded because the ultimate stakes involve the very survival of those Berman calls "the people of God" under assault by an all-consuming evil.

The second dimension of fundamentalist doctrine may be called *messianic* or *millennial*: while the ideology cannot promise to triumph, it is confident that in the case of victory a *Golden Age* will ensue. The result is an argument in favor of *utopian violence*, a struggle to the death whose sacrifices are to be redeemed by triumph over iniquity. Whatever the ideology, this period will unquestionably be enlightened and peaceful.

The third dimension of the fundamentalist argument consists in standardized arguments that debunk without investigation any criticism of the apocalyptic or millenarian visions. We may call this the *demagogic aspect* of the ideology, a set of assertions that allows objections to be rejected without being examined in terms of any rules of evidence or procedural right. At first inspection, the demagogic features of fundamentalism may seem to be of relatively minor importance, given that it is the apocalyptic and millenarian visions that require an extended defense and hence enjoy pride of place in analyzing an ideology. But in practice, successful demagoguery is vital to whipping up paranoid and self-righteousness emotional commitment and so maintaining group unity under a creedal banner.

Liberal Fundamentalism?

The question then arises: Could liberal democracy—whose embrace has some-times been referred to as a "secular religion"—lend itself to such a perversion of what for so long has been its progressive, humanist character? Are there forms of the liberal internationalist argument that fit the categories of apoca-lyptic, millennial, and demagogic thought?

Most surely there are. That said, we must be careful not to tar an entire approach to world affairs with a single brush. Just as many liberal interna-tionalists did not become liberal hawks, rejecting as they did the arguments of both the neoconservatives and the neo-Wilsonians, so too most liberal hawks did not, or have not yet, become liberal fundamentalists. Nevertheless, given the intellectual "advances" made by liberal internationalism thanks to the American academy in the 1990s, the structure of the doctrine increasingly lent itself to an extremist formulation. Especially in the aftermath of the shock of 9/11, perpetrated as it was by religious fanatics, we should not be surprised that arguments for a liberal Jihad were soon heard, calls for a holy war that pitted the House of Liberal Democracy against the outside world of barbarian terrorists, as if Armageddon itself were on the horizon.

For the apocalyptic vision of political life basic to fundamentalist thought, a viewpoint that divides the world into the civilized, peaceful "us" (a people of God or of Kant), and the barbaric, warlike "them" (a people of Satan or of Hobbes), no better concept could be fashioned than democratic peace theory. Here we have the liberal imperialist argument developed by the neo-Wilso-nians in the 1990s that the Kantian system that typifies the world of the indus-trial liberal democracies is by virtue of its very nature "post historic," a "zone of peace," a "pacific union." As such, it stands in sharp contrast to the Hobbes-ian world of unbridled violence, still mired in history, whose essential charac-ter makes it not only despotic internally but aggressive externally. According to the terms of this theory, reviewed in some detail in Chapter 4, totalitarian governments especially are to be distrusted, for by the logic of their system they are populist and militarist, centered on a mobilizing political party run according to a cult of the personality and bent on war. Domestic problems among the barbarians may be solved by oppression, or better by projection onto enemies in the liberal world, who by their very nature are fitting scape-goats for the aggressions generated by totalitarian repression.

Aware of the dangers posed to them by the existence of such pathologi-cal political systems, the democracies would be well advised to be on their guard, indeed to take the initiative if the situation seems to warrant it to pre-serve their way of life. The result is a reformulation of theories of "just war," a development that marks as well the resurgence of a form of argument for the superiority of certain cultural forms over others that bears disquieting resem-blance to the race theories of the late nineteenth century that ultimately led to the fascist militarism of the 1930s.[8] Thanks to its pretense to being a science, a development Hannah Arendt warns us especially to mistrust, democratic peace theory bids us take the offensive in the form of a crusade against the barbarians living in the state of nature and necessarily hating us with every fiber of their benighted being.

Secure in the deliberations of neoliberal international jurists in the 1990s, as we saw in the preceding chapter, non-democratic states may be declared illegitimate, pariahs of the international system. When they do so, the emi-nent liberal political philosopher John Rawls can be cited for justification. In fact, a warrant may be issued by the democratic world to attack such govern-ments if they are suspected of gross and systematic violation of human rights or if they are attempting to acquire weapons of mass destruction. Preemptive wars launched against authoritarian or totalitarian states are thus explicitly recognized as justifiable by neoliberal internationalist jurisprudence, a posi-tion made all the more legitimate by democratic peace theory's premature elevation to the status of being a science.

Finally, given the allegedly universal appeal of democratic values, a matter reviewed in Chapter 5, such a crusade was not itself a clash of civilizations for the self-evident reason (for those who subscribed to this logic) that the major-ity of the peoples of the world want to live in liberal democracies and hence are simply being liberated from tyrannical systems of government, culture, and family life on terms that for the most part they themselves already embrace. True, a period of rehabilitation may be necessary in order to remake them into people of freedom and peace. But the "generational commitment" the Bush administration has repeatedly called for to steel us to our responsibilities should in due course make of them what some of their traditional values, as well as the inherent desire for freedom, will allow them to become: peace-lov-ing peoples as we are.

In circumstances of this sort, where absolute evil is on the march, half measures are doomed to failure. Unpleasant means, including torture of the enemy, may be necessary. Our own civil liberties may have to be sacrificed. Who wills the ends, wills the means. Not that such measures are all losses. Manning the battlements may well bring a gain in a patriotic pride in the achievements of liberal democracy and market capitalism. That said, any talk that suggests the nature of the enemy may be more complicated or less demonic than the fundamentalist sees it, is ruled out of order, just as is any suggestion that the character of the forces of light may be less than immaculate.

Hence, the repeated reference in liberal fundamentalist declarations to the "totalitarian," "Islamofascist," "pathological," and "evil" character of the enemy we confront in the Middle East, at the same time that we are the wholly innocent victims. The Dark One's limits, his internal divisions, his likely evolution are not specified, for his compass is presumed to be vast, his threat critical as he tries to establish through a terrorist "World War IV" (sometimes referred to, depending on the author, as World War III) a "global caliphate" that only a fully mobilized America can hope to defeat. Paranoid oversimplification and demonization, with the explicit intent to polarize and militarize conflict, are thus part and parcel of the fundamentalist's stock in trade. Nor is it difficult to find liberal internationalists aplenty, in the neoconservative camp especially, who deal in the currency of such talk with random abandon. The pages to follow will offer Paul Berman, Thomas Cushman, Richard Perle, Charles Krauthammer, William Kristol, and Michael Ledeen as exhibits A, B, C, D, E, and F.[9]

The millennial aspects of democratic peace theory are also abundantly apparent. In the promise of making war unthinkable among market democracies, liberal democratic theory promises a golden era of peace after the struggle against the Great Satan of hostile totalitarian orders has been won. Consider the European Union. With its integrated markets, democratic governments, and multilateral organizations progressively pooling sovereignty, the EU has deepened the character of liberalism in Europe, increased the general prosperity, and made war unthinkable. Similarly, the North American Free Trade Agreement has increasingly consolidated the mutual well-being of Canada, Mexico, and the United States (as well as other countries that participate, or are expected to, in its terms). With the expansion of the European Union and NATO into Central and Eastern Europe, the "pacific union" is enlarging, the zone of democratic peace gaining in strength in the process, Kant's hopes for perpetual peace coming closer and closer to fruition. The result is what we have seen the liberal philosopher John Rawls call reason for hope, enough to reconcile us to a largely cynical and amoral world if the notion of a Society of Peoples can be sustained as a realistic utopia.

The demagogic possibilities of democratic peace theory should be evident as well. Those who deny the dangers that confront us, or who fail to appreciate the messianic promise the doctrine reveals, are lacking in the appropriate level of patriotic commitment or nationalist pride. By an ironic twist, an *internationalist* doctrine in a time of imperialism becomes the basis of a *nationalist* appeal. It is our national responsibility to dominate the world. Not America, but Pax Americana, is for us, as it is for others, the last, best hope of earth.

In such circumstances, how can domestic opposition in such a war of ideas be seen as other than stemming from cowardice and personal selfishness (themselves born of the contradictions of life in liberal democracy that empowers self-interest and mindless hedonism)? These are ills that defy the uplifting moral rewards of commitment to a cause greater than to self, ills that stifle a healthy patriotism, indeed a healthy cosmopolitanism. The highest form of patriotism becomes the highest form of internationalism, personal dedication to a doctrine of freedom, prosperity, and above all peace that will benefit all humanity and redound to the glory of the United States.

In a word, thanks to the developments of neoliberal internationalist ideology in the 1990s into a particular form of imperialism, the way was open to making it into an extremist nationalist creed. The apocalyptic dimension: in the name of defending the civilized world, the barbarian world could come under preemptive assault in a modern day version of just war. The millennial dimension: victory thanks to utopian violence could convert the defeated peoples into liberal democrats given that for the most part they already subscribed to the "universal appeal" of democracy, ushering in a golden age, the era of Kant's perpetual peace, Rawls' Society of Peoples, in all a pacific union of market democracies existing in a zone of democratic peace. The demagogic dimension: woe unto those who questioned such an ambition—theirs would be cowardice and dishonor, not heroism and the joy of living, and perhaps dying, for such a noble cause, worthy of any sacrifice, our honor to carry forward.

Liberal Fundamentalism and the Bush Doctrine

The emergence of liberal fundamentalism from within liberal internationalist discourse remains a minority affair. To date, most liberals have not subscribed to such a perspective, nor am I prepared, given how it has been used to call the Bush Doctrine itself fundamentalist. The danger of the doctrine being interpreted in such a manner most certainly is manifest, but in the president's hands at least, such a potential has not as yet been fully realized. Let us consider, first, the troubling aspects of the president's discourse as it stood through most of 2006, then the reasons not to rush to judgment on his position.

The worrisome features of the president's public remarks are abundant. Take first the Manichean and apocalyptic character of any fundamentalist creed. The tone was there as when the president asserted at West Point in June 2002, "We are in a conflict between good and evil, and America will call evil by its name." In this speech, Bush called for the "moral clarity" to see that like "imperial communism...our enemies are totalitarians, holding a creed of power with no place for human dignity." The American flag, by contrast, "will stand not only for our power, but for freedom. Our nation's cause has always been larger than our nation's defense. We fight, as we always fight, for a just peace—a peace that favors human liberty...we will extend the peace by encouraging free and open societies on every continent." Or as he declared on October 6, 2005, addressing the National Endowment for Democracy (NED), "freedom is once again assaulted by enemies determined to roll back generations of democratic progress. Once again, we're responding to a global campaign of fear with a global campaign of freedom. And once again, we will see freedom's victory."

By the second half of 2006, a confluence of events made President Bush's sense of urgency even more pronounced. The combination of the Israeli invasion of Lebanon in July 2006, designed to crush the Shi'a movement Hezbollah, accentuated the concern that Iran (a major sponsor of Hezbollah) might develop nuclear weapons. The opening of a new session of the UN General Assembly and the fifth anniversary of the attack of 9/11 all took on new meaning as a result of the Iranian question and the national elections to be held in November. The evident Republican strategy to prevail at the urns was to accentuate the sense of danger that Islamic fundamentalism posed to the United States and to rally the country in the name of democratic freedoms at home and abroad.

Accordingly, on September 5, 2006, the president warned that Islamic extremists intended to create a "caliphate [that] would be a totalitarian Islamic empire encompassing all current and former Muslim lands, stretching from Europe to North Africa, the Middle East, and Southeast Asia." Reminding his public that world opinion had failed to respond to Lenin and Hitler as early as they should have, he declared that, "if we don't uphold our duty to support those who are desirous to live in liberty, fifty years from now history will look back on our time with unforgiving clarity and demand to know why we did not act." The solution: "defeating their hateful ideology and spreading the hope of freedom.... So America has committed its influence in the world to advancing freedom and liberty and democracy as the great alternatives to repression and radicalism…freedom is once again contending with the forces of darkness and tyranny…. This is the great ideological struggle of the twenty-first century—and it is the calling of our generation."

At the same time as his speech, the president announced the publication of a National Strategy for Combating Terrorism. Two days later, Bush reiterated his message:

> The war on terror is more than a military conflict—it is the decisive ideological struggle of the twenty-first century. And we're only in its opening stages. To win this struggle, we have to defeat the ideology of the terrorists with a more hopeful vision. So a central element in our strategy is the freedom agenda. We know from history that free nations are peaceful nations. We know that democracies do not attack one another…. We will replace violent dictatorships with peaceful democracies. We'll make America, the Middle East, and the world more secure.

The process of projecting on to one's fundamentalist opponent one's own exaggerated ambitions is one of the dangerous ironies of this confrontation. So in his State of the Union Address of January 2006, for example, Bush declared, "Their aim is to seize power in Iraq and use it as a safe haven to launch attacks against America and the world." As he had already phrased it in October 6, 2005 (and would again on November 11, 2005 and September 5, 2006), "the militants believe that controlling one country will rally the Muslim masses, enabling them to overthrow all moderate governments in the region, and establish a radical Islamic empire that spans from Spain to Indonesia." Yet apparently, Bush had forgotten that in the reasoning that lay behind the invasion of March 2003, his own team had meant to use Iraq in precisely the same way—as the first step in the conversion of what was repeatedly referred to as "the Broader Middle East" to liberal democratic government and open markets. And would the Bush administration have stopped with the Middle East had its crusade proved successful there? "We're facing a radical ideology with inalterable objectives, to enslave whole nations and intimidate the world…they have endless ambitions of imperial domination and they wish to make everyone powerless except themselves," he affirmed on November 11, 2005. Doubtless, the president was correct. But let us ask ourselves: did the neoconservative thinking behind the Bush Doctrine's vision of America's "benevolent hegemony" (what the neoliberals baptized "the zone of democratic peace") amount to a project any less grand?

The result of the combination of concepts flowing from neo-Wilsonian thinking has been to give an edge to the Bush Doctrine that can appropriately be called a millennial message backed by utopian violence. Standing on the bedrock of democratic peace theory analyzed in Chapter 4, the war party repeatedly made references to the golden age of peace that would emerge for all the world once the scourge of totalitarianism in all its forms had been replaced by market democracy. The "single sustainable model for national success: freedom, democracy, and free enterprise" as the National Security Strategy of 2002 put it, was also the framework for world peace. American military primacy, a force "beyond challenge," would be its backing. As the president declared in the letter that prefaced the NSS 2002:

> We will extend the peace by encouraging free and open societies on every continent.... Today the United States enjoys a position of unparalleled military strength and great economic and political influence. In keeping with our heritage and principles...we seek...to create a balance of power that favors human freedom; conditions in which all nations and all societies can choose for themselves the rewards and challenges of political and economic liberty.... America will act against such emerging threats before they are fully formed. We cannot defend America and our friends by hoping for the best...the only path to peace and security is the path of action.

The implication of utopian violence was to be repeated many times, most famously perhaps in Bush's assertion in his Second Inaugural Address of January 2005 that, "it is the policy of the United States to seek and support the growth of democratic movements and institutions in every nation and culture, with the ultimate goal of ending tyranny in our world."

There could be a demagogic dimension to the Bush Doctrine as well. Anti-imperialists have always warned that the empire would consume the republic. None, therefore, would take at face value the president's assertion on January 26, 2005 that, "the nation's commitment to expanding liberty at home" was indelibly linked to "promoting liberty abroad...America is at its best when it leads toward an ideal." Most worrisome, perhaps, was the way the president's liberal internationalist message overlaid the emotions aroused by deep wellsprings of Jacksonian nationalism (a sort that reaches for a gun as it gets out of bed) and fervent evangelical Christian religiosity in the United States.[10] Another serious terrorist attack, a national disaster of some other sort, be it economic or environmental, and the ingredients for a witches' brew have been assembled that might be mixed with dangerously volatile consequences. The Bush Doctrine may yet become in the hands of the White House what it already is understood to be in the minds of some in the war party whose ambitions range even further than "from Spain to Indonesia."

Knowledgeable commentators as different as Kevin Phillips and Madeleine Albright are persuasive when they link the president's pronouncements to Christian evangelical thinking.[11] Phillips points out, for example, that the president's speeches may be "double-coded," meaning that a secular message translates easily into religious thinking. If we superimpose the ostensibly secular democratic peace theory and democratic transition theory developed by social scientists in the 1990s onto Christian evangelical concepts, the way in which they synergistically interact may be disquieting to contemplate. As the president put it speaking before NED on November 6, 2003, "Liberty is both the plan of Heaven for humanity, and the best hope for progress here on Earth."

The stage is set, then, for what is today a relatively mild form of fundamentalism on the president's part to become much more virulent. His evangelical supporters will surely stand with him if it happens. For example, consider the remarks of the Reverend Jerry Falwell, Chancellor of Liberty University, senior pastor of a Baptist congregation in Virginia, whose comments were defended by the Republican-hopeful candidate for president, the Reverend Pat Robertson. Falwell found the attack of 9/11 to be God's punishment on the United States for permitting abortion, gay rights, and the activities of the American Civil Liberties Union: "what we saw on Tuesday [9/11], as terrible as it is, could be minuscule if, in fact, God continues to lift the curtain and allow the enemies of America to give us probably what we deserve."

> The abortionists have got to bear some burden for this because God will not be mocked.... I really believe that the pagans, and the abortionists, and the feminists, and the gays and the lesbians who are actively trying to make an alternative lifestyle, the ACLU, People for the American Way, all of them who have tried to secularize America, I point the finger in their face and say "you helped this happen."[12]

In no meaningful way that I can see is this curse, for that is what it amounts to, essentially different than that cast by a legion of neoconservatives, from Max Boot to Richard Perle, from William Kristol to Robert Kagan, from Paul Wolfowitz to Michael Ledeen. These neoconservatives have proclaimed over and over again (and unlike Falwell and Robertson never have rescinded their comments) that it was the culpable weakness of the years from Bush senior to Clinton that invited the attack of 9/11. The curse of history on "weakness," itself the product of a lack of courage and "moral clarity," was the terrorist attack 9/11. The curse of the evangelicals and that of the secular theorists may be melded into one as the fundamentalist steam engine gains power.

Yet for all the evidence that points to the potential for the Bush Doctrine becoming a fundamentalist charter to wage "World War III or IV" (depending on the alarmist), as of late 2006 we had not yet arrived at that point. One litmus test was that the president had not indicted all of Islam as our enemy. "Islam is Peace," Bush entitled his remarks on September 17, 2001. Thereafter, the president consistently took pains to differentiate the small minority of fanatic Muslim terrorists from the mainstream— denouncing "the perversion by a few of a noble faith into an ideology of terror and death," as he put it characteristically in his State of the Union Address in January 2006. Or as he responded on ABC News on October 26, 2004, when asked if he thought Muslims and Christians worship the same God: "I think we do. We have different routes of getting to the Almighty."[13]

In saying this, the president set himself clearly apart from many of the extremist religious voices in the United States supporting his war, as well from secular liberal fundamentalists, all who sounded convinced that our enemy was ultimately an undifferentiated diabolical religion, aggravated by oppressive forms of statecraft, from which anti-Western terror must necessarily flow. For example, on October 6, 2002, *60 Minutes* aired a program where Jerry Falwell announced, "Mohammed was a terrorist." On January 13, 2003, the Christian Coalition of America released a survey (presumably of its own members) in which 91.5 percent of the respondents found that Islam was not "a divine religion," 88 percent found that Islam was not a "religion of peace," and 75 percent supported war with Iraq. Or again, on May 14, 2003, the Christian Broadcasting Network reported approvingly on a "messianic pastor who works and prays for reconciliation between Jews and Arabs" whose conclusion, nonetheless, was that, "there is no provision in the Bible for a Palestinian state. 'Very simply, if we look into the scripture, we will find no such reality, no such promise.'" Consider, finally, the statement by Billy Graham's son and apparent successor, Franklin, saying in the aftermath of 9/11, Islam was "wicked, violent, and not of the same God."[14] If statements such as these are the litmus test of what it means to be a fundamentalist, then George W. Bush was most certainly not in their ranks.

In the same mode, a check of the conservative Human Events Book Service in April 2006, found a long series of books being advertised for its readers, which presumably did not include the president. Among its selections, surely none of which would have been endorsed by Bush:

- *The Politically Incorrect Guide to Islam and the Crusades* by Robert Spencer, described by HEBS as follows:

  > When PC propagandists assure us that jihadist terror doesn't reflect "true" "peaceful" Islam, they're not only wrong, they're dangerous— because they lull America and the West into letting their guard down against their mortal enemy. And not only do the self-appointed "experts" lie elaborately and persistently about Islam—they have also replaced the truth about Christian Europe and the Crusades with an all-pervasive historical fantasy that is designed to make you ashamed of your own culture and heritage—and thus less determined to defend it.

- *Defeating Jihad, How the War on Terror May Yet Be Won In Spite of Ourselves* by Serge Trifkovic
- *Eurabia* by Bat Ye'or (a volume on the Arab takeover of most of Western Europe)
- *The Myth of Islamic Tolerance* by Robert Spencer, ed.
- *Islamic Imperialism: A History* by Efraim Karsh
- *The West's Last Chance* by Tony Blankley
- *Holy War on the Home Front* by Harvey Kushner
- *War Footing: 10 Steps America Must Take to Prevail for the Free World* by Frank Gaffney[15]

These examples could be multiplied many times over to the same end: providing evidence that fundamentalists trade in demonizing an entire culture toward an effort to polarize the situation, leading to a final conflict that could engulf the planet.

At times, as on June 28, 2005, the president did indeed label in a blanket manner this country's enemies as terrorists who "murder in the name of a totalitarian ideology that hates freedom, rejects tolerance, and despises all dissent. Their aim is to remake the Middle East in their own grim image of tyranny and oppression—by toppling governments, by driving us out of the region, and by exporting terror." Indeed, in a period covering October–November 2005, President Bush used especially harsh terms to describe apparently anyone who opposed the American conquest of Iraq, favoring the term "evil" above all others. This said, well through 2006, the president never approached the rhetoric of his warmongering Christian evangelical supporters, just as he also resisted neoconservative and liberal hawk fundamentalist urgings that the United States in effect be mobilized root and branch, day and night, for a struggle without an evident end in which our most cherished values and institutions were in imminent danger. That he sounded the alarm is without question, but that he promoted paranoia and panic, or called for purges in places high and low, most certainly was not the case.

Time will tell. For the moment, while President Bush has been roundly accused of walling himself off from his critics, he has not been charged with conducting witch-hunts against his opponents in ways that could be called demagogic. To the contrary, his personal manner has been determinedly correct, often to the regret of his fundamentalist supporters who apparently might like to see the critics of their war lose many of their civil liberties. "I will never question the patriotism of somebody who disagrees with me," the president declared on August 20, 2006, "we'll continue to speak out, in a respectful way, never challenging somebody's love for America when you criticize their strategies or their point of view." To be sure, Homeland Security and the Patriot Act may be setting the stage for what eventually could be a different reality. As we have seen, in the run-up to the fifth anniversary of 9/11, the November elections, and United Nations deliberations over Iran's nuclear program, the president escalated his rhetoric, which was amplified even more by Vice President Cheney and Secretary of Defense Rumsfeld as they joined the president in declaring the need for victory in Iraq and denouncing the danger of Iran's program of nuclear development. Cheney and Rumsfeld also dealt much more harshly with domestic critics of administration policy than did the president himself.[16] As noted in Chapter 2, by this point writers such as David Cole, Mark Danner, Elizabeth Drew, Frank Rich, and Seymour Hersh had been warning for some time about the threat of American imperialism to the country's civil liberties. Despite these warning signs, to date, in my opinion we are not at the point when we can claim a fundamentalist assault on traditional liberties.

The question was how the Democrats would rise to the challenge in the elections of 2006 and 2008. If they tried to outbid the Republicans as the war party, they were likely to fail, for how could one outdo the president's rhetoric? If they failed to back the president, they could be labeled "appeasers," much like those, President Bush reminded his listeners, who refused to take Lenin and Hitler seriously when something might have been done to crush them in their infancy.

Whatever the desire of the Democratic electorate by the fall of 2006 to find a quick way out of Iraq, one possibility was that the Democrats would pledge to complete what the Republicans had begun by more aggressive stewardship of the national interest. Writing in *The Weekly Standard* on August 14, 2006, William Kristol broached the idea of "creating a broader and deeper governing party, with Lieberman Democrats welcomed into the Republican fold, just as Scoop Jackson Democrats became Reaganites in the 1980s." Perhaps, Kristol suggested, President Bush could name Joseph Lieberman secretary of defense in early 2007, after which he could run as the Republican vice presidential nominee in the 2008 elections.

Whereas Kristol would have the Republicans co-opt hawkish Democrats, Thomas L. Friedman would have the Democrats realize the Republican agenda by showing that the administration's rhetoric was hollow. Democrats could prosecute the war more effectively. On August 16, 2006, writing in the *New York Times*, Friedman declared the Republican Party to be "a fraud:...you will the ends, but you won't will the means." By September 8, Friedman was suggesting a "national unity coalition," apparently under Democratic leadership, so as to do what "Bush-Cheney-Rumsfeld" had failed to do: "They told us we are in the fight of our lives against a new Islamic fascism...[they] summoned us to D-Day and gave us the moral equivalent of the invasion of Panama."

What none of these hawks, be they Democrats or Republicans, would admit was that the invasion of Iraq had been a disastrous mistake, surely the greatest error made by deliberate political calculation in the history of American foreign policy. But for the war party, this was water under the bridge. Now the president bid the country to press forward to victory, an undertaking whose cost and duration had no apparent limit, while he coupled his determination with asserting that Iran would not be permitted to develop advanced nuclear technology. Many leading Democrats could be found at his side.

Still, if the danger of liberal fundamentalism in Washington was genuine, one should not exaggerate the danger. Just as one should not confuse President Bush with his evangelical Christian followers, so he was not identical with his neoconservative supporters either. For example, in a large-scale "Symposium" published in *Commentary* in November 2005, a number of neoconservatives weighed in on the question of whether the president was truly living up to the terms of the doctrine that bore his name. Here was a collection of fundamentalists not at all certain that President Bush was still their man.[17]

Thus, for Max Boot, the doctrine "has been largely successful." That said, Boot reminded his readers that Iran and North Korea remained to be dealt with—the other two members of the "axis of evil"—worried about Syria, and was bothered that "Pakistan, Egypt and Saudi Arabia appear not to have gotten the message."

For Eliot Cohen, not enough had been done to alert us to the dangers of Islam as a religion: "Anodyne formulations like 'a perversion of a great religion' or 'a few extremists' do not capture the power of this movement. There is a great need for a sober, detailed and educated rhetoric about whom we are fighting. Happy talk to the Muslim world about what nice people Americans are is not only no substitute—it fools only those who utter it."

Frank Gaffney agreed. In the "global conflict imposed upon us by a dangerous totalitarian ideology that has properly come to be known as Islamofascism...the administration has largely refused to go beyond euphemisms like 'terror' and 'an evil ideology.' The unwillingness to declare Islamofascism the force that drives our foes" means that we have not taken on "the nation that is arguably most responsible for the worldwide spread of Islamofascism: Saudi Arabia."

So too Robert Kagan lamented that the White House "has not applied its 'doctrine' very broadly or systematically...for instance to North Korea and Iran....the administration has almost entirely ignored the quashing of what little democracy remains in Russia and it no longer makes more than the barest pretense of caring about the lack of democratic reform in China." Kagan opened his statement asking, "Is there a Bush Doctrine?" He concluded it asking, "whether I support the Bush Doctrine and an expansive vision of America's role in the world. I do. The question remains whether there is a Bush Doctrine to support. The answer is still unknown."

William Kristol's contribution to the symposium closely paralleled Kagan's. Kristol was unsure of the future trajectory of the doctrine and pointed again to lands where it needed to be exercised, including Syria, Saudi Arabia, China, North Korea, and Iran.

By the time of this symposium, it was already becoming clear that the question of the moment was the proliferation of nuclear technology to Iran. Richard Perle sounded the alarm most clearly: "While Tehran and Damascus work hard to undermine the fledgling Iraqi democracy and American influence in the region, the administration dithers.... Soliciting cooperation from duplicitous Iraqi Baathists, making deals with Kim Jong Il, indecision on Iran, seemingly limitless patience with Syria's support for the insugency in Iraq, pretending the Saudis are our friends...these are the products of your tax dollars at work. A cast of thousands of bureaucrats has been blunting or deflecting the president's best instincts."

Such fundamentalist citations from the ranks of the neoconservatives could be multiplied but only to the same end message: chief architects of the Bush Doctrine could lament what they saw as its faulty implementation in the hands of the president. Was this welcome evidence that the president was not the extremist many of his closest supporters were?

The supreme test remained to be passed sometime later with Iran. When in the spring of 2006, Secretary of State Rice announced that "the United States understands that Iran is not Iraq," Kristol framed the matter for many neoconservatives: "Much of the U.S. government no longer believes in, and is no longer acting to enforce, the Bush Doctrine…the United States of America is in retreat."[18]

With the backing of the Bush administration for the Israeli invasion of Lebanon in July 2006 all of this was to change. On July 31, *The Weekly Standard* published three pieces in praise of the president. But the question remained: Would Washington conduct a sufficiently vigorous campaign to deny nuclear weapons technology to Iran if that meant the use of armed force? On this question hung the answer to the relationship of the neoconservatives and the Bush administration in the fall of 2006. However comforting the president's statements might sometimes be, it was actions, not words, that ultimately would count.

In sum, by late 2006, if elements of the Bush Doctrine could be seen as seeding fundamentalist thinking, nonetheless the apocalyptic, millenarian, and demagogic features of the doctrine simply did not amount to an ideology of utopian violence with the implication of an increasingly authoritarian—much less totalitarian—government at the helm of such an effort. Consequently, we must look elsewhere to see liberal fundamentalism calling today for Jihad, the exercise of seemingly unlimited utopian violence in a struggle against absolute evil for the sake of a tomorrow of freedom and peace.

Christian fundamentalists and right-wing Zionists may be found aplenty to fill the bill. Yet to date no one has fulfilled the role of providing such an example so well as the secular leftist Paul Berman, who sees his mission as the quashing of fundamentalist extremism in the name of liberty through unrelenting warfare justified by the terms of what is immediately perceptible as a liberal Jihad.

The Case of Paul Berman

On the eve of the invasion of Iraq in March 2003, Paul Berman published *Terror and Liberalism,* widely agreed to be one of the most influential statements in the liberal imperialist canon at the time and still today. In his short, impassioned book, Berman describes in apocalyptic terms the menace facing the West in ways that link terrorism to two kinds of evil emanating from the Middle East. One is Islamic fundamentalism, of which the Taliban or the

Iranian Revolution could be expressions, although Berman is more interested in the teaching of Sayyid Qutb and his influence on Wahabi religious thought in Saudi Arabia. The other is the secular totalitarian system set up by Saddam Hussein in Iraq. Different though these two sources of terror might be—one of religious fanaticism, one of the secular state despotism—both have demonstrated a capacity to inflict enormous human suffering. Berman's reaction is to call for a progressive campaign on the part of liberal democrats to combat what he sees as these combined dangers, taking the battle to the enemy so as to give rise to a "new liberal birth of freedom…a chance to undo the whole of Muslim totalitarianism."

Given Berman's distance from the corridors of power—he identifies himself as to the left of the Democratic Party and expresses little but contempt for the Bush administration for not making the liberating cast of its invasion of Iraq a more prominent feature—he has the authority of someone who is not supporting the invasion for some ulterior motive. And Berman has a talent for writing. His take no hostages, give no quarter style of confronting the seriousness of the challenge from the Middle East—multifaced and root and branch—conveys a powerful emotion capable of being readily transfused into an America traumatized by the attack of 9/11—wondering why it happened and what could be done to end the danger.

Perhaps the most compelling aspect of Berman's book is that it evokes so powerfully the human capacity for evil. Genocide or enslavement—such has seemed throughout history to be the story of the human race when one group with power and a clear-set identity confronts another. No civilization has been spared—either from an existential challenge to its existence from outside forces, or from groups within itself calling for the destruction or total domination of others. To pretend otherwise—to act as if the human capacity for evil were not a continuing threat today, even after the victories over fascism and communism in the terrible struggles of the twentieth century—would be to ignore the most basic lesson that history can teach us. On this point, Berman is surely right.

Berman's book thus touches a responsive chord in many hearts. We know humanity's capacity for evil from the events of the twentieth century. Apocalypses happen. We have been witness to the barbarity of the attack of 9/11, we know of assaults launched by Muslim terrorists in Israel and Russia, and against each other as Sunnis especially have persecuted Shi'a. We are aware as well of violence stemming from the basest of motives within the Muslim world itself—most notably in the prolonged war launched by Saddam Hussein against Iran in 1980, but also in the excesses of the Iranian Revolution and the Taliban rule in Afghanistan against their own people. At first reading, then, Berman's call to arms makes intuitive sense—we must not lower our guard and relax on our laurels after the travails of the twentieth century. Today's challenge comes from the Middle East.

Just as Pearl Harbor had finally made the American public understand we could not avoid war with fascism, so 9/11 should have resolved doubts as to the danger extremism in the Middle East posed to the liberal democratic community. But to Berman's dismay (though not completely to his surprise), many do not see the handwriting on the wall. Hesitations about the Iraq War are bad enough in the United States, but Berman's particular contempt is reserved for our European allies. So he compares Europe to a "comfortable burgher, blinking stupidly and wondering about dinner." "Keep your head down," would be their motto:

> Sweden symbolized the left-wing version, and Switzerland, the right-wing version.... And yet, this sort of loftiness was, in the end, hard to distinguish from the base, cowardly, greedy, and self-absorbed motives described variously by Nietzsche and his heirs. The Swedes and the Swiss achieved wonderful things with their own societies...but the survival of both places owed entirely to the fighting spirit of other people. During the years of Nazi triumph, Sweden and Switzerland played roles that were, all in all, contemptible. Neutrality seemed to them better than defeat.... But they could hope that other people would ensure that Hitler lost. And other people did. Entire Polish cities fought virtually to the last man so that Sweden and Switzerland could go on perfecting their social systems.[19]

Here is Berman as liberal internationalist demagogue. To oppose the war is to be like the Swedes or the Swiss confronted with Hitler. The challenge for Berman is to rally the democratic world to the struggle against a new form of evil manifest in the terrorism of the Middle East, whether it be of the religious sort that has struck Israel, Russia, the United States and places in Western Europe (not to speak of it acting internally within the Middle East), or of the sort wherein despots like Saddam subject their own populations to exactions rare in the annals of human history.

Berman sees the task as daunting. As Francis Fukuyama had pointed out in the early 1990s, liberal society breeds a sort of anti-heroism, a me-first-ism, a confidence that negotiated compromise is possible, an empathy with the position of the other, an "I'm okay, you're okay" outlook—a set of habits and values that can minimize the sacrifices called for in the war on terror. In a word, liberals are weak, and in their weakness contemptible. Consequently, Berman understands his mission as mobilizing public opinion for the struggle to come, enlisting himself in the "war of ideas," "a war of persuasion" to be fought by reminding the liberal democratic world of the glory of its heritage and pointing out the seriousness of the menace it once again faced. And in this struggle he finds the Bush administration quite wanting because it has not waged the war of ideas powerfully enough. It has not been as militantly committed for reasons of high moral purpose as Berman the high priest of liberal fundamentalism demands.[20]

Should the challenge be embraced, Berman promises a millennial outcome, the third dimension of fundamentalist thinking. On the one hand, the West itself could be redeemed by a heroic defense of its ideals and institutions. Here is the message Berman propagates in 2005 in his book *Power and the Idealists*. Still imbued with the need to recognize the global danger of totalitarianism despite the end of the Cold War, our author divides the world into "resisters" and "collaborationists." It does not take much imagination to guess on which side the supporters and the opponents of the Iraq War stand in this simplistic dichotomy.[21]

Berman readily imagines the bright future that beckons once the forces of American imperialism have lifted from the backs and minds of the Muslim world the tangled forces that had for so long held them back from the promise of freedom. In a breathtaking, utopian affirmation of the promise the American conquest of the Middle East might make true, he writes:

[We need to be a force] devoted to a politics of human rights and especially of women's rights, across the Muslim world, a politics of ethnic and religious tolerance, a politics against racism and anti-Semitism; no matter how inconvenient that may seem to the Egyptian media and the House of Saud; a politics against the manias of the ultra-right in Israel, too, no matter how much that might enrage the Likud and its supporters; a politics of secular education, of pluralism and law across the Muslim world; a politics against obscurantism and superstition; a politics to out-compete the Islamists and Baathi on their left; a politics to fight against poverty and oppression; a politics of authentic solidarity for the Muslim world, instead of the demagogy of cosmic hatred. A politics, in a word, of authentic solidarity for the Muslim world, instead of the demagogy of cosmic hatred. A politics, in a word, of liberalism, a "new birth of freedom".…. The reality of the Terror War…[is that it is a] clash of ideologies…a chance of encouraging a new liberal birth of freedom…a chance to do what had been done in Germany, Italy, and Japan…. A chance to undo the whole of Muslim totalitarianism.

On this topic, the war of ideas, I'm happy to be a laptop general.[22]

The prospect of the degree of violence necessary for the pursuit of this utopian ambition is unsettling to contemplate. The reader may not be surprised to learn that Paul Berman has repeatedly expressed himself as distrustful of President Bush's ability to lead such a crusade. In his writings of early 2003, he lambasted the White House for its failure to hoist high enough the banner of freedom under which the invasion would be led. Writing in early 2005, Berman somewhat modified his views, finding that by late 2003 the president had sharpened his rhetoric, raising higher the standard of freedom. But by late 2005, Berman was once again disappointed in the level of the president's determination to promote the doctrine that bore his name. Alarmed that "the administration has launched public-relations programs in the Muslim world, which have been laughable," he lamented that Bush "has sometimes recast the ideological battle in terms that might seem appropriate to a rustic Christian preacher, all of which suggests a somewhat casual or non-committal attitude." What Berman championed instead was the effort "to mount a campaign of ideas—a campaign to identify the totalitarian doctrines and expose their flaws...on the eye-catching and ambitious scale that our current predicament would seem to require."[23]

The irony, of course, is that Berman's version of liberal internationalism is very much of the form of the fundamentalism he denounces. Absolute evil (Middle Eastern in inspiration) confronts the people of God (the liberal democratic world). Because of hedonism, selfishness, and moral relativism (born of boorish liberals), the people of freedom refuse adequately to defend themselves. An enlightened elite (Berman at their head) calls them to the battle stations invoking, to repeat his charge, "the chance to undo the whole of Muslim totalitarianism" with as result "a new birth of freedom." All the ingredients of fundamentalism are up-front and present: the apocalyptic vision, the messianic promise, the demagogic attacks on those who beg to differ. As the well-known psychiatrist Robert Jay Lifton perceptively noted (although not with reference to Berman):

> [W]e are experiencing what could be called an apocalyptic face-off between Islamist forces, overtly visionary in their willingness to kill and die for their religion, and American forces claiming to be restrained and reasonable but no less visionary in their projection of a cleansing war-making and military power. Both sides are energized by an intense idealism; both see themselves as embarked on a mission of combating evil in order to redeem and renew the world; and both are ready to release untold levels of violence to achieve that purpose.[24]

Is what Berman calls for so different from the evil he claims we face? Our fundamentalism will respond to theirs. They have "death cults," Berman tells us, whereas we will presumably have Nietzschean "cults of the will to power" ably summed up in the Bush Doctrine, to which Berman does not subscribe because it does not pitch the crusade high enough in the confrontation between "a new liberal birth of freedom" and absolute evil. Should we follow Berman's counsel and mobilize ourselves in the populist, nationalist militarist fashion he favors—with a healthy dose of religious blessing, given the character of the American political system and the two parties increasingly becoming as one—the empire he calls for may devour the republic whose virtues he claims to want to serve and expand to others.

Consider the extraordinary breadth and depth of the crusade Berman proposes to lead. In the name of his progressive ideals, Berman would ride roughshod over the lives of hundreds of millions. Not only are governments and economies to be remade, but the very stuff of culture will be reworked. This is "a clash of ideologies...the war between liberalism and the apocalyptic and phantasmagorical movements that have risen up against liberal civilization" he tells us. Again and again, he returns to the emancipation of women, calling the Afghan War "the first feminist war in all of history."[25] Yet, whatever the evils of the orders he would destroy, how can he be confident that the chaos his wars of liberation would unleash would not breed more evil still?

As the Iraq War broke, Paul Berman became a Horseman of the Apocalypse. His thinking is fundamentalist, first, by virtue of the stark light in which it presents the alternatives—its apocalyptic and Manichean features—in which the children of light are under siege from the forces of evil. It is fundamentalist, second, by virtue of its confident call to arms—its millenarian and messianic appeals combined with utopian violence—that imagines here and now a world of perpetual peace and freedom. And it is fundamentalist, third, given its demagogic assertions thoroughly denigrating anyone (especially in his book the pusillanimous Europeans) who fails to enlist in what promises to be an undertaking of a kind perhaps never seen before in human history as it involves not simply conquering vast numbers of foreign peoples but also converting them root and branch to different institutions and practices based on cultural assumptions Berman himself knows to be unfamiliar in the Middle East and beyond. Recall Berman's "ur-myth" leading to fundamentalist terror cited above. Has he not, by his own definition, adopted the character of his enemy?

After his book *Terror and Liberalism* was in press, and to sustain the faith in the days before the war, Berman published a piece in the *New Republic* in which he turned for inspiration in the battle to come to Abraham Lincoln and the Gettysburg Address. Here Lincoln saw beyond the horror of the battlefield to the hope that the sacrifices there would give rise to a new birth of freedom. In Berman's words, Lincoln:

> chose to radicalize the U.S. republic because he knew that, in order to survive, liberal democracy needed to arouse among its own citizens a greater commitment than ever before to the cause of universal freedom—in fact, an absolute commitment, which could only mean a commitment unto death…. Liberal democracy was going to endure…by taking on grander and more radical goals than ever before—by becoming more revolutionary, not less; by offering, in some form or another, liberty and solidarity to the entire world.[26]

For a last time, let us invoke Berman against himself. Writing a review of Francis Fukuyama's book *America at the Crossroads* in 2006, Berman lashed out at the neoconservatives, who, he claimed, "all along indulged a romance of the ruthless—an expectation that small numbers of people might be able to play a decisive role in world effects, if only their ferocity could be unleashed… this very weird and self-defeating combination of idealism and brass knuckles." Yet who better to represent what he calls "the romance of the ruthless" more than once in this essay than Berman himself? As if to underscore his self-deception, Berman concluded his piece explaining why people are eager to join the Islamic Jihad.

> They are eager for ideological reasons, exactly as in the case of fascists and other totalitarians of the past. These people will be defeated only when their ideologies begin to seem exhausted, which means that any struggle against them has to be, above all, a battle of ideas—a campaign to persuade entire mass movements around the world to abandon their present doctrines in favor of more liberal ones…the most important problem of all [is] the problem of murderous ideologies and how to combat them.[27]

Berman is right, to be sure, but we might understand his point more broadly: in hands such as his, the murderous ideology that must be struggled against in the battle of ideas is not only Islamic terrorism, but liberal imperialist fundamentalism as well, whose capacity for utopian violence has not been better expressed than by Paul Berman himself. If the "war of ideas" that he repeatedly calls for is to begin, what better place than with the apocalyptic, millenarian, demagogic fundamentalism of the man whose self-described mission, ironically enough, is to root out just this kind of thinking?

The Fundamentalist International

Paul Berman is far from an isolated example of the rise of liberal internationalist fundamentalism expressed in terms any student of Jihadist thinking would immediately recognize as a form of extremism leading to utopian violence. His message is frequently cited as a statement of purpose that has enlisted considerable support for the war. Consider, as one example, a 2005 volume of twenty-four essays edited by Thomas Cushman, a professor of sociology at Wellesley College and editor-in-chief of the *Journal of Human Rights*. In "Terror and Liberalism", Berman called for the creation of "a Third Force neither realist or pacifist—a Third Force devoted to the politics of human rights"—and Cushman offers Berman's statement cited at length above as to how he would "undo the whole of Muslim totalitarianism" as his inspiration in editing his own book.[28]

Cushman announces that "the contributors to this volume represent the voices of a Third Force of liberal internationalism. They understand the limitations of the current system of global governance, which tolerates gross violations of human rights.... For most of the authors, the liberal internationalist case for the war was not made strong enough by the Bush administration." Although Cushman concedes that the invasion on the grounds of destroying Saddam's weapons of mass destruction proved "empirically unfounded," he recites at length the despot's crimes against humanity and concludes, "The war can be seen as morally legitimate on grounds of basic human rights as embodied in the Universal Declaration of Human Rights, which is the ethical basis for the international world order."[29]

Cushman relies on Berman to articulate the apocalyptic and millenarian dimensions of fundamentalist thinking to which he too subscribes. His own special aptitude is to lampoon in a demagogic fashion critics of the war. He declares that his "volume serves as an important historical document...one that remains principled and idealistic rather than descending into a vortex of cynical realism, appeasement, moral indifference, tolerance of tyrants, and the denial of human rights." Without offering a single documented example, Cushman assures us that his book will offer, "pointed critiques of the liberal left opposition to the war, much of which is contradictory, reductionistic, logically flawed, or excessively emotional, and irrational. Even the most sober and reflective critics of the war occupied a stage that also displayed demonstrators toting placards of Bush with a Hitler mustache, waving Iraqi and Cuban flags, and passing out copies of the *Protocols of the Elders of Zion*."

Cushman even goes so far as to cite Orwell's line that "pacifism is objectively profascist." Hence, "If one agrees with Paul Berman that the West is at war with the forces of Islamofascism, then those who do not recognize this point or take it seriously are, objectively, part of the problem of fighting successfully against it."[30] That is, they are traitors.

Others have come by their own lights to conclusions similar to Berman's. Take the case of Richard Perle and David Frum, both neoconservatives housed at the American Enteprise Institute, the former influential in the Bush Pentagon, the latter for a time a speechwriter for the president. In a book with the ambitious title *An End to Evil: How to Win the War on Terror,* they declare that "our survival as a nation" is in the balance: "For us terrorism remains the great evil of our time and the war against this evil, our generation's great cause.... There is no middle way for Americans. It is victory or Holocaust."[31]

An End to Evil contains many more such apocalyptic statements, all to one end: a massive threat faces the United States against which the only choice is victory or death. No distinctions can be made as to the variety of dangers confronting us. Each and all they must be destroyed. Various internal elements of our way of life are undercutting our resolve. While lifting the state of siege is possible, it will take a tremendous effort, to be redeemed by the scope of the eventual triumph. The book is replete with apocalyptic assertions that may be read as deliberate efforts to demonize the other, polarizing and heightening emotions for an eventual Armageddon.[32]

> [I]f you are an Iranian mullah clutching on to billions in stolen oil wealth, or a Saudi imam terrified of the loss of your congregants, or a Palestinian would-be dictator rallying your people to suicide instead of trade and cooperation—the excitement and appeal of American life is your deadliest enemy....
>
> [T]he terrorists espouse an ideology of conquest just as the Nazis and Soviets did; and as we defeated the Nazis and the communists by championing freedom not only for ourselves but also for Germans and Russians, so we must now do the same for the Islamic people who are both terrorism's prime constituency and its principal victims.

If our authors turn to what they label "militant Islam," they nonetheless make no effort to separate this branch of the Muslim world from the rest. Instead we are told "the roots of Muslim rage are to be found in Islam itself." "Mullahs preach jihad from the pulpits of mosques from Bengal to Brooklyn." The fact that neither Iraq nor Syria was under the control of militant Islam but instead of secular forces, or that theocratic arguments among the Shi'a do not resemble those among the Sunni, does not detain them for a minute. And the hydra-headed danger is proliferating everywhere including "a growing infrastructure of extremism inside this country and in Canada." Virtually all American Muslim religious leaders and organizations are suspect. And if Islam is itself not enough to create this mortal danger, then the barbaric oppression of Middle Eastern governments may be invoked to give rise to "an enraged populace ready to transmute every frustration in its frustrating daily life into a fanatical hatred of everything 'un-Islamic.' This fetid environment nourishes the most venomous vermin in the Middle East swamp."[33]

If more proof is needed of Islam's fallen state, Perle and Frum invoke the status of Muslim women. They devote an entire section to this, concluding: "Women's oppression contributes to terror.... A society that treats women like slaves will teach its men all the cruelty and violence of the slaveholder."[34]

Given such a threat, the response must be appropriately bold. In addition to dealing with Hamas and Hezbollah, the countries the United States may need to attack, according to Perle and Frum, would appear to include Libya, Syria, Saudi Arabia, Iran, and North Korea. In later pages, Pakistan, China, Russia, and the United Nations all come up for concern as well.

Given such a vast apocalyptic menace, what possible hope can we have for salvation? Exactly like Berman, Perle and Frum are silent on just how their remedy—they propose "democracy"—will provide a solution to a challenge of the magnitude they have depicted, although they do discuss the matter briefly. Their one concrete idea comes in the form of regretting that the incarnation of the hopes of the Iraqi people in Ahmad Chalabi was sabotaged by the CIA and the State Department. The lesson they draw is that these bureaucracies need to be purged, for they committed the invasion's "most serious mistake" when they acted for "the pettiest of reasons" because "he was not a puppet they could easily control."[35] Yet despite the magnitude of the adversities we face, our authors nonetheless provide a millenarian promise, a calm after the storm, in the very last lines of their book:

> A world at peace; a world governed by law; a world in which all people are free to find their own destinies. That dream has not yet come true, it will not come true soon, but if it ever does come true, it will be brought into being by American armed might and defended by American might, too. America's vocation is not an imperial vocation. Our vocation is to support justice with power. It is a vocation that has earned us terrible enemies. It is a vocation that has made us, at our best moments, the hope of the world.[36]

As for those who oppose their viewpoint, Perle and Frum are character-istically demagogic. Never once are the critics given a single serious reason for their opposition to the war. Instead they apply typical masculine terms of abuse, finding those opposed to the war are "losing their nerve" or "quivering." They doubt such critics' "patriotism or good faith." They blame "lax multicul-turalism" for permitting Muslims to organize unsupervised and unchallenged in the United States. They take out after the French, who showed not only "cow-ardice" but "gleefully smashed up an alliance [NATO] that had kept the peace of the world for half a century." Why? Given all we have done for France and Europe in the twentieth century, "Now at least they could be free of the United States and the horrible burden of gratitude." Their remedy? That Washington support the expansion of the European Union so as to dilute French influence, then "force European governments to choose between Paris and Washington" while "we must do our utmost to preserve our British ally's strategic indepen-dence from Europe." Their ultimate demagogic insult: critics who tie the war to concern for Israeli security thanks to "the myth of the neoconservative cabal in the halls of power in Washington" are by implication anti-Semites.[37]

Yet another influential neoconservative fundamentalist is Charles Kraut-hammer. Rallying the troops for Iraq in February 2004 at the American Enter-prise Institute, Krauthammer waxed apocalyptic, announcing the struggle with "Arab-Islamic totalitarianism, both secular and religious" to be "existen-tial...a fight to the end—extermination, or even better, conversion." Sound-ing very much like Berman, he announced that we must get to the "roots of Arab-Islamic nihilism. September 11 felt like a new problem, but for all its shock and surprise, it is an old problem with a new face...a return to history, the twentieth-century history of radical ideologies and existential enemies." In fact, this time the challenge may be graver still: "On September 11, we saw the face of Armageddon again, but this time with an enemy that does not draw back. This time the enemy knows no reason."[38]

Writing late in 2004 in answer to criticism from Francis Fukuyama that he exaggerated the degree of threat posed to the United States by Islamic terror-ists, Krauthammer responded by escalating his rhetoric. If his fault had been to say that Islamic terrorism was as great a threat as America had faced with Hitler or Stalin, Krauthammer agreed he was wrong—such an equivalence would be mistaken because the Muslim threat was actually *far worse*.

[R]adical Islam is not just as fanatical and unappeasable in its anti-American-ism, anti-Westernism and anti-modernism as anything we have ever known.

It has the distinct advantage of being grounded in a venerable religion of over one billion adherents that not only provides a ready supply of recruits—trained and readied in mosques and madrassas far more effective, autonomous and ubiquitous than any Hitler Youth or Komsomol camp—but it is able to draw on a long and deep tradition of zeal, messianic expectation and a cult of martyrdom.

Hitler and Stalin had to invent these out of whole cloth. Mussolini's version was a parody. Islamic radicalism flies under a flag with far more historical depth and enduring appeal that the ersatz religions of the swastika and the hammer and sickle that proved so historically thin and insubstantial.[39]

For Krauthammer, as for Perle and Berman, whatever the dimension of the adversary, the millenarian answer nevertheless beckoned. "Where is it written that the Arabs are incapable of democracy?" he asks. His goal: "to vindicate the American idea by making the spread of democracy, the success of liberty, the ends and means of American foreign policy." The banner he would fly: "democratic globalism," the democratization of the Muslim world based on the conviction "that the spread of democracy is not just an end but a means, an indispensable means for securing American interests." "Democratic globalism sees as the engine of history not the will to power but the will to freedom."

Yes, as in Germany and Japan, the undertaking is enormous, ambitious and arrogant. It may yet fail. But we cannot afford not to try. There is not a single, remotely plausible, alternative strategy for attacking the monster behind 9/11…. It's not Osama bin Laden; it is the cauldron of political oppression, religious intolerance and social ruin in the Arab-Islamic world—oppression transmuted and deflected by regimes with no legitimacy into virulent, murderous anti-Americanism.[40]

And later that year:

America was pursuing democratization in Europe, East Asia, South and Central America—everywhere except the Arab world. Democratization elsewhere was remarkably successful and was the key to stability and pacification. The Arab exception proved costly. On 9/11, we reaped the whirlwind from that policy and finally understood that it was untenable. We could continue to fight Arab/Islamic radicalism by catching a terrorist leader here, rolling up a cell there. Or we could go to the heart of the problem and take the risky but imperative course of trying to reorder the Arab world. Success in Iraq would be a singular victory in the war on radical Islam. Failure in Iraq would be a singular defeat.[41]

Krauthammer's demagogic side was revealed during this period as he continued his counterattack on Francis Fukuyama. Fukuyama doubted that the threat posed by Islamic terrorism to the United States was "existential," although it might be to Israel, doubted that the democratization of the Middle East was a realistic goal to pursue, and warned that getting the struggle against America's enemies right would not be helped by a perspective as basically flawed as Krauthammer's, one that was "unrealistic in its overestimation of U.S. power and our ability to control events around the world." Krauthammer chose as his whipping stick, Fukuyama's reference to Israel as the country genuinely under the gun and the deeper source of his concern. He observed that this was "a novel way of Judaizing neoconservatism." By implication calling Fukuyama anti-Semitic, Krauthammer unloaded:

> His is not the crude kind, advanced by Pat Buchanan and Malaysia's Mahathir Mohamad, among others, that American neoconservatives (read: Jews) are simply doing Israel's bidding, hijacking American foreign policy in the service of Israel and the greater Jewish conspiracy. Fukuyama's take is more subtle and implicit. One is to understand that those spreading the mistaken idea that the War on Terror is existential are neoconservatives so deeply and unconsciously identified with the Jewish state that they cannot help seeing the world through its eyes.[42]

Perhaps the best known of the neoconservatives is William Kristol, cofounder of both the Project for the New American Century and *The Weekly Standard*, where his many editorials have defined the common position of a phalanx of liberal internationalist jihadists, none more articulate than Kristol himself. Kristol's millennial phase was most vividly expressed in the 1990s when, working with Robert Kagan, he expressed his confidence in the democratic peace theory that we have seen resurface endlessly in the arguments behind the Iraq War. As we saw in chapters four and five of this book, in the widely cited article they published in *Foreign Affairs* in the summer of 1996, Kristol and Kagan are sure that the United States can easily dispatch the various "monsters" prowling the sidelines of the international system during the 1990s, in the process bettering the lot of humanity in general while promoting basic American security concerns. Among the countries they would take on were not only the tyrannies of Iraq and Iran but also Cuba, China, North Korea, and the Balkans. A collateral benefit to the expansion of what they call America's "benevolent hegemony" would be "an elevated patriotism" at home: "The re-moralization of America at home ultimately requires the re-moralization of American foreign policy."

Only after 9/11 can we speak with assurance of Kristol's apocalyptic vision coming to the fore. In the run-up to the invasion, Kristol explained, quoting the president, the nation faced:

> "a world of chaos and constant alarm" where "outlaw regimes" sponsor terrorism and acquire and trade in horrific weapons…the nature of the regime is crucial, rather than some alleged underlying geographically or economically or culturally determined 'national interest.' The priority of the political order implies a morally informed American foreign policy. Thus a brutal tyranny like Saddam's is evil, Bush said, or else "evil has no meaning."[43]

With the conquest going well, Kristol could announce, "the war in which we are presently engaged is a fundamental challenge for the United States and the civilized world…. The liberation of Iraq was the first great battle for the future of the Middle East. The creation of a free Iraq is now of fundamental importance…. But the next battle…will be for Iran. We are already in a death struggle with Iran over the future of Iraq…. On the outcome of the confrontation with Tehran, more than any other, rests the future of the Bush Doctrine…and the prospects for a safer world."[44]

Given the stakes, Kristol was on hand to see that the president did not backslide. Thus, in February 2006, when President Bush expressed some sympathy with international Muslim outrage against Danish cartoons most of this community saw as blaspheming the Prophet Mohammad, Kristol denounced the "cartoon jihad."[45]

> This is a moment of truth in the global struggle against Islamic extremism. Will Hamas succeed in creating a terror state on the West Bank? Will a terror-sponsoring Iranian regime succeed in its quest for nuclear weapons? Will Danish imams succeed in intimidating Europe—or the free world as a whole?… Robert Frost said of liberals that they're incapable of taking their own side in a fight. We will see how deeply a degenerate form of liberalism has penetrated our souls. Will we anguish? Or will we fight?

What should be done? "Moral seriousness means political seriousness…. Make a real effort to destabilize Ahmadinejad in Iran. Do what it takes to defeat Zarqawi and secure Iraq. Stand with Denmark and moderate Muslims against the radical mob. This is no time for dishonorable retreat. It is time for resolve and competence."[46]

Kristol excelled at demagoguery as well. In the run-up to invasion, he and Kagan attacked the French for their "increasingly notable propensity to appease vicious dictators" and their "aggressive pacifism."[47] Like an evangelical saying we were attacked for our sins, he proclaimed that 9/11, "was the product of two decades of American weakness in the face of terror and three decades of American fecklessness in the Middle East.... But that era—in which the American stance was one of doubt, weakness, and retreat, in which we failed to affirm our most cherished principles or even stand up for ourselves—came to an end on September 11, 2001."[48]

In the preceding review of intellectuals whom I believe to be fundamentalists, I have limited myself to men generally considered to have a reasoned position and wide influence, and therefore to possess ideas worth analyzing. But behind these individuals stands a battalion of thinkers of lesser distinction, whose tone is more shrill yet. Consider just one example, that of Michael Ledeen, a resident fellow of the American Enterprise Institute routinely cited in reports on neoconservative thinking as a man with influence. In December 2001, Ledeen sounded once again the fundamentalist note declaring that:

> we must keep our fangs bared, we must remind them [the terrorists] daily that we Americans are in a rage, and we will not rest until we have avenged our dead, we will not be sated until we have had the blood of every miserable little tyrant in the Middle East, until every leader of every cell of the terror network is dead or locked securely away, and every last drooling anti-Semitic and anti-American mullah, imam, sheikh, and ayatollah is either singing the praises of the United States of America, or pumping gasoline, for a dime a gallon, on an American military base near the Arctic Circle.[49]

In a book published the following year, Ledeen vaunted what he repeatedly called "our revolutionary power:... Creative destruction is our middle name.... Our enemies have always hated this whirlwind of energy and creativity which menaces their traditions.... They must attack us in order to survive, just as we must destroy them to advance our historic mission."[50]

I rest my case. Out of a liberal internationalism creed that once, now long ago, was an anti-imperialist doctrine dedicated to freedom and to peaceful relations among peoples, the scourge of war and state sponsored terror can arise, defended by the terms of an argument perverted by a will to power into an insidious doctrine of world domination.

Let me repeat that few neo-Wilsonians, and presumably no traditional Wilsonians, walked the bridge thrown up by liberal fundamentalists into a

Jihad, which was mainly a neocon affair. Yet as the reader surely understands by now, a cadre of intellectuals exists in the country for whom this war is a fundamentalist mission. The Muslim world is demonized into an undifferentiated aggressively pathological whole, while the West is seen as immaculate in its conduct (attacked for what it is, not for what it does) as well as "existentially" threatened. However, by virtue of its superior ways, America can rouse the civilized world to action, which means taking the battle to the enemy and, difficult though it may be, bring the freedoms of our making to the dawn of an enlightenment in those parts of the world where it is still dangerously lacking. Those who disagree are answered not with an analysis of their argument but instead with a smear on their masculinity, or their honor, or with the suggestion that anti-Semitism explains a perspective that does not patriotically answer the call to arms.

The Jewish Question

Among the hard fought battles in the war of ideas has been the allegation that neoconservative Jewish American intellectuals have engineered the conquest of Iraq and contemplated the domination of the greater Middle East as a way of assuring Israeli security in the region, without regard for American interests. By 2006, many commentators had made such charges, implicitly if not explicitly. The inevitable response has been that the critics are anti-Semites, or that in their criticism of Israel they are engaging in "the new anti-Semitism," covering their ethno-religious prejudices in their attacks on the Zionist state.

No sooner had the Iraq War begun than charges were heard that this was a conflict inspired by Jewish American concerns for Israeli security, as defined by the Likud party in Israel.[51] The implication was that the Bush Doctrine was not to be taken at face value, but was a camouflage for another set of purposes, of which the defense of Israel, under siege by a rising tide of Muslim fundamentalism, was the most important.

The evidence assembled had the veil of plausibility. The Bush Doctrine rather faithfully reflected neoconservative thinking, and leading neoconservatives were virtually all American Jews deeply committed to the security of Israel, usually as defined by the "get tough" ("peace through strength") policies of the Likud party. In addition, the Israel Lobby in Washington was without peer in influencing the conduct of American foreign policy in the Middle East, and it generally took its marching orders from Jerusalem, which favored the American invasion of Iraq. Could it then be that the elaborate arguments about democratic peace theory, the character of legitimate state sovereignty, and the like were all an elaborate ideological screed covering the real intentions of the neocon movement, a project that pivoted on ensuring Israel's position in the Middle East, including its claims on occupied Arab lands that some Jewish expansionists insisted on calling Judea and Samaria?[52]

There are serious problems with taking this argument as more than a marginal explanation of the reasons behind the American invasion of Iraq, one not to be dismissed entirely out of hand, but most certainly not to be embraced wholeheartedly either. First, none of the major policy makers was a neoconservative or even Jewish. As any account of the thinking and character of President Bush, Vice President Cheney, or Defense Secretary Rumsfeld would quickly reveal, these officials were able very much on their own to call for a bold policy in the Middle East to set right the attack of 9/11. To make them pawns of other people's thinking is to underestimate their temperaments by a long chalk indeed.

A second objection to the proposition that neoconservative reasoning was primarily premised on coming militarily to Israel's defense is that the group that made up this school of thought had a range of thinking for more than a generation that suggests any such charge is badly reductionist. What is true is that in the 1940s, at the origins of what we today call neoconservative thinking, lay a deep-set anti-totalitarian bias. At its origins, neoconservatism was also dedicated to liberal democracy and supportive of an aggressive role for the United States in international affairs for the sake of the promise of democracy worldwide. To be sure, neoconservatism was from its inception pro-Israel as well. But to reduce the tenets of its intellectual arguments to Zionism alone is quite untenable, as virtually anyone who has studied the length and the breadth of this school's thinking would surely attest. Yes, neoconservatism was Zionist. But it was also super-patriotic and cosmopolitan in its defense of liberal democracy, dedicated to a vision of the United States as a beacon of hope in a world where not only Jews remained in danger, but the promise of liberal democracy itself.

Whether it was in opposition to the anti-war movement on the left, or to plans for détente emanating from Henry Kissinger to the right, the neoconservatives of the 1970s wanted the United States to have primacy militarily and to defend democracy worldwide. They thus opposed becoming overly trustful of the Chinese, just as they argued against détente with the Soviet Union. By the 1990s it was completely in line with their tradition of thinking that they would oppose a fascistic militarist like Saddam Hussein every bit as much as they would oppose a fascistic Slobodan Milosevic or Hugo Chavez, or take an antagonistic stance toward the communist leadership of North Korea.

Of course Israel's interests would be served by a resolute American commitment to democratic governments the world around. The meaning of the Holocaust and concern about the well-being of the Jewish state was most certainly a prominent theme in neoconservative thinking. But to imply that these super-patriots who in a cosmopolitan manner were friends of liberal democracy the world around were exclusively, or even primarily, motivated by a first loyalty to a Likud-like definition of what was good for Israel is as simplistic as saying that because the president and the vice president had been heads of petroleum companies, the invasion of Iraq was about nothing more than the pursuit of oil.[53]

A final reason to object to singling out the Jewish identity of so many neoconservatives as the basis of their thinking about the Middle East is that the opposition they posited as necessarily arising between the liberal democratic world and the world of authoritarian and totalitarian governments has an intellectual integrity to it that must be debated on its own terms. Whatever the problems of democratic peace theory as it emerged in the 1990s, it was not constructed by neoconservatives but by neoliberals, it was not designed to serve Israeli interests, and it may have enough truth to it that its message should be heeded, or at least debated, not disregarded in favor of seeking out some ulterior reason America went to war in the spring of 2003.

In this respect, it would be preposterous to say that Bruce Russett, Andrew Moravcsik, and John Rawls—all champions of democratic peace theory (Moravcsik to a lesser degree perhaps) as a framework for American foreign policy, as we saw in Chapter 4—were stalking horses of the Likud party in the United States. And yet here are three sophisticated thinkers who came to the conclusions we have seen with respect to democratic peace theory that it should play a part in American thinking about the world.

Or again, what would we say of those who suggested that American Jews in the 1930s were overly sensitive to the rise of Hitler in Germany? Of course they were sensitive, but it would have well behooved more Americans to have listened to their concerns after 1933, rather than trying to appease the Nazis and telling the Jews to be quiet. The question of the inevitability of antagonism between liberal democracies and totalitarian systems must be debated on its own terms, not treated as a camouflage for some other agenda.

These assertions made, the association of many right-wing American Jews concerned with Israel's security and support for the Iraq War is undeniable.

Some of the neoconservatives—those associated with Richard Perle and Douglas Feith in authoring the 1996 "Clean Break" position paper for Benjamin Netanyahu, for example—come immediately to mind as perhaps thinking how to turn to Israel's benefit the American response to 9/11. Again, arguments by *The Weekly Standard* that regularly justified whatever repression the Israeli government was meting out to the Palestinians as no more than what the Americans were doing in Afghanistan or Iraq seemed intended to serve the policies of a Greater Israel. Or again, there were the various think tanks in Washington working on world affairs that consistently called for the United States to support Israel in terms of that country's definition of its security needs: the Center for Security Policy, the Jewish Institute for National Security Affairs, the Washington Institute for Near East Policy, the Foundation for the Defense of Democracies, to which should be added their many supporters in more mainstream arenas including the American Enterprise Institute, the Hudson Institute, and the Heritage Foundation. Finally, there was the support of Israel itself for the war and the impact this had on what is universally considered the most powerful foreign policy lobby in Washington, the American Israel Public Affairs Committee.

In a word, that there was an important element of Jewish right-wing activism in favor of the invasion of Iraq for reasons that had to do with Israel's security appears incontrovertible.[54] But I repeat: this kind of evidence does not mean that the Bush Doctrine is essentially a screed for right-wing Israeli interests. That the domestic Israel Lobby, and Israel itself, supported the war is evident; that most neoconservatives almost surely had Israel's security needs in mind when they called for war is likely; that here is to be found the complex of the reasons the invasion of Iraq took place would be a badly exaggerated charge.

Where I believe one can attribute a more primary responsibility to some Jewish thinking about the war effort, however, is with the birth of liberal fundamentalism after 9/11. There should be no doubt that the Muslim extremists who attacked that day were anti-Zionists, as was Saddam Hussein. There is no doubt that Israel is even more endangered by this kind of hatred than the United States. I find it easily understandable and defensible that not only Jews worldwide but that many of the rest of us who sympathize with the existence of a Jewish state would be seriously concerned by the challenges to this country's very existence emanating from the Middle East. If "Never Again" is to be a meaningful statement, then where better should it be invoked than against

the inveterate hatred of Israel and the Jewish diaspora that one sees so dangerously widespread today in the Muslim world?

Unfortunately, the liberal fundamentalists, Jewish or other, who would
defend the liberal democratic world against this assault from Islamist or
Muslim secular extremists, act much as those who would indeed destroy
us if they could. However, an overreaction to the threat, a demonizing of
Islam far and wide for launching a world war in the effort to establish "a
global caliphate," the affirmation of an existential evil that must be met with
whatever force we can marshal against it, the bashing of critics at home or
in Europe who reject the arrogance that lay behind the Bush Doctrine—all
this makes an effective response to the dangers of the moment less likely to
be adopted.

"Never Again" is a meaningful phrase, there must be no doubt about it. But
used in the service of whipping up paranoid hysteria, it could well become the
banner of a self-destructive fear and righteousness that by a terrible irony of
history becomes an evil in its turn.

Conclusion

In its transformation from a hegemonic to an imperialist ideology during
the 1990s, liberal internationalism became a danger to the very values it pro-
fessed to champion. Whatever progressive features it undeniably possessed
needed henceforth to be weighed against the damage it might plausibly inflict.
By allowing an unprecedented act of imperial aggression on the part of the
United States to justify itself in the language of democracy promotion, liberal
internationalism has seriously damaged its own cause.

Much worse may be to come if the categories of thought engendered by
neo-Wilsonian reasoning fully metamorphoses into a liberal Jihad.

Linked to a populist militarism sometimes called Jacksonianism, reinforced by elements of Christian evangelical thinking anticipating Armageddon, urged forward by those committed to the call "Never Again" whatever
the cost, associated with neoconservatives who have always had American
supremacy over the world system as their fondest desire, liberal internationalism has the capacity to become as dangerous as the fundamentalist doctrines
it did so much to defeat in the twentieth century. That it should dishonor its
great tradition by the betrayal of its own promise would be the moment the
Devil would indisputably get his due. The question for today is whether this
moment is at hand.

NOTES

Preface

[1]   Tony Smith, *America's Mission: The United States and the Worldwide Struggle for Democracy in the Twentieth Century*. Princeton, NJ: Princeton University Press, 1994.

[2]   Samuel P. Huntington, *The Clash of Civilizations and the Remaking of World Order*. New York: Simon & Schuster, 1996.

[3]   For a discussion of the definition of "imperialism," see Tony Smith, *The Pattern of Imperialism: The United States, Great Britain, and the Late-Industrializing World since 1815*. New York: Cambridge University Press, 1981; introduction. For reflection on the course of empire, see Charles S. Maier, *Among Empires: American Ascendancy and its Predecessors*. Cambridge, MA: Harvard University Press, 2006.

[4]   John Rawls, *The Law of Peoples*. Cambridge, MA: Harvard University Press, 1999.

[5]   For the use of Rawls by self-described liberal partisans of the Iraq War, see for example, Thomas Cushman, *A Matter of Principle: Humanitarian Arguments for War in Iraq*. Berkeley and Los Angeles: University of California Press, 2005, introduction by Cushman and chapter 6 by Mehdi Mozaffari.

[6]   Ronald Steel, *Temptations of a Superpower*. Cambridge, MA: Harvard University Press, 1995.

Introduction

[1]   For equivalent extravagant ambitions on the military field, see Michael Gordon and Bernard Trainor, *Cobra II: The Inside Story of the Invasion and Occupation of Iraq*. New York: Pantheon, 2006. Thomas E. Ricks, *Fiasco: The American Military Adventure in Iraq*. New York: Penguin, 2006.

[2]   George Packer, ed., *The Fight is for Democracy: Winning the War of Ideas in America and the World*. New York: HarperCollins, 2003, pp. 14-15.

[3]   Will Marshall, ed., *With All Our Might: A Progressive Strategy for Defeating Jihadism and Defending Liberty*. New York: Rowman & Littlefield, 2006. Peter Beinart, *The Good Fight: Why Liberals—and Only Liberals—Can Win the War on Terror and Make America Great Again*. New York: HarperCollins, 2006. The Euston Manifesto retrieved September 5, 2006 from http://eustonmanifesto.org/joomla/content/view/84/49.

4   Retrieved May 5, 2006, from www.townhall.com/opinion/columns/clifford-may2005/03/17/14830.html.

5   Retrieved June 12, 28, 2006, from www.defenddemocracy.org.

6   Posters distributed at Tufts University, spring 2006.

7   Claudia Rosett, "How Corrupt Is the United Nations?" *Commentary* 121 (4), April 2006.

8   Retrieved June 2, 2006, from http://zope06.v.servelocity.net/hjs.

9   Thomas L. Friedman, *Longitudes and Attitudes: Exploring the World After September 11.* New York: Farrar, Straus and Giroux, 2002. Entries in this book are by date.

10   Avishai Margalit and Ian Buruma, "Occidentalism," *The New York Review of Books* 49 (1), January 17, 2002.

11   United Nations Development Program, *Arab Human Development Report 2004.* New York and Geneva: United Nations Publications, 2005. See also as indicative of this thinking, Rashid Khalidi, *Resurrecting Empire: Western Footprints and America's Perilous Path in the Middle East.* Boston: Beacon Press, 2004, chapter 2.

12   Shibley Telhami, "What Arab Public Opinion Thinks of U.S. Policy." The Saban Center for Middle East Policy, the Brookings Institution, December 2005.

13   Pew Research Center, "The Spread of Anti-Americanism," *Global Opinion* 7, 2005.

14   Ole R. Holsti, "Promotion of Democracy as a Popular Demand?" In Michael Cox, et al., *American Democracy Promotion.* New York: Oxford University Press, 2000.

15   Andrew Kohut, "How the United States Is Perceived in the Arab and Muslim Worlds." Testimony before the U.S. House of Representatives, November 10, 2005. Kohut is Director of the Pew Research Center. Chicago Council on Global Affairs, "Americans on Promoting Democracy," September 29, 2005. See also Chaim Kaufmann, "Threat Inflation and the Failure of the Marketplace of Ideas," *International Security*, 29 (1), 2004.

16   Reinhold Niebuhr, *Beyond Tragedy: Essays on the Christian Interpretation of History.* New York: Scribner's, 1937.

Chapter 1

1   For the Monroe through the Reagan Doctrines, see H. W. Brands, ed., "Presidential Doctrines," *Presidential Studies Quarterly*, 36 (1), March 2006.

2   "Defending and Advancing Freedom: A Symposium," *Commentary,* November 2005. See also Norman Podhoretz, "In Praise of the Bush Doctrine," *Commentary,* September 2002.

3   Andrew J. Bacevich, *American Empire: The Realities and Consequences of U.S. Diplomacy.* Cambridge, MA: Harvard University Press, 2002; Bacevich, *The New American Militarism: How Americans Are Seduced by War.* New York: Oxford University Press, 2005. Also Bacevich, "Why Read Clausewitz When Shock and Awe Can Make a Clean Sweep of Things?" *London Review of Books*, 28, June 11, 2006. Also Michael Gordon and Bernard Trainor, *Cobra II: The Inside Story of the Invasion and Occupation of Iraq.* New York: Pantheon, 2006; and Thomas E. Ricks, *Fiasco: The American Military Failure in Iraq.* New York: Penguin, 2006.

4   All presidential statements in this book have been downloaded from the White House website, www.whitehouse.gov, which is arranged by date. After the next presidential election, President Bush's addresses will be available on a variety of internet sources as well as in book form.

5   The term "unipolarity" was first introduced by the neoconservative Charles Krauthammer in "The Unipolar Moment," *Foreign Affairs*, Winter 1990/91. See also Krauthammer, "The Unipolar Moment Revisited," *National Interest*, Winter 2002/03.

6   Stefan Halper and Jonathan Clarke, *America Alone: The Neo-Conservatives and the Global Order*. New York: Cambridge University Press, 2004, chapter 4. James Mann, *The Rise of the Vulcans: The History of Bush's War Cabinet*. New York: Penguin, 2004, chapter 13.

7   Patrick E. Tyler, U.S. Strategy Calls for Insuring no Rivals Develop In a One-Superpower World, *New York Times*, 3/08/1992.

8   Richard Cheney, "Defense Strategy for the 1990s: The Regional Defense Strategy," January 1993. Retrieved August 17, 2006, from www.informationclearinghouse.info/pdf.naarpr_Defense.pdf.

9   William Kristol and Robert Kagan, "Toward a Neo-Reaganite Foreign Policy," *Foreign Affairs*, 75 (4), July-August 1996.

10   Robert Kagan and William Kristol, *Present Dangers: Crisis and Opportunity in American Foreign and Defense Policy*. San Francisco: Encounter Books, 2000. Thomas Donnelly, et al., "Rebuilding America's Defenses," The Project for a New American Century, 2000. See also, Kristol and Kagan in "America Power for What? A Symposium," *Commentary*, January 2000.

11   Niall Ferguson, *Colossus: The Price of America's Empire*. New York: Penguin, 2004.

12   Charles Krauthammer, "Democratic Realism: An American Foreign Policy for a Unipolar World," American Enterprise Institute, February 2004.

13   Paul Kennedy, *The Rise and Fall of the Great Powers*, New York: Vintage, 1987.

14   Paul Kennedy, "The Eagle Has Landed," *Financial Times*, February 2, 2002.

15   Cheney, op. cit.

16   Condoleezza Rice, "Campaign 2000: Promoting the National Interest," *Foreign Affairs*, 79, 1, January-February 2000.

17   Debate transcript, *New York Times*, October 12, 2000.

Chapter 2

1   James Mann, *Rise of the Vulcans: The History of Bush's War Cabinet*. New York: Penguin, 2004, chapter 16. Michael Lind, *Made in Texas: George W. Bush and the Southern Takeover of American Politics*. New York: Basic Books, 2003. Ivo H. Daalder and James M. Lindsay, *America Unbound: The Bush Revolution in Foreign Policy*. Washington, DC: Brookings Institution Press, 2003. Joan Didion, "Cheney: The Fatal Touch," *The New York Review of Books*, October 5, 2006. Garry Wills, "A Country Ruled by Faith," *The New York Review of Books*, November 16, 2006.

2   Stefan Halper and Jonathan Clarke, *America Alone: The Neo-Conservatives and Global Order*. New York: Cambridge University Press, 64ff. See also, Gary Dorrien, *Imperial Designs: Neoconservatism and the New Pax Americana*. New York: Routledge, 2004, 143; and Dorrien, *The Neoconservative Mind: Politics, War, and the Culture of Ideology*. Philadelphia: Temple University Press, 1993.

3   Dorrien, ibid., 2004, 153.

4   Dorrien, ibid., 2004, 143; Halper and Clarke, op cit., 64ff, 103ff.

5   For an earlier period, see Irving Kristol, *Neoconservatism: The Autobiography of an Idea*. New York: Free Press, 1995. See also Joseph Dorfman, *Arguing the World: The New York Intellectuals in Their Own Words*. New York: Free Press, 2000; but especially the film of the same name by Dorfman, 1997. Also valuable on the early period are John Ehrman, *The Rise of Neoconservatism: Intellectuals and Foreign Affairs, 1945-1994*. New Haven, CT: Yale University Press, 1995; and Murray Friedman, *The Neoconservative Revolution: Jewish Intellectuals and the Shaping of Public Policy*. New York: Cambridge University Press, 2005.

6   On a "convergence" of Straussian with neoconservative ideas, which nonetheless does not
    mean a merger of one in to the other, see Robert Devigne, *Recasting Conservatism: Oake-
    shott, Strauss, and the Response to Postmodernism.* New Haven, CT: Yale University Press,
    1994, 59ff. For an effort to see the links—and also the disconnects—between Straussian
    and neoconservative thinking so far as Bush administration policy is concerned, see Anne
    Norton, *Leo Strauss and the Politics of American Empire.* New Haven, CT: Yale Univer-
    sity Press, 2004, chapters 10-13 especially. For the argument that Straussian thinking had
    a direct impact on American imperialism after 9/11, see Shadia B. Drury, *The Political
    Ideas of Leo Strauss.* New York: Palgrave Macmillan, new ed., 2005, "Introduction to
    the Updated Edition: Straussians in Power: Secrecy, Lies, and Endless War." For a more
    skeptical analysis, see Steven B. Smith, *Reading Leo Strauss: Politics, Philosophy, Judaism.*
    Chicago: University of Chicago Press, 2006, chapter 8. For an excellent assessment of neo-
    conservative thinking prior to the end of the Cold War, which shows Strauss's minor influ-
    ence, see Dorrien, op. cit., 1993. See also Leo Strauss, *Natural Right and History.* Chicago:
    University of Chicago Press, 1953, 190ff. I appreciate professor Devigne's discussion of
    these matters with me in July 2006.

7   Francis Fukuyama, *America at the Crossroads: Democracy, Power, and the Neoconservative
    Legacy.* New Haven, CT: Yale University Press, 2006, 29f, but see too 21ff.

8   Steven Smith, op. cit., 200f; emphasis in original.

9   Justin Vaisse, *Le mouvement neoconservateur aux Etats-Unis.* These de l'Ecole Doctorale
    d'Histoire, Institut d'Etudes Politiques de Paris, November 2005. This book will be pub-
    lished in English by Harvard University Press late in 2007.

10 Michael Lind, *Made in Texas: George W. Bush and the Southern Takeover of American Poli-
    tics.* New York, Basic Books, 2003, chapters 5–6. See also Lind's statement in *The New States-
    man,* April 7, 2003. Lind is currently a senior fellow at the New American Foundation.

11 Ronald Reagan, Address to Members of the British Parliament, June 8, 1982. Retrieved
    August 2006, from www.reagan.utexas.edu/archives/speeches/1982/60882a.htm.

12 Tony Smith, "American Liberalism and Soviet 'New Thinking,'" in Pierre Melandri and
    Serge Ricard, eds., *Les Etats-Unis et la fin de la guerre froide.* Paris: L'Harmattan, 2005.

13 Retrieved June 2006, from www.newamericancentury.org.

14 Paul Wolfowitz, "Statement Before the U.S. House International Relations Committee
    on U.S. Options in Confronting Iraq," 2/25/1998, and "Statement Before the U.S. House
    National Security Committee," 9/16/1998; Dorrien, op. cit, 2004, 66ff; Mann op. cit., 81,
    235, 367f.

15 Richard A. Clarke, *Against All Enemies: Inside America's War on Terror.* New York: Free
    Press, 2004, 30f, 231f.

16 Kanan Makiya, *Republic of Fear: The Politics of Modern Iraq.* Berkeley: University of Cali-
    fornia Press, 1998, first ed., 1989.

17 The PNAC letter comes from its website newamericancentury.org; the Perle speech was
    before the Philadelphia-based Foreign Policy Research Institute, at its annual dinner,
    2001. Retrieved spring 2006, from www.fpri.org.

18 Sam Tanenhaus, "Bush's Brain Trust," *Vanity Fair,* July 2002; Paul R. Pillar, "Intelligence,
    Policy, and the War in Iraq," *Foreign Affairs,* 85, 2, March-April 2006; Mark Danner, *The
    Secret Way to War: The Downing Street Memo and the Iraq War's Buried History.* New
    York: New York Review of Books, 2006.

19 Seymour M. Hersh, *Chain of Command: The Road from 9/11 to Abu Ghraib.* New York:
    HarperCollins, 2004. Thomas Powers, "The Failure," and "How Bush Got It Wrong," *New
    York Review of Books,* September 23, 2004 and April 29, 2005. David Cole, *Terrorism and*

the Constitution: Sacrificing Civil Liberties in the Name of National Security. New York: New Press, 2002; Mark Danner, *Torture and Truth: America, Abu Ghraib, and the War on Terror.* New York: New York Review of Books, 2004.

[20] Lawrence F. Kaplan and William Kristol, *The War Over Iraq: Saddam's Tyranny and America's Mission.* San Francisco: Encounter Books, 2003.

[21] Ibid., 118-121.

[22] Max Boot, "Myths about Neoconservatism," in *Foreign Policy*, 2004, reprinted in Irwin Stelzer, *The Neocon Reader.* New York: Grove Press, 2004, 46; and Joshua Muravchik, "The Neoconservative Cabal," from *Commentary*, September 2003, reprinted in Stelzer, 256. Charles Krauthammer, "The Neoconservative Convergence," *Commentary*, July-August 2005.

[23] For Israel's and the Bush administration's hopes to march on to Tehran after Lebanon, see Seymour M. Hersh, "Watching Lebanon: Washington's Interests in Israel's War," *New Yorker*, August 21, 2006.

[24] Jonathan Monten, "The Roots of the Bush Doctrine." *International Security* 29 (4), Spring 2005.

[25] Kaplan and Kristol, op. cit., 2003, chapter 6 and 63, 112f; Paul Berman, "What Lincoln Knew About War," *New Republic*, March 03, 2003; Michael Ignatieff, "Who Are Americans to Think that Freedom Is Theirs to Spread?" *New York Times*, July 26, 2005.

[26] Tony Smith, *America's Mission: The United States and the Worldwide Struggle for Democracy in the Twentieth Century.* Princeton, NJ: Princeton University Press, 1994.

[27] See the coverage of the debate among historians in Lloyd E. Ambrosius, "Woodrow Wilson and George W. Bush: Historical Comparisons of Ends and Means in their Foreign Policies," *Diplomatic History* 30 (2), June 2006. Smith, op. cit., 1994, chapter 4.

[28] Robert Kagan, *Of Paradise and Power: America and Europe in the New World Order.* New York: Knopf, 2003, 85, 93-94. Apparently, out of these lines a book was born. According to the publisher's description of Kagan's *Dangerous Nation*, scheduled to appear after my book is in press, "Even before the birth of the nation, Americans believed they were destined for leadership. Underlying their ambitions…was a set of ideas and ideals about the world and human nature. [Kagan] focuses on the Declaration of Independence as the document that firmly established the American conviction that the inalienable rights of all mankind transcended territorial borders…American nationalism, he shows, was always internationalist at its core." In short, it would appear that for Kagan, America has always been neoconservative but had to await the coming of this conscious movement (under his auspices in part) to find its identity self-consciously formulated.

[29] See, for example, Joshua Muravchik, *Exporting Democracy: Fulfilling America's Destiny.* Washington, DC: American Enterprise Institute Press, 1991; Max Boot, "What Next? The Foreign Policy Agenda Beyond Iraq" *The Weekly Standard*, May, 5, 2003.

[30] David Rieff, *A Bed for the Night: Humanitarianism in Crisis.* New York: Simon & Schuster, 2002.

[31] For a critical survey of liberal support for military intervention in the Middle East, see Frank Rich, "Ideas for Democrats?" *New York Review of Books*, October 19, 2006; and Tony Judt, "Bush's Useful Idiots," *London Review of Books*, September 21, 2006.

Chapter 3

[1] Andrew J. Bacevich, *American Empire: The Politics and Consequences of U.S. Diplomacy.* Cambridge, MA: Harvard University Press, 2002, 2.

[2] John Lewis Gaddis, *Surprise, Security and the American Experience.* Cambridge, MA: Harvard University Press, 2004.

3   Ibid., 31, 13, emphasis in original.

4   Ibid., 93.

5   Ibid., 115f, 89.

6   John Lewis Gaddis, "Grand Strategy in the Second Term," *Foreign Affairs* 84 (1), January-February 2005.

7   Gaddis, op. cit., 2004, 93, 116, 118.

8   Matthew Spalding and Patrick J. Garrity, *A Sacred Union of Citizens: George Washington's Farewell Address and the American Character.* Lanham, MD: Rowman & Littlefield, 1996, 113f.

9   Stanley Elkins and Eric McKitrick, *The Age of Federalism: The Early American Republic, 1788-1800.* New York: Oxford University Press, 1993.

10   Tony Smith, *America's Mission: The United States and the Worldwide Struggle for Democracy in the Twentieth Century.* Princeton, NJ: Princeton University Press, 1994, chapter 3.

11   Ibid., chapter 4.

12   David Fromkin, *A Peace to end All Peace: The Fall of the Ottoman Empire and the Creation of the Modern Middle East.* New York: Holt, 1989.

13   Tony Smith, "Making the World Safe for Democracy," *Diplomatic History* 23 (2), Spring 1999.

14   G. John Ikenberry, *After Victory: Institutions, Strategic Restraint, and the Rebuilding of Order after Major Wars.* Princeton, NJ: Princeton University Press, 2001. See also, Ikenberry, *Liberal Order and Imperial Ambition: Essays on American Power and International Order.* Princeton, NJ: Princeton University Press, 2006.

15   Daniel C. Thomas, *The Helsinki Effect: International Norms, Human Rights and the Demise of Communism.* Princeton, NJ: Princeton University Press, 2001.

16   Tony Smith, "American Liberalism and Soviet 'New Thinking'," in Pierre Melandri and Serge Ricard, eds., *Les Etats-Unis et la fin de la guerre froide.* Paris: L'Harmattan, 2005.

17   Archie Brown, *The Gorbachev Factor.* New York: Oxford University Press, 1996.

18   Smith, op. cit, 1994, chapter 10.

19   Compare George Bush and Brent Scowcroft, *A World Transformed.* New York: Knopf, 1998, to Lawrence F. Kaplan and William Kristol, *The War Over Iraq: Saddam's Tyranny and America's Mission.* San Francisco: Encounter Books, 2003, chapter 4.

20   Smith, op. cit, 1994, 312ff.

21   Bill Clinton, "U.S. Trade With China Opens a Door for Freedom," *New York Times,* September 25, 2000.

22   Kaplan and Kristol, op. cit, 2003, 5. Robert Kagan and Kristol, eds., *Present Dangers: Crisis and Opportunity in American Foreign and Defense Policy,* San Francisco: Encounter Books, Introduction. David Wurmser, *Tyranny's Ally: America's Failure to Defeat Saddam Hussein.* Washington, DC: American Enterprise Institute Press, 1999.

23   Micheal Ignatieff, "The Rights Stuff," *New York Review of Books,* June 13, 2002.

24   Kimberly Zisk Marten, *Enforcing the Peace: Learning from the Imperial Past.* New York: Columbia University Press, 2003, 37.

25   Walter Russell Mead, *Special Providence: American Foreign Policy and How It Changed the World.* New York: Knopf, 2001, chapter 6; John B. Judis, "The Chosen Nation: The Influence of Religion on U.S. Foreign Policy," Policy Brief, Carnegie Endowment for International Peace, 37, March 2005; John B. Judis, *The Folly of Empire: What George W. Bush Could Learn from Theodore Roosevelt and Woodrow Wilson.* New York: Scribner, 2004.

Chapter 4

1   Samantha Power, *"A Problem from Hell:" America and the Age of Genocide.* New York: Basic Books, 2002, 503-504.

2   *Wall Street Journal*, September 2, 1993.
3   Francis Fukuyama, "The End of History?" *National Interest* 16, Summer 1989.
4   Francis Fukuyama, *The End of History and the Last Man*. New York: Maxwell Macmillan, 1992, xi.
5   Ibid., chapter 26.
6   For an extended list, see Larry Diamond, "Promoting Democracy in the 1990s: Actors and Instruments, Issues and Imperatives." Carnegie Commission on Preventing Deadly Conflict, December 1995.
7   Piki Ish-Shalom, "The Democratic Peace Thesis in the Israeli-Palestinian Conflict: Uses and Abuses." Hebrew University of Jerusalem, Leonard Davis Institute, 96, 2005.
8   Michael Doyle, "Kant, Liberal Legacies and Foreign Affairs," *Philosophy and Public Affairs* 12, Summer and Fall 1983; Doyle, "An International Liberal Community," in Graham Allison and Gregory F. Treverton, eds., *Rethinking America's Security: Beyond the Cold War to New World Order*. New York: Norton, 1991; Doyle, *Ways of War and Peace: Realism, Liberalism, and Socialism*. New York: Norton, 1997, part two. On Doyle's place in neoliberal theory, see Bruce Russett, *Grasping the Democratic Peace: Principles for a Post-Cold War World*. Princeton, NJ: Princeton University Press, 1993, chapter 1, fn. 1, 139.
9   Jack S. Levy, "Domestic Politics and War: Realism, Liberalism, and Socialism," *Journal of Interdisciplinary History* 18 (4), 1988, 622.
10 Bruce Russett and John Oneal, *Triangulating Peace: Democracy, Interdependence, and International Organizations*. New Haven, CT: Yale University Press, 2001.
11 Ibid., 272.
12 Ibid., 30.
13 Andrew Moravcsik, "Taking Preferences Seriously: A Liberal Theory of International Politics," *International Organization*, 51 (4), Autumn 1997.
14 Andrew Moravscik, "Liberal International Relations Theory: A Scientific Assessment," in Colin Elman and Mariam Fendius Elman, eds. *Progress in International Relations Theory: Appraising the Field*. Cambridge, MA: MIT Press, 2003.
15 John Rawls, *The Law of Peoples*. Cambridge, MA: Harvard University Press, 1999, chapter 5.
16 Ibid., 14f.
17 Ibid., 127f.
18 Matthew Frye Jacobson, *Barbarian Virtues: The United States Encounters Foreign Peoples at Home and Abroad, 1876-1917*. New York: Hill and Wang, 2000.
19 Russett, op. cit., 1993, 136.
20 Natan Sharansky with Ron Dermer, *The Case for Democracy: The Power of Freedom to Overcome Tyranny and Terror*. New York: Public Affairs, 2004, 88; emphasis in original.
21 Fareed Zakaria, *The Future of Freedom: Illiberal Democracy at Home and Abroad*. New York: Norton, 2003.
22 Larry Diamond, "The Global Imperative: Building a Democratic World Order," *Current History* 93 (579), January 1994.
23 Diamond, op. cit., 1995, 7.
24 Larry Diamond, "Building a World of Liberal Democracies," in Thomas H. Henriksen ed., *Foreign Policy for America in the Twenty-first Century*. Stanford, CA: Hoover Institution Press, 2001, 50, 73.
25 Russett and Oneal, op. cit., 184ff, 297ff.
26 Tony Smith and Larry Diamond, "Was Iraq a Fool's Errand?" *Foreign Affairs* 83 (6), November/December 2004.

Chapter 5

[1]   Freedom House, *Freedom in the World: The Annual Survey of Political Rights and Civil Liberties*. New York: Freedom House, various years.

[2]   George Packer, *The Assassins' Gate: America in Iraq*. New York: Farrar, Straus and Giroux, 2005, 12f. Paul Berman, *Power and the Idealists: Or the Passion of Joschka Fischer and Its Aftermath*. Brooklyn, New York: Soft Skull Press, 2005, 173ff.

[3]   Samuel P. Huntington, *Political Order in Changing Society*. New Haven, CT: Yale University Press, 1968. Huntington, *The Third Wave: Democratization in the Late Twentieth Century*. Norman, OK: University of Oklahoma Press, 1991.

[4]   Giuseppe Di Palma, *To Craft Democracies: An Essay on Democratic Transitions*. Berkeley and Los Angeles: University of California Press, 1990.

[5]   Nancy Bermeo, "Shortcuts to Liberty." *Journal of Democracy* 2 (2), Spring 1991.

[6]   Alexander Wendt, *Social Theory of International Politics*. New York: Cambridge University Press, 1999, 1, 113ff and chapter 5.

[7]   Francis Fukuyama, *America at the Crossroads: Democracy, Power, and the Neoconservative Legacy*. New Haven, CT: Yale University Press, 2006, 54f.

[8]   Juan J. Linz and Alfred Stepan, eds., *The Breakdown of Democratic Regimes*. Baltimore, MD: Johns Hopkins University Press, 1978.

[9]   Guillermo O'Donnell, et al., eds., *Transitions from Authoritarian Rule: Tentative Conclusions About Uncertain Democracies*, written jointly by the editors, and Adam Przeworski, "Some Problems in the Study of the Transition to Democracy" in the volume entitled *Comparative Perspectives*. Baltimore, MD: Johns Hopkins University Press, 1986.

[10] Larry Diamond, et al., eds., *Democracy in Developing Countries: Vol. 4, Latin America*. Boulder, CO: Rienner, 1989, 89, xxiiiff.

[11] Larry Diamond, et al., eds., *Politics in Developing Countries: Comparing Experiences with Democracy*. Boulder, CO: Rienner, 1995, 2.

[12] Ibid. Introduction.

[13] Larry Diamond, "Can the Whole World Become Democratic? Democracy, Development, and International Policies." University of California, Irvine, CSD Paper, March 2005. Retrieved spring 2004, from http://repositories.cdlib.org/csd/03-05.

[14] Diamond, Ibid., 5, 7, 10, 13.

[15] Afro Barometer, Briefing Paper 1, April 2002. Retrieved February 2005, from www.globalbarometer.org.

[16] Gabriel Almond and Sidney Verba, *The Civic Culture: Attitudes and Democracy in Five Nations*. Boston: Little, Brown, 1965.

[17] Larry Diamond, "Iraq and Democracy: The Lessons Learned," *Current History*, January 2006. For a strong antidote to these proposed lessons, see Rory Stewart, *The Prince of the Marshes and Other Occupational Hazards of a Year in Iraq*. New York, Harcourt, 2006.

[18] John Boli and George M. Thomas, eds., *Constructing World Culture: International Nongovernmental Organizations since 1875*. Palo Alto, CA: Stanford University Press, 1999; Jack Donnelly, *Universal Human Rights in Theory and Practice*, 2nd ed. Ithaca, NY: Cornell University Press, 2003; Elizabeth Borgwardt, *A New Deal for the World: America's Vision for Human Rights*. Cambridge, MA: Harvard University Press, 2005.

[19] Thomas Risse, et al., eds., *The Power of Human Rights: International Norms and Domestic Change*. New York: Cambridge University Press, 1999, opening chapter by Risse and Sikkink, and concluding by Risse and Ropp.

20 Noah Feldman, *After Jihad: America and the Struggle for Islamic Democracy*. New York: Farrar, Straus and Giroux, 2003, 11-12. For something of an antidote to this thinking, see Daniel A. Bell, *East Meets West: Human Rights and Democracy in East Asia*. Princeton, NJ: Princeton University Press, 2000.

21 "Democracy, Closer Every Day," *New York Times*, September 24, 2003; "A New Democracy, Enshrined in Faith," *New York Times*, November 13, 2003; "Political Islam: Global Warming," book review, *New York Times*, February 8, 2005; "Muslim Democrats? Why Not!" *Wall Street Journal*, April 8, 2003; "Operation Iraqi Democracy," *Wall Street Journal*, July 15, 2003.

22 David Rieff, *A Bed for the Night: Humanitarianism in Crisis*. New York: Simon & Schuster, 2002, chapters 3, 8; Michael Barnett, "Humanitarianism Transformed," *Perspectives on Politics* 3 (4), December 2005.

23 Barnett, Ibid.

24 Cited in American Council for Voluntary International Action. Retrieved summer 2006, from www.Interaction Org/Forum2003. The Agency for International Development website as of summer 2006 was www.usaid.gov.

25 The National Endowment for Democracy, "About Us." Retrieved June 2006, from www. ned.org.

26 Retrieved April 2006, from www.wmd.org/about/secretariat.html.

27 Retrieved April 2006, from www.democracyatlarge.org; www.ifes.org.

28 Retrieved April 2006, from www.ccd21.org.

29 Thomas Carothers, "The Backlash Against Democracy Promotion," *Foreign Affairs* 85 (2), March-April 2006. For an estimate of over $2 billion, not counting private subscriptions, see Thomas O. Melia, "The Democracy Bureaucracy," *American Interest*, Summer 2006. See also the Congressional testimony of Carl Gershman, "The Backlash Against Democracy Assistance," June 8, 2006. National Endowment for Democracy, op. cit.

30 Freedom House, *Monitor* 20 (1), Winter/Spring 2003. Retrieved March 2006, from www. freedomhouse.org. By contrast, for a position that steered clear of the war, see George Soros, *The Age of Fallibility: The Consequencesof the War on Terror*. New York: Public Affairs, 2006.

31 Natan Sharansky with Ron Dermer, *The Case for Democracy: The Power of Freedom to Overcome Tyranny and Terror*. New York: PublicAffairs, xviii, 88, 17.

32 Lawrence Kaplan and William Kristol, *The War Over Iraq: Saddam's Tyranny and America's Mission*. San Francisco, CA: Encounter Books, 2003.

33 Packer, op. cit., 115.

34 Peter Boyer, "The Believer: Paul Wolfowitz Defends His War," *New Yorker*, November 1, 2004, 731.

35 Bill Keller, "The Sunshine Warrior," *New York Times*, September 22, 2002.

36 Mark Bowden, "Wolfowitz: The Exit Interviews," *Atlantic Monthly*, July-August 2005.

37 Jeffrey Goldberg, "Breaking Ranks," *New Yorker*, October 31, 2005.

38 Packer, op. cit., 115; James Mann, *The Rise of the Vulcans: The History of Bush's War Cabinet*. New York: Penguin, 2004, 75; Stephen F. Hayes, "The Visionary," *Weekly Standard*, May 9, 2005.

39 Condoleezza Rice, speech at Princeton University, Woodrow Wilson School of Public and International Affairs, September 30, 2005. Retrieved October 2006, from www.state.gov/secretary/rm/2005/54176.htm.

40 Blair's website containing his speeches during his term as prime minister is www.number-10.gov.uk.

41 James Dobbins et al., *America's Role in Nation-Building: From Germany to Iraq*. Santa Monica, CA: Rand, 2003.

[42] Ibid., xixff.

[43] Niall Ferguson, "The Empire Slinks Back," *New York Times*, April 27, 2003.

[44] Niall Ferguson, *Colossus: The Price of America's Empire*. New York: Penguin, 2004, 28-29.

[45] Niall Ferguson, "Empires with Expiration Dates," *Foreign Policy*, September-October 2006.

[46] David Rieff, *At the Point of a Gun: Democratic Dreams and Armed Intervention*. New York: Simon & Schuster, 2005, 163ff. See also, Rieff, "We Are the World," *Nation*, August 3, 2006.

[47] Michael Ignatieff, "The Burden of Empire," *New York Times*, January 5, 2003; Ignatieff, "The Rights Stuff," *New York Review of Books*, June 13, 2002.

[48] In addition to other citations, see also in the *New York Times*, Michael Ignatieff, "Why Are We in Iraq? (And Liberia? And Afghanistan?)," September 7, 2003; "The Year of Living Dangerously," March 14, 2004; "Democratic Providentialism," December 12, 2004; "The Uncommitted," January 30, 2005; "Who Are Americans to Think that Freedom is Theirs to Spread?" June 26, 2005.

[49] Condoleezza Rice, "Transforming the Middle East," *Washington Post*, August 7, 2003.

[50] Tony Smith, *America's Mission: The United States and the Worldwide Struggle for Democracy in the Twentieth Century*. Princeton, NJ: Princeton University Press, 1994, chapter 5.

[51] Vali Nasr, *The Shia Revival: How Conflicts Within Islam Will Shape the Future*. New York: Norton, 2006.

[52] Edward D. Mansfield and Jack Snyder, *Electing to Fight: Why Emerging Democracies Go to War*. Cambridge, MA: MIT Press, 2005.

[53] Ibid., 13.

[54] Thomas Carothers and Marina Ottaway, eds., *Uncharted Journey: Promoting Democracy in the Middle East*. Washington, DC: Carnegie Endowment, 2005. F. Gregory Gause, "Can Democracy Stop Terrorism?" *Foreign Affairs* 84 (5), September-October 2005.

Chapter 6

[1] David Rieff, *At The Point of a Gun: Democratic Dreams and Armed Intervention*. New York: Simon & Schuster, 2005, 159f.

[2] Samuel P. Huntington, *Who Are We? The Challenges to American National Identity*: New York: Simon & Schuster, 2004, 326, 270. Martha C. Nussbaum, *For Love of Country: Debating the Limits of Patriotism*. Boston: Beacon Press, 1996.

[3] Kofi Annan's speeches may be found on multiple sites through google.com. In the summer of 2006, his September 1999 speech appeared in 102 books reproduced in google as well as http://globalpolicy.igc.org/secgen/. Annan's Nobel speech can be found in many places, including http://nobelprize.org/nobel_prizes/peace/ retrieved August 2006.

[4] Mario Bettati, *Le droit d'ingérence: mutation de l'ordre international*. Paris: Jacob, 1996. On the more general issue of the nature of sovereignty, see Stephen D. Krasner, *Sovereignty: Organized Hypocrisy*. Princeton, NJ: Princeton University Press, 1999, chapter 4; also Krasner, "Sharing Sovereignty," *International Security* 29 (2), Fall 2004.

[5] Thomas M. Franck, "The Emerging Right to Democratic Governance," *American Journal of International Law* 86 (1), January 1992.

[6] Thomas M. Franck, "Is Personal Freedom a Western Value?" *American Journal of International Law* 91 (3), July 1997.

[7] Thomas M. Franck, "Are Human Rights Universal?" *Foreign Affairs* 80 (1), January-February 2001.

[8] See the equivocal language used in Thomas M. Franck, *Recourse to Force: State Action against Threats and Armed Attacks*. New York: Cambridge University Press, 2002.

9   International Commission on Intervention and State Sovereignty, "The Responsibility to Protect." Ottawa, Ontario: International Development Research Centre, 2001, sections 2.16-18, 2.25-27.

10   Ibid., section 2.1.

11   Ibid., Part 4, "The Responsibility to React," includes "six criteria for military intervention"; emphasis in original.

12   Ibid, sections 2.11-2.29; 3,21, and Part 5.

13   United Nations, "In Larger Freedom." United Nations General Assembly, September 2005, executive summary III; section 153.

14   Michael Ignatieff, "The Burden." *New York Times*, January 5, 2003.

15   Michael Ignatieff, "Who are Americans that Think that Freedom is Theirs to Spread?" *New York Times*, June 6, 2005.

16   David Kennedy, *The Dark Side of Virtue: Reassessing International Humanitarianism.* Princeton, NJ: Princeton University Press, 2004, chapter 8. For a discussion critical of efforts to justify the invasion of Iraq under international law, and that sets the effort within an Anglo-American historical context, see Philippe Sands, *Lawless World: America and the Making and Breaking of Global Rules from FDR's Atlantic Charter to George W. Bush's Illegal War.* New York: Viking, 2005.

17   Ignatieff, op. cit., "The Burden."

18   Anne-Marie Slaughter and Lee Feinstein, "A Duty to Prevent," *Foreign Affairs* 83 (1), January-February 2004.

19   Ivo Daalder and James Steinberg, "The Future of Preemption," *Los Angeles Times*, December 4, 2005; and *American Interest*, Winter 2005.

20   Amitai Etzioni, *From Empire to Community: A New Approach to International Community.* New York: Palgrave Macmillan, 2004, 126ff, 134f. Not surprisingly, Anne-Marie Slaughter praised Etzioni's book because it was "not afraid to tackle the very real challenge of creating genuine institutions to govern a potential global polity." Retrieved October 19, 2006 from The Communitarian Network at George Washington University, comnet.gwu.edu.

21   Citations in this section came from the PPI website. Retrieved spring 2006, from www.ppionline.org.

22   Will Marshall, "A Smarter Fight," October 21, 2005. Retrieved spring 2006, www.ppionline.org. Madeleine Albright, "Promoting Democracy: 14 Points for the 21st Century." Princeton University, keynote address at the Woodrow Wilson School, April 29, 2006.

23   Philip Gordon, "America, Europe and the Challenge of Bringing Democracy to Iran." Brookings Institution, December 16, 2005.

24   Will Marshall, ed., *With All Our Might: A Progressive Strategy for Defeating Jihadism and Defending Liberty.* Lanham, MD: Rowman & Littlefield, 2006.

25   Ibid., Introduction by Will Marshall and Jeremy Rosner, 5f.

26   Ibid., 6f.

27   Pollack in Ibid., 34ff.

28   In addition to individual writers and the PPI, evidence for this assertion could be found during the summer of 2006 on two liberal blog websites, where many of the intellectuals vying for position within the Democratic Party could be found: Democracy Arsenal (sponsored by the Century Foundation and the Center for American Progress) and America Abroad (sponsored by TPMCafe).

29   The Euston Manifesto, Retrieved September 5, 2006, http://eustonmanifesto.org/joomla/content/view/84/49.

30   New American Liberalism, "Foundational Statement," Retrieved October 31, 2006, www.newamericanliberalism.org.

[31] Peter Beinart, *The Good Fight: Why Liberals—and Only Liberals—Can Win the War on Terror and Make America Great Again*. New York: HarperCollins, 2006.

[32] Beinart, op. cit., chapter 4 on the menace of totalitarian Islam; 116ff, 137ff, 154ff on out-doing the Republicans in nation building in the Middle East; and on entering into conflict in such a way that "our faith in ourselves" is redeemed, 140, 201ff. As he puts it, "nation build-ing—defined as 'the use of armed force in the aftermath of a crisis to promote a transition to democracy'—remains central to American security, and to liberalism's hopes for a better world" (198). For an enduring review of the bankruptcy of Democratic ideas on foreign policy before the election of November 7, 2006, including scathing commentary on Beinart, see Frank Rich, "Ideas for Democrats?" *New York Review of Books*, October 19. 2006.

[33] Larry Diamond, *Squandered Victory: The American Occupation and the Bungled Effort to Bring Democracy to Iraq*. New York: Holt, 2005.

[34] Rahm Emanuel and Bruce Reed, *The Plan: Big Ideas for America*. New York: Public Affairs, 2006.

[35] Efforts to de-legitimate liberal thinking in general are already gathering in intensity. See, especially, Tony Judt, "Bush's Useful Idiots," *London Review of Books*, September 21, 2006. See also from the radical tradition, Noam Chomsky, *Failed States: The Abuse of Power and the Assault on Democracy*. New York: Metropolitan, 2006; from the liberal left tradi-tion, Stephen Kinzer, *Overthrow: America's Century of Regime Change from Hawaii to Iraq*. New York: Times Books, 2006; and from the realist tradition Christopher Layne, *The Peace of Illusions: American Grand Strategy from 1940 to the Present*. Ithaca, NY: Cornell University Press, 2006, chapter 6.

[36] Thomas O. Melia, "The Democracy Bureaucracy," *American Interest*, Summer 2006.

Chapter 7

[1] Tony Smith, *America's Mission: The United States and the Worldwide Struggle for Democ-racy in the Twentieth Century*. Princeton, NJ: Princeton University Press, 1994, chapter 5.

[2] Francis Fukuyama, *America at the Crossroads: Democracy, Power, and the Neoconserva-tive Legacy*. New Haven, CT: Yale University Press, 2006. Richard Haass, *The Opportu-nity: America's Moment to Alter History's Course*, New York: PublicAffairs, 2005. Michael Mandelbaum, *The Case for Goliath: How America Accts as the World's Government in the Twenty-First Century*. New York: PublicAffairs, 2005; and Mandelbaum, *The Ideas that Conquered the World: Peace, Democracy, and Free Markets in the Twenty-First Century*. New York: PublicAffairs, 2002.

[3] Peter Beinart, "A Fighting Faith: An Argument for a New Liberalism," *New Republic*, December 13, 2004.

[4] Tony Smith, *Thinking Like a Communist: State and Legitimacy in the Soviet Union, China, and Cuba*. New York: Norton, 1987, Introduction, chapter 1.

[5] Hannah Arendt, *The Origins of Totalitarianism*. New ed. New York: Harcourt, 1966 (first ed., 1951), 486.

[6] Ibid., 470f.

[7] Paul Berman, *Terror and Liberalism*. New York: Norton, 2003, 47ff.

[8] Matthew Frey Jacobson, *Barbarian Virtues: The United States Encounters Foreign People at Home and Abroad, 1876-1917*. New York: Hill and Wang, 2000.

[9] Concern for redundancy does not allow consideration of yet another member of this club, Norman Podhoretz. See his "World War IV: How It Started, What It Means, and Why We Have to Win," *Commentary*, September 2004; and Podhoretz, "The War Against the World War IV," *Commentary*, February 2005.

10 Walter Russell Mead, *Special Providence: American Foreign Policy and How It Changed the World*. New York: Knopf, 2001, chapter 5.

11 Madeleine Albright, *The Mighty and the Almighty: Reflections on America, God, and World Affairs*. New York: HarperCollins, 2006; Kevin Phillips, *American Theocracy: The Peril and Politics of Radical Religion, Oil, and Borrowed Money in the 21st Century*. New York: Viking, 2006, part two.

12 Jerry Falwell, *New York Times*, September 15, 2001. See also "Jerry Falwell" in Wikipedia. Retrieved August 2006, from http://en.wikipedia.org/wiki/Jerry_Falwell.

13 For analyses that make clear distinction among Muslims, see William Dalrymple, "Inside the Madrasas," *New York Review of Books*, December 1, 2005; and Max Rodenbeck, "The Truth About Jihad," *New York Review of Books*, August 11, 2005.

14 Christian Coalition of America Press Release, January 17, 2003. Retrieved April 20, 2003, from www.cc.org/becomeinformed; Christian Broadcasting Network, John Waage, "Ignoring God's Road Map for the Holy Land," retrieved May 14, 2003, from www.Cbn.org/cbnnews; *60 Minutes*, October 8, 2002, retrieved October 9, 2002, from www.cbsnews.com. Peter Boyer, "The Big Tent," *New Yorker*, August 22, 2005.

15 Human Events Book Service. Retrieved April 24, 2006, from www.hebookservice.com/products.

16 The vice president's website is with the president's at www.whitehouse.gov. As of summer 2006, the most complete website for the secretary of defense was www.defenselink.mil/speeches.

17 "Defending and Advancing Freedom: A Symposium," *Commentary* 120 (4), November 2005.

18 *Weekly Standard*, May 6, 2006.

19 Berman, *Terror and Liberalism*, op. cit., 166-167.

20 Ibid., 84ff.

21 Paul Berman, *Power and the Idealists: Or the Passion of Joschka Fischer and its Aftermath*. Brooklyn, New York: Soft Skull Press, 2005.

22 Berman, *Terror and Liberalism*, op. cit., 184, 189f, 199.

23 Berman in "Defending and Advancing Freedom: A Symposium," *Commentary* 120 (4), November 2005.

24 Robert Jay Lifton, *Superpower Syndrome: America's Apocalyptic Confrontation with the World*. New York: Thunder's Mouth Press, 2003, 1f.

25 Berman, *Terror and Liberalism*, op. cit., 183, 195.

26 Paul Berman, "What Lincoln Knew About War," *New Republic*, March 3, 2003.

27 Paul Berman, "Neo No More," *New York Times*, March 26, 2006.

28 Thomas Cushman, ed., *A Matter of Principle: Humanitarian Arguments for the War in Iraq*. Berkeley: University of California Press, 2005, Introduction.

29 Ibid., 4, 2.

30 Ibid., 6, 4, 22.

31 David Frum and Richard Perle, *An End to Evil: How to Win the War on Terror*. New York: Random House, 2003, 41, 9.

32 Ibid., 276ff.

33 Ibid., 4, 48, 82, chapter 4, 161.

34 Ibid., 171ff.

35 Ibid., on democracy 158ff; on purges, chapter 7, 37f. Also Ben Wattenberg on PBS Think Tank, "Richard Perle: The Making of a Neoconservative," November 14, 2002.

36 Ibid., 279.

37 Ibid., on being unmanly 4, 12; on being unpatriotic, 15; on being a "lax multiculturalist," 93; on dealing with the Europeans 2451ff; on charges of anti-Semitism, 190f.

38   Charles Krauthammer, "Democratic Realism: An American Foreign Policy for a Unipolar World." Washington, DC: American Enterprise Institute for Public Policy, February 12, 2004. See too Krauthammer, "The Unipolar Moment." *Foreign Affairs* 70 (5), Winter 1991; "The Unipolar Moment Revisited," *National Interest*, Winter 2002/2003.

39   Charles Krauthammer, "In Defense of Democratic Realism," *National Interest*, Fall 2004. Also, Francis Fukuyama, "The Neoconservative Moment," *National Interest*, Summer 2004.

40   Krauthmmer, op. cit, February 12, 2004.

41   Krauthammer, op. cit, Fall 2004.

42   Fukuyama, "Letter to the Editor," *National Interest*, Winter 2004; Krauthammer, "Letter to the Editor," *National Interest*, Spring 2005.

43   *Weekly Standard*, February 10, 2003.

44   *Weekly Standard*, May 12, 2003.

45   *Weekly Standard*, March 20, 2006.

46   *Weekly Standard*, March 6, 2006.

47   *Weekly Standard*, February 3, 2003.

48   *Weekly Standard*, April 28, 2003.

49   Michael Ledeen, *National Review On Line*, December 7, 2001.

50   Michael Ledeen, *The War Against the Terror Masters: Why It Happened, Where We are Now, How We'll Win*. New York: St. Martin's Press, 2002, 212f.

51   Patrick Buchanan, "Whose War?" *American Conservative*, March 24, 2003.

52   See Stephen M. Walt and John J. Mearsheimer, "The Israel Lobby and U.S. Foreign Policy," Working Paper at the Kennedy School of Government, Harvard University, RRWP06-011, March 2006; Tony Smith, *Foreign Attachments: The Power of Ethnic Groups in the Making of American Foreign Policy*. Cambridge, MA: Harvard University Press, 2000, chapters 1, 4. Michael Massing, "The Truth About 'the Israel Lobby'," *New York Review of Books*, June 8, 2006; "Does the Israel Lobby Have Too Much Power?" Roundtable in *Foreign Policy*, July-August 2006. Aryeh Neier, The Attack on Human Rights Watch," *New York Review of Books*, November 2, 2006. Tony Judt, "Bush's Useful Idiots," *London Review of Books*, September 21, 2006.

53   Anatol Lieven, *America Right or Wrong: An Anatomy of American Nationalism*. New York: Oxford University Press, chapter 6; Judith A. Klinghoffer, *Vietnam, Jews and the Middle East*. New York: Saint Martin's Press, 1999.

54   Richard Perle, et al., "A Clean Break: A New Strategy for Securing the Realm," The Institute for Advanced Strategic and Political Studies, Jerusalem and Washington, 1996; Robert Kagan and William Kristol, "A Green Light for Israel," *Weekly Standard*, August 27, 2001. Stefan Halper and Jonathan Clarke, *America Alone: The Neoconservatives and the Global Order*. New York: Cambridge University Press, 2004, 103ff.

INDEX